A

WO

L

AWOL

TALES FOR TRAVEL-INSPIRED MINDS

Edited by Jennifer Barclay and Amy Logan

 Vintage Canada

VINTAGE CANADA EDITION, 2003

Collection and Introduction Copyright © 2003 Jennifer Barclay and Amy Logan

Published in Canada by Vintage Canada, a division of Random House of Canada Limited, in 2003. Distributed by Random House of Canada Limited, Toronto.

Vintage Canada and colophon are registered trademarks of Random House of Canada Limited.

Eveery reasonable effort has been made to trace ownership of copyright materials. Information enabling the Publisher to rectify any reference or credit in future editions will be welcomed.

Pages 269 and 270 constitute a continuation of the copyright page.

National Library of Canada Cataloguing in Publication

AWOL : tales for travel-inspired minds / edited by Jennifer Barclay and Amy Logan.

ISBN 0-679-31215-3

1. Voyages and travels. I. Barclay, Jennifer II. Logan, Amy

G465.A86 2003   910.4   C2002-904567-3

www.randomhouse.ca

Text design by Bill Douglas at The Bang

Printed and bound in the U.S.A.

10 9 8 7 6 5 4 3 2 1

I am a part of all that I have met;
Yet all experience is an arch wherethro'
Gleams that untravell'd world, whose margin fades
For ever and for ever when I move.

Alfred, Lord Tennyson, "Ulysses"

CONTENTS

INTRODUCTION

What you hold in your hands is a treasure trove of travel tales from people gone AWOL—*absent without leave* from their usual circumstances; true stories to inspire those who replenish their spirits by getting out there.

For most of us, home is safe and comfortable—it's hard to lose our bearings on the daily trek to work by car or subway. Travel is a state of being that brings us moments of beauty and unusual challenge. It can change our perspective, make us less materialistic, more willing to mix with different kinds of people. It can scare us and confuse us at the same time as it makes us feel most alive. Travelling without an agenda, with time for meandering, is often the hardest and most rewarding form of adventure: it can lead us away from the beaten path toward something unexpected.

Travel and writing have always gone hand in hand. The urge to inscribe moments of a journey onto paper can be irresistible, while many of us wander because of a story we've read. For us, the editors, the travel stories that fire our imagination resonate with the peculiar magic of being in a particular place at a particular time. Like fiction, these tales capture something emblematic or beautiful in their characters or description or direction. Like travel, they assume various shapes. They are illustrations of another reality; of how each place yields different things to every traveller, depending on why you go, whom you meet, who you are.

In compiling this book, we looked for stories that showed the author altered by getting away from the familiar, whether across the globe or a few hours from home; we looked for humour, emotional honesty, beautiful style, a zest for life, an absorption in the surroundings conveying a strong sense of place, stories that surprised. Each piece was chosen for something special it portrayed to our travel-inspired sensibilities. All had to be original, never published before, and all had to be true—the truth, of course, often being stranger than fiction.

Deliberately approaching an unusual mix of writers—some new, others established, among them poets and novelists and journalists—we were overjoyed at the positive response. Not only did these writers have AWOL stories to share, they were excited about this collection coming together. People who treasure "getting away" have plenty of stories to tell about what they have seen and learned out there; and more often than not, they want to hear about other people's travel exploits.

In compiling this collage of stories and visuals, we included the offbeat, the irreverent and the provocative, to keep the concept as unconfined as the travel we enjoy. Out on the road, alliances both strong and bizarre form. The travellers in this book fall in love, make marriage proposals, are subjected to strange courtships. They are thrown together with people they'd never meet back home, make new friends and discard identities they have acquired among people they know. They learn to travel with babies and teenagers. They also long for privacy and isolation, a chance to get away from the pack and breathe deeply.

Storytelling is at its best when it includes the traveller as a character, perhaps astonished, perhaps dismayed, but always learning along the way. We enjoy the picture of the young traveller setting out to experience the big wide world, looking for love and adventure, the world and its stories there "for the taking," as Scott Gardiner puts it. There is an infectious enthusiasm in Mark Jarman's romp through Europe, Hemingway filling his head, or in Deirdre Kelly's opportunistic hunt for excitement in Paris.

In some of the longer pieces, writers who have lived in other countries reveal deeper observations: Karen Connelly trying to switch off what she knows, to merely listen and learn in Burma; Camilla Gibb feeling guilt over the hardship she leaves behind in Ethiopia; David Manicom wondering how he can appreciate societies as old as coal when he comes from a country still hesitant about its own identity. Jamie Zeppa paints a powerful picture of the culture shock of returning to Canada after years in Bhutan.

All the writers are from Canada. Canadians are always looking beyond their borders, and many of these authors have already published extraordinary travel books. Combining freshness with intelligence, Canadian travel writing remains under-promoted, in spite of the national appetite for memoir and for travel itself. Short pieces that are unconventional, personal and opinionated rarely reach Canadian readers by way of the mainstream press unless written by celebrities.

Many of these tales were pulled from travel journals, personal stories that, until now, never had an appropriate forum.

A recurring theme that jumps out as being Canadian is multicultural heritage. Simona Chiose feels wealthy when spending pesos in Cuba, yet the poorest villages remind her of Romania, where she grew up. Nikki Barrett has to go through a claustrophobic tour of Robben Island to realize that her African childhood has been overwritten by her more recent North American experience. If Canadians find pieces of their identity by travelling the world—the quest for identity is the only journey, said Northrop Frye—their sense of self is no less complex or mysterious when they come back.

For us travel addicts, there is a simple pleasure in stepping on unknown ground: the smells and tastes of a new place; the struggles with unfamiliar languages and customs; the knowledge that when you wake up, there will be new people to meet, that life might take you in an unexpected direction. This book shows how the delicious moments of travel—in Brazil, India, China, Greece, Iceland, Thailand, Australia, the United States or Canada—can inspire in many different ways. Because these stories are personal, they don't aim to tell the full story about a place, just one juicy slice of experience.

This is a book for those of us who are happy to live with no fixed address, and those of us who are inspired by sitting back and reading about it. However you do it—go AWOL!

Jennifer Barclay and Amy Logan

MONKS ON MOPEDS
Laurie Gough

The midnight boat to the island of Koh Phangan was full of hippies. Not friendly hippies, but people who liked to dress the part. They didn't smile. For such a ragged, dreadlocked, motley crew, they took themselves extremely seriously. I lay awake on the deck for most of the night and let my thoughts sink into the deep purple sky over Thailand. I was thrilled to be in a country I had read so much about, a country so ancient and storied, the Venice of the East, filled with temples of dawn and northern hill tribes. I recalled what I had seen earlier that day on the train through the southern tip of Thailand: jagged mountains, jungles, rubber plantations and giant Buddhas that sat contemplatively in rice paddies.

When the boat reached the island in the morning, I found a bamboo hut to rent on the beach. Over the next ten days I discovered Koh Phangan's outstanding features: nasty dogs that bite your ankles wherever you go, the most delicious food in the entire world (noodles with ginger, chilies, cashews, shrimp in coconut milk, sticky rice), full-moon parties where foreign tourists eat magic mushrooms and fly to solitary planets where conversation is neither required nor even possible, and wandering old men who use their thumbs as instruments of torture.

A Danish woman recommended the Thai massage administered by elderly men who stroll the beaches, soliciting willing victims. When the eighty-year-old masseur offered to ply his trade on my body, I eagerly complied, overjoyed at the idea of soothing my aching shoulders, which had heaved a far too heavy backpack far too long. Just before he began, I noticed his thumbs. These were no ordinary thumbs but appendages of astounding proportions, mutated digits, round and flat, the size of dessert spoons. Clearly he had spent his life cultivating his thumbs for the art of massage.

While I lay on the sand, the man with the thumbs prodded and poked his way from my feet up my legs with cruel and unyielding force, even took unnecessary jabs at my knees, showing no mercy at my protests. I had been far less tense before the massage began. He applied his thumbs to the deepest reaches of my body, surely causing irreparable damage to my life-giving organs. By the time he reached my stomach, I was overcome with self-pity. His thumbs forced down into my stomach with such a weight, they seemed to touch the ground beneath me. I couldn't keep my eyes off his face, which was severe, determined and hardened.

Clearly, massage was serious business to this man, and flinching was for sissies. Clearly, I was a sissy. When he tried to grab hold of my tongue, I clamped my teeth to prevent the intrusion. Then, in a strange and dreadful moment, the giant thumbs were boring into my ears. No one had ever done such a thing, and I stopped the thumbs at that point, but not before I heard something pop. Afterwards, I went for a swim in the sea and couldn't get the water out of my ears for two days. The thumbs had carved a small cave in my inner ear for water to sit in, resulting in a painful ear infection that lasted two weeks.

Thailand didn't seem to hold the romance and mystical intrigue I had imagined.

From the moment I arrived in Bangkok, I was shoved up against a human tide, jostled by bodies of every description. Every time I walked out of my guest house, I encountered monsoons of activity: human, animal and vegetable. On the streets, I watched people who had fallen half-mad into the gutters of life. Vacant, destitute faces begged for acknowledgement of their existence. Children with rakes for bodies stared at me with eyes bigger than all the world's darkest secrets. Mangy dogs ate rotten vegetables off the roads. I gazed into the rich, brown, beautiful faces of the women who sold me combs, cheap soap and pineapples on the sidewalks. I wandered through night markets that sold pig heads, red coiled intestines in glass jars, dripping animal appendages, green leafy vegetable shoots, smoked fish and pyramid mounds of spices. In these markets, every passing scent was either sublime or rank.

Small shops and sidewalk stalls in Bangkok are run by old men with cataracts, who have seen too much and give none of it away. They would wrap my passion fruit carefully in yesterday's newspaper, fold all the edges as if it were a wedding present. I watched monks on mopeds, sometimes two on a bike, race down the streets, their saffron robes flowing behind them as they sped through the chaos. Glorious smiles, shaved heads, and Doc Martens on their feet.

Bangkok endures annual floods and an eternal stickiness—a stickiness in the air, in the rice, in the sex sold on the streets. This is the city where Japanese businessmen come for sex holidays, whole planeloads of them seeking out the young Thai girls from the hill tribes, whose starving parents sell them into prostitution. Young boys sell themselves for movie tickets. Street life sharpens to a razor's edge on which few can balance.

It seemed to me that Bangkok lay smouldering under a blue haze of exhaust fumes and smog: the city of perpetually honking horns. Wheels and people are everywhere, all spinning like the city and your head, spinning fast toward the Western world of chaos, Coca-Cola and Internet cafés.

To cross a street in Bangkok is to risk your life. Pedestrians have no rights. I would always have to wait for a flood of rickshaws and careening cabs, tuk-tuks, bikes and buses to cease, and sometimes I waited half an hour. Sidewalks end abruptly with cement walls in your face, and they're full of gaping holes, wide-open sewage holes that are gateways to the underworld. I worried for the children and dogs who might slip in silently. Somewhere in that city, lost souls must wander in the sewers, like filthy fallen angels.

I took a bus north out of Bangkok. I wanted to breathe oxygen again. Just outside a village, I stayed at a guest house run by a woman with too many children to count. Sumalee started working before the sun came up and didn't stop until after it set. She cooked, cleaned, gardened, took care of her children, and in the evenings, if she had foreign guests, she practised other languages. She loved singing and knew all the words to "Over the Rainbow." Although she said she didn't keep track, she thought she was close to thirty-five years old. When I asked where her husband was, she told me, very poetically I thought, that he was experimenting with different hearts.

In the lantern-lit evening, I watched the rich communal life of Sumalee's family. As in many non-Western countries, everyone is related and no one is ever alone. Mothers are never isolated and burdened with small, bored children. Children have many mothers, most of them cousins, aunts and older sisters. Social intimacy comes at the cost of privacy, however. Everybody in that extended family seemed to know each other's business. They also seemed to know intimate details about every person in the village.

A week later, I camped in the countryside near a wide glassy river. All night long I gagged from the sickly sweet stench of a burning pile of organic matter and garbage near my tent. I had seen these fires from bus and train windows all over the country. So overpowering were the fumes that I tried to put out the fire, and when that didn't work, I uprooted and moved my tent in the middle of the night. To think I had left Bangkok because of its noxious fumes. Smoke choked even the country skies in an eternal season of burning. Where was the ancient soft pure air of Thailand?

In Chiang Mai, I hooked up with my Canadian friend Charlie. We stayed at the Be Happy Guest House, run by an elderly couple who fed us sticky rice and vegetables with fish sauce. After dinner we explored Chiang Mai and discovered the Be More Happy Guest House, just down the street. If only we'd known. The next morning when we were eating breakfast at an outdoor restaurant, a little boy came by, holding a cage full of birds. "Give me five baht and I'll let the birds go," he said to us. We refused to pay the wildlife kidnapper's ransom and he moved on to other tourists at the next table.

Charlie and I continued north. In Chiang Rai, everyone and his brother tried to get us to go on a hill tribe trek. These treks were all the rage. Ride elephants into the past, see hill tribe people untouched by the modern world, they advertised. A Dutch couple, recently returned from one of the more popular expeditions, told us they had walked ahead of their group and arrived at the hill tribe station an hour before they were expected. Through the trees they watched the hill people preparing for the visitors by changing from their ordinary ragged clothes into bright costumes, traditional elaborate hats, and jewellery.

Charlie and I decided to do our own exploring of northern Thailand. We rented a motorcycle in Chiang Rai and set off early one morning into the hills. On the main road north we learned the only law of Thai highway travel: might is right. Every vehicle larger than our motorcycle bullied us over to the extreme edge of the road, beside the gutter. We drove on the shoulder—one dead dog and we'd be dead too—and let the wailing, streaking, hurtling consciousness of the highway leave us in the dust.

Soon we escaped the main highway and, on our rickety motorcycle with its sputtering engine, began to follow switchback roads that led into the sky. Thai soldiers had warned us of the danger in the green terraced mountains leading to the Golden Triangle, danger from drug dealers and thieves, communist terrorists and Laotian soldiers who might fly out of the hills to attack travellers at any time. Higher up into

TO CROSS A STREET IN BANGKOK IS TO RISK YOUR LIFE.

the clouds, the mountains become tough and weather-worn, like the skin of the barefoot people who stood and watched us from the roadside. These northern hills were inhabited by ten thousand lives, people eking out their existence in tattered dirt villages that cling to the sides of mountains like bats to cave walls.

When our motorcycle needed a rest, we stopped in a village where we saw a woman smoking opium from a pipe as she breast-fed her baby. She looked fifty but was probably much younger. I smiled at her and she thrust her hand out toward me. "Five baht to make picture," she said.

Farther up the road we found a Buddha statue inside a cave. The cave was deliciously cold and tranquil after the thick heat of the day. A monk from a nearby temple came to greet us. He wore biker sunglasses and an orange robe; tattoos laced his forearms. In broken English, he told us about his simple life in the hills and how much happier he was now than when he was young. "Life is a handful of days, then poof," he blew on his hands, "then it's all over." He laughed and bowed for us as he turned to leave. His jack-o'-lantern robe ruffling in the wind as he walked up a wooded path was a scene of golden beauty.

Charlie and I searched most of the afternoon for the Golden Triangle. Considered by some to be one of the most exotic places in the world, and long a centre for drug trafficking, the infamous Golden Triangle is found at the intersection of the Mekong and Ruak rivers, forming the borders between Burma, Laos and northern Thailand. Road signs were extremely poor and misleading and we got lost several times. So desolate were the roads, many of them ending abruptly into a dead open nowhere, we thought the Golden Triangle must be remote and unvisited.

We rounded a corner and found ourselves on a gleaming paved highway full of honking horns. The first sign of the Golden Triangle was a slick, air-conditioned Japanese tour bus glistening in the sun. I was reminded of Niagara Falls. Cameras clicked incessantly at the small triangular island on the Mekong River. Pepsi and Coke competed for attention like ten-year-old brats. Posters of half-naked Thai women advertised orange pop. A little girl dressed in hill tribe garb asked if I wanted to take her picture for five baht, and pouted when I said no.

We fled and got lost again as we headed south, drawn off the beaten tourist track onto smaller, narrower roads. After a while, we found ourselves snaking through a different kind of countryside. An emptiness seemed to clutch hold of the rolling land around us, but it wasn't lonely or barren. The villages we passed in this new and different land were rich with details of seemingly simple and joyful lives. The people were evidently not accustomed to outsiders, and they stared, waved, smiled and laughed as we passed them on the road. A little girl ran when she saw us and hid behind a tree.

Outside one village, some water buffalo crossing the road forced us to stop and wait. The farmer ran behind the beasts to hurry them off the road. He grinned sheepishly, embarrassed about interrupting our journey. "No problem," Charlie said to the man with a wave of his hand.

"No problem?" said the water buffalo herder. "No problem, no problem," he continued to say over and over. He started laughing. He laughed so hard he doubled over and held his stomach. I wondered if this was the first time he'd actually heard an English speaker use the phrase. Perhaps he had heard it once in a movie. "No problem, no problem," continued the man. Once his water buffalo had crossed and we drove on, I turned around to see the laughing man running toward his house, probably to tell his family what he'd heard.

Soon after, we realized we were seriously lost. Our map was entirely useless, and it was getting dark. In the next village, we stopped to ask a boy the way to Chiang Rai, but he didn't have a clue what we were saying. Frightened, he ran away to his house. An older man came along and didn't understand us either. Soon a gathering of people surrounded us, the lost *falangs*. Repeatedly we said, "Chiang Rai," pointed to our map, pointed ahead and then behind us on the road, trying to discern which way to go. Either the villagers didn't know the way to Chiang Rai or we weren't pronouncing it correctly. Then, we looked up from the map and saw two teenage boys dragging a younger boy by his shirt across the road. Proudly, they deposited him in front of us. The little boy's eyes shone at our decrepit motorcycle. Very slowly, he said, "Where . . . you . . . want go?" The villagers had given us their prize linguist.

The boy pointed the way back for us, and on seeing the boy do this, the whole village pointed the way back for us too. The whole village pointed. It set off inside me a surge of sweet gratitude. The handful of days we're given on earth exploded on the road before us into a thousand shards of light. The way back would be easy to find. The way back would be paved in Judy Garland songs.

No problem.

Laurie Gough is the author of Island of the Human Heart: A Woman's Travel Odyssey *(entitled* Kite Strings of the Southern Cross *in the rest of the world), finalist for the Thomas Cook Travel Book Award and winner of* ForeWord Magazine*'s Silver Medal for Travel Book of the Year. She also contributes to salon.com, the* Globe and Mail, *the* Los Angeles Times *and numerous travel anthologies. She has just moved to Wakefield, Quebec, where she's writing her next book.*

INCIDENT AT RANKIN INLET
Peter Unwin

Stories tend not to unfold in the Arctic the same way they do in the south. The contours are different, and the outcomes are different too. At one time off Rankin Inlet, an Inuit woman in a small boat needed to relieve herself. Her husband begged her not to urinate in the water, arguing that this would offend the gods. Desperate, she called upon a spirit to help her. The spirit agreed to help but demanded the woman forfeit her life.

In the south, there would be no deal. But in the Arctic, the woman agreed. The spirit at once transformed a nearby iceberg into an island for her convenience, and having relieved herself, she died moments later while crawling on her hands and knees on the cobble beach.

That shining piece of rock is called Marble Island. Made almost entirely of quartz, it glows a brilliant white beneath clear skies. In 1721, a gold-seeking expedition led by James Knight, consisting of two ships and twenty-five men, landed on the island. During the course of the next two years, scurvy, starvation and mortal

Boats are scattered in clusters, as if waiting for the tide to float them.

A Taste from Canada's Arctic

Teriyaki Caribou STICK

20 g

Tundra Brand

Quality Foods from the People of the Land

INGREDIENTS: CARIBOU, SALT, DEXTROSE, SOYA SAUCE, MONOSODIUM GLUTAMATE, SPICES, GARLIC POWDER, SODIUM ERYTHORBATE, SODIUM NITRITE, NATURAL SMOKE.
INGREDIENTS: CARIBOU, SEL, DEXTROSE, SAUCE AU SOJA, GLUTAMATE MONOSODIQUE, ÉPICES, POUDRE D'AIL, ERYTHORBATE DE SODIUM, NITRITE DE SODIUM, FUMÉE NATURELLE.

Prepared at:
Keewatin Meat & Fish Ltd.
Rankin Inlet, NT X0C 0G0

conflict with the "Eskemays" turned the site into one of the grimmest locations in the history of Northern exploration. The entire expedition vanished; no survivors, no skeletons, not even any graves were ever found.

Today on the island's western tip, whales are still flensed by men and women wielding *sivaks* and *ulus*, the gendered knives of the Inuit. Visitors approach the island on their hands and knees in deference to a legendary woman who needed to pee, and perhaps to the many others who have died horrible deaths here and whose stories have never been told.

Twenty miles away on the mainland lies the modern settlement of Rankin Inlet. In a rock field just outside of town, a few dog carcasses in various stages of decomposition are scattered about. Some have the red plastic casing of a shotgun shell lying next to them. Scampering everywhere are the *siskiit*, a nervous, corpulent ground squirrel the size of a terrier, the preferred target of Inuit boys who hurl stones at them with astonishing accuracy.

Out on the land sit several large rusted compressors with evidence of people having overnighted in them: a few berths bolted to the walls, a television antenna, three or four small windows—small enough to keep the polar bears from getting in—blowtorched out of the side. Other examples of Inuit adaptability are near at hand, including a snowmobile's cracked Plexiglas windshield sewn exquisitely back together with wire. This sort of ingenuity is legendary in the Arctic. An Inuk in the 1950s was said to have opened the back of a thirty-five-millimetre camera for a traveller and fixed the broken timing mechanism, having never seen a camera before in his life.

The town is named after the British naval officer John Rankin. History remembers him as the man who lied about the Northwest Passage. He swore not only that it existed at this latitude (sixty-four), but that Christopher Middleton, his commanding officer and one of history's finest navigators, was deliberately concealing it for his own profit.

Rankin Inlet is a windswept settlement of prefabricated buildings mounted on rocks. The wind is legendary and scours the ancient bedrock while venting itself continuously southward. There are no flags in Rankin Inlet, only half flags, the ends torn to shreds. It is said here that flags snapping loudly but straight out indicate winds of thirty-five kilometres. A snapping flag inclined upward means winds of more than thirty-five kilometres. Boats are scattered in clusters, like the houses, down by the waters of Hudson Bay, as if waiting for the tide to float them.

Unlike the neighbouring coastal communities of Arviat and Whale Cove, which were established in the 1950s to save the Inuit from starvation following a change in the caribou migrations, Rankin Inlet began as a mining town. According to the *1998 Nunavut Handbook*, the Inuit were "very hard workers and much appreciated by the mine owners." In plain English, Inuit men received half the wages of the white miners and were required to eat in separate lunchrooms. The mine closed in 1962. The

THERE ARE NO FLAGS IN RANKIN INLET, ONLY HALF FLAGS, THE ENDS TORN TO SHREDS.

giant shaft head that dominated Rankin Inlet burnt to the ground in the mid-1980s. Today there is a nasty, ongoing lawsuit concerning who exactly owns the rights to the land and the nickel that lies beneath the ground.

Across the street from this abandoned mine is the Northern Store, formerly owned by the Hudson's Bay Company, a massive prefabricated shed that sells everything from T-shirts to white rolled slabs of whale fat labelled *Muuktuuk*. In a small stall off the side is a combination pizza parlour, fried chicken restaurant and video store. An enormous walrus head is mounted above the videos. The place is packed with Inuit children. A few fries are getting eaten, and more kids file in and look about the room the way grown men enter a tavern.

Inuit children are granted a freedom rare in the south. At Iqaluit, in a friend's house, following a dinner of frozen peas, instant mashed potatoes and fresh caribou, I watched a powerful boy of five begin to push a broken stereo console across the living room floor. The women played cards and smoked cigarettes. The men smoked and watched, transfixed, a documentary on the hunting techniques of large jungle cats. They had watched this same video many times and fell into a familiar reverential silence in the moments leading up to the kill. Finally the boy, with a great deal of proud grunting, managed to shoulder the cabinet to the lip of the landing and send it crashing down the flight of stairs. The noise was deafening. No one in the room even looked up. Another time, at Arviat, a seven-year-old boy, clutching a ticket, boarded the twin-prop Saab on which I was travelling, and took a seat. The flight attendant spent ten minutes attempting, in English, to find out who he was. "Who's your mommy?" she asked repeatedly. But the boy did not speak English, he spoke Inuktitut. After skidding sideways through ferocious Arctic "bubbles," the plane landed. The little Inuit boy had been playing unconcernedly throughout with a plastic spoon. At Rankin Inlet he skipped down the runway and disappeared.

Conversation among the boys and girls crowded into the only fast-food place in town is mostly in Inuktitut, although a few phrases of English filter through, "Johnny, you rich man now hey? You rich man?"

I manage to buy a hamburger, but the accomplishment is marred by my insistence on mustard. The girl behind the counter views my request with some skepticism. She sees no reason for putting mustard on a hamburger; she sees little reason for a hamburger. There is a good chance she prefers *eeqoonak*, walrus meat aged three months under a rock and eaten raw, preferably from a sheet of plywood on the gymnasium floor at the community centre. After engaging in a whispered conversation with her co-worker, she eventually provides me, proudly, with salt.

I am seated at a plastic table, eating my salted hamburger, when I notice a two-year-old with black tangled hair. She's staring at me, either because I am one of the *quallnaat,* "white people," or because I have red hair. It must be the hair. There have been *quallnaat* here since 1540 when fool's gold brought Martin Frobisher and a crew of twelve boys, each armed with a jackknife, a *poignard*, and a Bible to fight the heathen.

The girl is quite mesmerized. She is sucking on a large Slurpee and clutching a penny in her left hand. It's the penny that fascinates her now. She presses it between her fingers as though it were a totem possessing magical power, pulsating in her hand. Then suddenly, her focus changes. She is no longer interested in the penny; there are other people, dozens of them. She knows every one of them. The people come in, go out, laugh, step around her, over her. In the midst of this activity, the penny falls to the ground and rolls tantalizingly down the aisle.

I've seen this story before. I've seen it in film clips and in life, perhaps even in dreams. I will get up and rescue the penny, then hand it back to her. Her mouth will

The wind is legendary, even tilting stop signs.

13

detach from the Slurpee, and she will smile gratefully at me. The large man, her father, will nod agreeably. By this act, I will fit in. I will demonstrate the truth of Waugh's dictum, "the tourist is the other fellow." Somehow the gesture will be made more touching by the valuelessness of the coin up here, where a stale lettuce the size of a baseball costs four dollars. My role is clear.

Instead I remain firmly seated. This is not the south, and stories do not have the same contours here. A man sits in the corner ten feet away from me; his face covered with stitches. Six weeks ago a polar bear removed the flesh from his skull. I'm told his face "was hanging off." Apparently this is what a polar bear does: attempts to crack a man's skull the way it cracks the head of a seal. The man's grandmother was killed in the attack. He escaped with a boy, in a small boat. It was the third time in his life that he had been attacked by a polar bear. Now he's eating a slice of pizza next to a rack of videos underneath an enormous stuffed walrus head.

I watch the penny as it continues to roll down the aisle and finally stops. No disappointed wail comes from the girl. She has lost interest in the penny and turns away. The urge to intercede and do something has washed over me and passed. I've withstood it and done nothing. Because of that, I'm free to watch the story unfold the way it's meant to.

Another man starts to reach for the penny. His moves are laboured. The man suffers from a serious skeletal injury; his legs and his spine are twisted. The complex gestures required for him to unfold his legs are excruciating to watch. At one point he's forced to use his hands to move his legs. Finally he manages to crouch down, lifting one leg awkwardly to accommodate the other. A grimace of pain flashes across his lips. He is virtually lying on the floor where the penny is. I'm holding my breath.

The same painful gestures are executed in reverse to get himself back up. This is done gradually, in stages. Through a series of agonizing gestures, he retrieves a penny that belongs to a very little girl.

The man rises to his feet and folds the penny in his hand. Then, with a quick look around, he shoves it into his pocket and limps from the building.

Peter's essays, poems and stories have appeared in a large number of publications, and his historical writing has been nominated for a National Magazine Award and two Western Magazine Awards. His first collection of short stories, The Rock Farmers, *received a Stephen Leacock Award nomination, and his novel,* Nine Bells for a Man, *tells the true story of Canada's largest inland marine disaster. He is currently working on* The Wolf's Head, *a book about Lake Superior.*

CHICKENS, GIRLS AND RUINS
Simona Chiose

Maurice was from Paris—all his life he had lived in Paris—but now he lived in Martinique. He had been married four times but would never do it again: "*Plus jamais.*" This much we knew after talking to him for maybe fifteen minutes. Paul and I were sitting at the only café on a long strip of Havana's Malecón; the café really just a few tables, chairs and umbrellas in front of an apartment building. Maurice had rolled in with a thin, light-skinned Cuban woman. "Is it possible to sit here?" he'd asked, and they joined us at our table.

Across the street, the sea lapped at the edges of the Malecón's stone wall. Wind and salt had eaten the pinks and oranges off the buildings lining the boulevard, and plaster was peeling off in chunks. Faded green and blue American Buicks and Cadillacs rattled by on the wide avenue. The whole city of Havana was like that, an elegant diva wearing a stained 1930s gown to a Warhol Factory party. Cuban writer Pedro Juan Gutiérrez says Havana is popular with tourists because they love ruins. Ruined mansions that once belonged to rich landowners, their once-glittering blue pools empty for forty years. Ruined homes with crumbling Roman columns turned into private restaurants and hotels catering to foreigners with pockets full of the American dollar. To Cubans, Canadians and Americans are indistinguishable.

Habaneros like Maurice's girl believe that foreigners will lead them out of the ruins.

"This girl came up to me," Maurice said in French, and he looked over to the girl dressed in green cargo pants and a grey tank top, "and asked me if I want to kiss her.

"'I don't know you,' I told her. And you know what she said to me? She said, 'You have the most beautiful blue eyes!'" Maurice threw back his head and sighed. "I could not resist. I'm sixty-nine years old. How could I resist? This is magnificent. This is love in Cuba."

Paul, who always forgets names but rarely owns up to it, asked, "What is your

THIS JOE USED TO WORK AS A UNITED NATIONS ECONOMICS EXPERT ON AFRICA. NOW HE'S RETIRED AND DRIVES A TAXI. HE LAUGHS AFTER HE TELLS ME THIS.

PAUL FAIRWEATHER

name again?" as if the story had made this stranger so interesting that his name had to be stored and remembered. Or maybe he wanted to know if the name held a clue to his luck. What was this place where love just walked up to you on the street?

Then Paul asked the girl's name again because he hadn't caught it when she was introduced. Neither had I, and I didn't the second time either. So later when we talked about Maurice, we referred to her as "the girl." Maurice called her that too. As in, "You see, with the girl, I'm not going to invite her to dinner tonight. She's beautiful, look at her, like a model," and here he vaguely waved his arm toward her until I nodded in appreciation at the treasure he'd landed. "But she does not interest me. I will bring my *copine*."

The *copine* he would bring to dinner that night was older. Maurice said they had met two years before, when he had first come to Cuba with a French aid group to

deliver medicine, and had become friends. She had been a schoolteacher. But we didn't catch her name either and Maurice kept calling her "love" or *copine*. She later became "the second girl."

The "girls" were *jinteras*, hustlers. Men are *jinteros*. All Cubans who sell themselves, or their services, from taxi rides to cigars, get the label. I love the harshness of its first syllable and how that edge glides into a promise in the second. But I hate that it takes only that one word to dismiss a person.

That afternoon, I occasionally used my pathetically broken Spanish to attempt to

Girls waiting at a local bar.

translate our conversation to "the girl." Perhaps because it made up for being too relaxed, too on holiday, to care about her name.

She didn't pay attention to what Maurice was talking about. Most of the time she lounged back in her chair, gazed at the ocean and picked at a plate of fried chicken. Maurice had bought her a plate of it with fries for about four dollars, and in exchange for this, a couple of beers and the vague possibility that he might hand more money her way, she was willing to while away the afternoon.

She told me she was a computer student at the university. There was no money in it. Like all the tourist books said, a professional would make less than fifteen dollars a month.

"But later, *muy tarde, es bueno por muy tarde,*" I said. If you have a computer degree you can travel, you can go to America, I said. At least for a while, send money home, I said. I didn't say what I was thinking, which was that she wouldn't have to spend her life selling compliments for a four-dollar plate of chicken. She told me she didn't want to leave Cuba. Only for a holiday maybe. Then she looked away from me.

I didn't say what else I was thinking, which was that if she spent that afternoon and many others like it studying maybe she could get a grant to at least study abroad. In a way, I was glad she was barely tolerating my advice. I could hear her thinking, "This woman thinks she's going to save me from all this, like every other American woman I've ever met. What do they know about life here? Fuck her." So after she brushed me off, we sat side by side in companionable, sullen, "fuck-you" silence, and I talked to Maurice.

After a few hours, the girl started whispering to Paul urgently in fluent English.

"She's saying that if I want pot, I just have to walk into the building. They're selling it upstairs," he whispered to me. From what she said, it was too expensive.

The sun was going down. A small bus pulled up and unloaded a group of tourists. They filled the empty chairs, talked loudly in German and sucked back cheap mojitos. At another table a couple chewed on the burnt skin of their chicken.

"Is the chicken good? *Te gusta?* Do you want bread?" Maurice kept asking the

Wind and salt had eaten the pinks and oranges off the buildings.

PAUL FAIRWEATHER

girl. "Yes, yes, no bread, okay? Everything's fine," she'd say to him, giving him only as much attention as he'd bought, and she'd go back to watching the sea.

Another day we meet a *jintero*. We come out of our *casa*, a nice room with big shuttered windows and hot water in a house belonging to a lovely Cuban lady. We would like to go to the beach east of town.

Outside, several men are leaning against the fence. They are there every day. "Taxi? Taxi?" they ask every time we pass by. This time I say, "*Si, taxi por Playas del Este?*"

An older man steps away. "*Si,*" he says. "*Por Playas?*"

I repeat, "*Si,* okay," and he gets ready to walk to where I imagine his car is parked.

"*Cuanto?*" I say, because though to them we are rich Yankees, back home we have no money.

"Ten dollars," he says.

"Ten dollars? *Todo?*"

"Yes."

"Okay."

Again, we barely catch his name. I don't know if the problem is the thick Cuban accent that layers their Spanish with sounds I've never heard before, but we're terrible at this. So we refer to him as Joe, the name I use for my landlord—a good stand-in for any older man who's on the short side and keeps his thoughts to himself. This Joe used to work as a United Nations economics expert on Africa. Now he's retired and drives a taxi. He laughs after he tells me this. I want to apologize, but instead I laugh, because in that moment of laughter, we're together in an absurd world. A UN rep driving two Canadians to the beach.

A moment later, though, I see more of his world. He drives through a ramshackle neighbourhood that reminds me of villages I saw in Romania when I was a child while holidaying with my parents in the Carpathians. Kids in ripped T-shirts emblazoned with 7 UP or Coke logos mill around. The windows of houses are missing panes. To someone who's never seen this kind of life before, it looks bad, like the background to a World Relief ad. Life goes on, though. Chickens peck at the side of the road. A woman is standing on her balcony, breast-feeding a baby. Poverty means life is led in public. These streets are a kind of democracy.

If I'd been born in the West, perhaps my love of the beach would have been tainted by the scenes I've just witnessed. Instead, because that suburb of Havana reminds me so much of being a child, I feel at home swimming in the bluest and warmest waters I've ever seen.

"*Mais por qué? Pagamos con dollares,*" I say.

I'm arguing with the guard at one of the entrances to the Coppelia ice cream park, the 1960s-designed fantasy in tribute to *helado*. They only offer two flavours, strawberry and chocolate, a fact memorialized in the movie of the same name.

"*Allí, allí,*" the guard says and points us to a small enclosure just inside the gate.

Coppelia is one of the only places where Habaneros can still pay in pesos. Foreigners are penned into the other park the guard is directing us to. The lineup to get into the one place in Havana where there are no tourists to make the Habaneros feel poor can stretch for blocks. Paul tries another approach. He strolls brazenly past a guard with his back turned. I follow.

We're in! We got into the ice cream park! I feel like Bonnie, but contain my guilty excitement lest I tip off the cops.

"*Tienes fresa, por favor?*" I ask once we're sitting down at a little metal table, surrounded by families eating bowls of ice cream.

"*No, chocolate,*" the waiter replies.

"Okay. *Dos chocolates.*"

I give the waiter a twenty-peso bill and he looks at me impatiently and tells me again how much it is. I press another twenty-peso bill into his hand and he hands it back and takes off. I don't understand numbers in Spanish. He comes back with a ridiculous amount of change and we figure out that the ice cream is sold in centavos, so we paid about fourteen cents.

Afterwards, emboldened, we stand on the street corner and wait for a peso taxi-cab to pick us up. They're all old 1950s cars and only stop for locals. None of them stop for us tourists. We'd upset the economics of the peso cabs. Or try and talk Spanish to them, or take too long to understand.

And yet I continue to feel that somehow I fit in here because I grew up in a Second World Communist country just like theirs. Of course I'm a Westerner now. If I wanted to, I could live three months out of the year here quite comfortably with my dollars. I wish I were truly rich and could afford to go to places where I wouldn't be benefiting from people's poverty. I wish that the Cubans wanted us here only to be hospitable, to show us their beautiful country, not because they need our money. I say that I wish, I wish, all these benevolent wishes, but I find myself so annoyed by the constant requests for "*Tienes* dollar, dollar?" that I decide I'm going to answer, "*No, tengo tenedor.*" I have a fork. An insult made harsher by its absurdity. A friend says that when you're in India for the first time, you are shocked by the beggars lining the streets. Soon enough, you learn to slap them away.

Finally we hail a dollar taxi—a newer Russian-made Lada. We're going to a baseball game at el Estadio Latinoamericano. Two pesos for a ticket. Wooden benches line the stadium. The audience is made up mostly of kids and young men. We sit behind a boy and girl about nine years old. The girl looks at the boy every once in a while and strokes his short brown hair. He looks straight ahead and eats peanuts out of a skinny paper cone.

I'm very happy. The stadium reminds me of the pleasures of my childhood, when going to see the circus and buying an ice cream during intermission was happiness. What else do people need but some peanuts, a lovely evening and a baseball game to be content? But paradoxically, all the exhortations of the West to live simply, to stop and enjoy the moment, ring hollow right now. Cubans have no choice but to extract happiness out of few possibilities.

An old man walks around with a blue Thermos. I run after him and ask for whatever it is he's got, handing him a couple of pesos. He gives me back a whack of centavos and, as I try to put them in my pocket, I drop the small paper cup he's made out of some sheets of school paper, and spill the homemade espresso he poured. He gives me another one for free and shakes his head at my ineptitude. And finally, frowned upon by this man, I can put all my judgments and liberal superiority and emotional largesse back into my suitcase to take right back home, because at least this one Cuban has no need of me.

Simona Chiose is the author of Good Girls Do: Sex Chronicles of a Shameless Generation. *She has written on culture, arts, travel and society and has worked as a television producer. She is working on a novel about globalization.*

TWO DAYS IN DALLAS
Charles Wilkins

When bedtime came at perhaps two in the morning, Bob informed me unselfconsciously that I would be sleeping "in the truck." He led me to a grove of cottonwoods where he kept the mouldering eighteen-wheeler in which, twice a week, he drove eight hundred miles round-trip between Dallas and Galveston to fetch bananas for a local transport firm. At the moment, there were forty-thousand pounds of Chiquitas in the trailer, awaiting delivery to the distribution terminal of a Texas supermarket chain. The trailer's refrigeration compressor was thrumming at a volume that obliterated conversation within twenty feet of the vehicle.

"You can go right up there in the back of the cab," Bob shouted. "It's comfy as hell!"

The prophetic words were barely out of his mouth when a deathly sounding wail erupted from the nearby scrub. "That's just Cleo!" Bob hollered. "Rosa cut back her horse meat cause she ain't doin nuthin!"

Cleo, I quickly learned, was a four-hundred-pound Bengal tiger that, in Bob's

Rosa and Bob.

27

words, "had had a cuppa coffee with the circus" but had been shipped back to Texas a month ago because "she had taken half the arm off her groom and was simply too vicious for the act." Cleo had "busted out" twice during the past couple of weeks, but Bob's wife, Rosa, a retired Mexican circus performer, had, both times, gotten her safely back in before she "killed anybody or ate up the dogs." Bob had fixed her cage, he reassured me, and, as we approached it, I could see, sure enough, that its hinges and locks were reinforced with what appeared to be an old coat hanger and a few bent screw nails.

At the truck, I protested that I wouldn't be able to sleep with the din from the compressor, and Bob shouted that I wouldn't even hear it above the truck's engine, which he would turn on in order to run the air conditioner in the cab. "Without it you'll suffocate!" he shouted. "And ya can't have them windows down, or the skeeters'll chaw ya to ratshit!"

All of which is how on a pestilently hot night in mid-August 2001, on a plot of backwater scrub, by a south-Dallas alligator preserve (and within sniffing distance of a famished tiger), I found myself staring forlornly from the window of a twenty-five-year-old Freightliner and eventually drifting into dreamland.

I had arrived in Dallas eight hours earlier, having been summoned to the city by an up-market law firm to give a deposition in a civil suit against a broke and dissolute circus owner whose elephant had killed a young animal groom in Timmins, Ontario, a year earlier.

Not that I know a thing about elephants. But in 1998 I had written about the killer in question in a book about my travels with the Wallenda Circus and was considered marginally less ignorant on the subject than any average cowpoke who might have been hauled in off the street.

I hasten to add that one of the enduring legacies of my time with the circus is my friendship with Bob Gibbs, a 370-pound animal trainer and banana-truck driver who had handled the elephants on the aforementioned travels and who had taken me on as a kind of educational project. Bob had been pestering me for months to visit him, and when the call came to give testimony in what the Dallas press had labelled "the elephant murder," I took it as an opportunity for a social call.

Bob met me at the airport, and when I had collected my luggage, he suggested we drive immediately to a south-Dallas taqueria where we could tank up on enchiladas and, if we were in time, catch the Sunday evening floor show.

Lead on, commander, and off we rattled in Bob's rusty Ford Escort, in the company of Bob's young friend Tony, a Mexican fruit picker who was in the United States illegally, living with nine other aliens in the squalid shack of a south-side used-car lot. Because Tony spoke no English, Bob felt free to tell me in his presence that he was "a bit thick" and that he had been brought into Texas by a Mexican "coyote" whom he was paying off at a rate of twenty dollars a week. One missed payment, Bob confided, meant broken kneecaps, a second "the bullet and the shallow grave."

CLEO HAD "BUSTED OUT" TWICE DURING THE PAST COUPLE OF WEEKS, BUT BOB'S WIFE, ROSA, A RETIRED MEXICAN CIRCUS PERFORMER, HAD, BOTH TIMES, GOTTEN HER SAFELY BACK IN BEFORE SHE "KILLED ANYBODY OR ATE UP THE DOGS."

None of which seemed to affect Tony in the least as he ogled the dancers and scarfed down tortillas crammed with finely chopped pig brains and cow stomach.

When eventually we dropped Tony at the used-car lot, the choice for me was whether to return to the four-star hotel suite that had been rented for me by the law firm or go with Bob to where he lives with Rosa in a tiny trailer on forty dusty acres that are the winter quarters of the fast-fading Clyde Brothers Johnson Circus.

Two roads diverged, as Frost wrote, and I took the one to the winter quarters, where a burned-out elephant barn rotted amidst dozens of derelict circus vehicles— garishly painted trucks, animal cages and house trailers—in an atmosphere that, at one in the morning, was as foreign, fetid and sinister as the hotel suite would have been familiar.

A light flickered in the trailer window where Rosa slept, and as we approached the place, a team of Chihuahuas inside began throwing themselves at the screen door, the sooner to reach Bob and lick the sweaty expanses of his stomach.

While I had expected to stay with Bob and Rosa, I realized on poking my head into the trailer that, with four Chihuahuas, six cats, several tons of circus memorabilia, and three or four weeks of unwashed dishes spread more or less uniformly across the floor, it wouldn't, as they say, be a fit.

"Whatever you do," Bob told me as we relaxed on a pair of defunct car seats in the yard, "don't say anything to Rosa."

"About what?" I said.

"About the way we live," he winced, gesturing with his head toward the trailer. "She's very sensitive about it."

Rosa's sensitivities had already been hammered that afternoon when one of her kittens had "exploded" during an electrical storm as it sat in a tree where it had gone to escape the alligators that occasionally wandered onto the property.

Being a nature lover, Bob was pleased to point out that just a hundred feet away was the north boundary of an unfenced alligator preserve. The gators, fortunately, were little danger to human beings—at least compared to the water moccasins, which emerged regularly from the preserve.

When I regained consciousness in the sleeping compartment of the truck and stuck my head out of the curtains, it was still dark, and we were roaring along a twelve-lane freeway on the way into Dallas. I retreated to my slab of sponge and emerged again only when we had entered the faux-Arctic caverns of Texas's largest food-storage terminal. I climbed from the truck in shorts and a T-shirt, amid union lumpers wearing down jackets, snow boots and toques. The place was perhaps three times the size of the Toronto SkyDome, and was stacked forty feet high with crates of cherries, mangoes and melons; lobster tails, T-bones and hams. We celebrated this abundance in the terminal's windowless snack bunker with a breakfast of instant oatmeal (prepared runny so that it could be consumed without spoons or milk) and pink-iced shirt cardboard whimsically presented as Kellogg's Raspberry Pop-Tarts.

The plan was to spend the day sightseeing with Rosa. However, when we returned to the trailer, she had disappeared with the car. As a result, I spent the better part of the next six hours in a hammock, watching for snakes, dozing fitfully and working up a fiendish appetite in the 103-degree heat. Bob sat nearby, in front of a twenty-four-inch fan, all but naked—a kind of mini Mont Blanc—while Chihuahuas scrambled over his belly and chest. At one point, he shooed the dogs to the ground, fired a two-quart water bottle at the trailer and hollered, "WHERE THE HELL IS THAT WOMAN?"

By the time Rosa appeared at about two p.m., his rage had dissipated, and he protested only mildly when she suggested that rather than beginning our tour right away we seek out an obscure Chicano butcher shop where she had been told she could buy ninety-nine-cent chickens that she intended to stew for the dogs.

We found those chickens after a mere two-hour search, and at about dinner hour Bob and Rosa dropped me at the Crowne Plaza Hotel on Stemmons Freeway, next to Parkland Hospital, where JFK died in 1963. As I climbed from the car, taking care to avoid the unwrapped fowl spread out at my feet under the air conditioning, Rosa called from the back seat that JFK was alive! She was sure of it, having read it in a Mexican tabloid.

"He's living in the Crowne Plaza!" piped Bob, to which Rosa responded that Bob should shut his rude trap, that the matter was between her and me.

At 9:30 that evening, I had coffee in the hotel restaurant with the lawyers who would be grilling me in the morning. They wore golf shirts and Dockers and informed me that their intent in the case was to show that the "killer elephant" was predisposed to violence, in which case her owners could be proven liable in the victim's death. To encourage my complicity, they showed me autopsy photos—horrible things, which would feature in my dreams for weeks to come, and which I told them I hoped would never be seen by the boy's parents.

The hearing the next morning was in a splashy downtown law office, replete with antique furniture and oriental carpets. Four lawyers, each with a million-dollar education, had read my book and seemed prepared to make me dance. But their questions were as dull as dishwater and sometimes downright silly. Did I have "a degree" in writing? Had I ever seen an elephant with a venereal infection?

I sat there thinking about Bob, who had left the farm in Missouri at the age of eleven for a career in the circus. And about Rosa, whose father, a circus clown, had, like the victim in Timmins, been stomped to death by an elephant when she was six years old. Her widowed mother had raised eight children on the proceeds from an "iron jaw" act, in which she did spins and acrobatics while hanging by her teeth in the top of the circus tent. By the age of twelve, Rosa herself was doing "iron jaw" and, by sixteen, had gained passage to America as a trapeze flyer with a troupe called the Flying Padillas.

A pretty, dark-haired court stenographer, tastefully dressed and with spectacular Texas frontage, sat within four feet of me, in such splendid secretarial posture that I could hardly stop glancing at her. When the session ended at noon, she recommended that I spend the hours until my flight at four P.M. visiting Dealey Plaza, site of the Kennedy assassination, where the famed Texas School Book Depository had been made into a tourist museum.

I did so, poring over the surrounding streets and sidewalks, the concourse, the "grassy knoll" and the famous picket fence. I went up into the book depository and stared out the window from where Lee Harvey Oswald—or somebody from some vantage point—had exploded the president's skull with what I was informed was a twelve-dollar rifle and a pair of dumdum bullets.

My cab to the airport cost me sixty dollars and was driven by an ex–Chilean freedom fighter, whose family had been slaughtered by brutes and whose appreciation of Dallas included its hard-assed attitude toward crime.

With an hour to spare at the airport, I phoned relatives in an affluent north-Dallas suburb. They seemed relieved that I was leaving, not arriving and, in the absence of anything to say, offered up a fulsome assessment of the Texas governorship and early presidency of George W. Bush—whose name they pronounced "Buish" or "Bewsh."

I told them I had spent a night in a banana truck in Seagoville, the response to which was that "Bewsh" had done a wonderful job making the state safe from wayward Chicanos and other riff-raff.

I inquired about the shadow that had been cast over Dallas by the assassination, and was informed that the city's shame had been eradicated by a fedora-topped football coach named Tom Landry, who had earned national redemption in the form of a series of NFL championships with the Dallas Cowboys. Even the site of the ignominy, Dealey Plaza and the Texas School Book Depository, had been transformed from a locus of guilt into a National Historic Landmark where the souvenir shop was proud to sell assassination postcards and T-shirts. The paved lot next door was unashamed to offer ASSASSINATION PARKING for approximately the price Oswald had paid for his mail-order rifle.

On a whim I phoned Bob and reached him as he rolled toward Galveston in the banana truck. I told him I'd visited Dealey Plaza, and he said, among other things, that Texas was "the meanest state in the union," and that whatever they had told me downtown, I should not believe for a moment that the assassination had been carried off by "some kookie little commie with a ten-dollar rifle and a couple'a grooved bullets."

I passed through security, thinking about tigers and alligators and water moccasins—and death by elephant and autopsy photos and Mexican "coyotes." And Chilean terror and the wonders of redemption.

I wrote a postcard home, bearing a recipe for "Texas Sweat" chili, and a half hour later was in the air, drowsy as I cruised above the clouds, and then asleep.

A screening agent for Canadian customs had asked me, among other things, if I had "anything to declare."

As a matter of fact I had. But it was not the sort of thing that I could comfortably declare in the Dallas/Fort Worth International Airport.

So I kept it to myself.

Charles Wilkins is the author of several books including The Circus at the Edge of the Earth *and* A Wilderness Called Home. *He lives in Thunder Bay, Ontario, where he is at work on a book about his 2002 walk from Thunder Bay to New York City.*

HER EYES FOLLOW
Camilla Gibb

I'm squatting in a white hallway, waiting in line for my medication—"Smartie time," the Glaswegian woman with the greasy hair ahead of me calls this nightly ritual. I'm turning my hands over and over, staring at the black of my palms, when the woman behind me interrupts my private agonizing to ask me how I burned my hands. I'm about to object, I'm working up to words:

They're not burnt. It's henna. Henna that my friend Nuria and I darkened with gasoline and then slathered on our palms and the soles of our feet so that we would look beautiful at her sister Nimute's wedding. We were bridesmaids last week, veiled and ululating in a city in the eastern highlands of Ethiopia.

I don't speak it—the story just sounds too implausible, like the stories of all the other people here. *Last week I was a bridesmaid. This week I am crazy.*

In the brief journey between the walls of an Ethiopian city and those of an English psychiatric hospital, I am alone. I take airplanes, drink much wine, compensating for a year of abstinence; blurring the passage and the borders between worlds as the blues and oranges of East Africa morph into the crushing, familiar grey that is Oxford, that is home.

Tulu and Biscutti.

Home is a swamp waiting to swallow. I've been neck deep in its mud before—depressed enough to have been hospitalized, wild enough to be diagnosed manic, depressed and wild enough that when I left to spend a year in Ethiopia to conduct anthropological fieldwork for my Ph.D. thesis I took two duffle bags: one full of clothes, the other full of pills because they didn't have lithium where I was going.

I've been back for a day now and I walk around Sainsbury's with the boyfriend who has waited for me all this time. I cry at the sight of chickens—pasty poultry suffocating under plastic—frozen vegetables, foul-mouthed toddlers, and fluorescent lights. I think of ritualized slaughter, halal meat stewed with fenugreek, peppers and pumpkins taken from the fertile earth beyond the city walls. Women huddled over a fire, food shared between hands. The fights that would break out over whose turn it was to suck the marrow from the bone. In the first month, that honour was mine, but for the next eleven, no longer a guest, I had to fight like everyone else.

Ted is beside me, and there is Marmite and Earl Grey tea and pasteurized milk for miles, but life's former essentials seem unnecessary now, unwanted.

We carry our bags full of pathetic vegetables down our street, passing door after closed door. Life here is the weak light behind shutters, the faint smell of cooking oil, graffiti and broken car-windows, and the footsteps of men making their way to the damp pub at the bottom of the hill. It begins to rain an English rain and I know that as tedious and protracted as this drizzle will be, my tears will outlast it—they will last through the night and into the next day when I have an out-patient appointment at the psychiatric hospital because my lithium levels have not been read in over a year.

I am resuming a weekly ritual from which I had been spared during my time in Ethiopia, the ritual of a crazy person. I am trying to explain to the row of doctors in front of me that I am not crying because I am crazy, but because I'm suffering from something that anthropologists call "reverse culture shock"—the disorientation of returning to your own culture as an alien.

"Does it look bleak? Does it look hopeless?" they ask.

"Honestly? Yes it does. It looks terribly sad, devoid of any colour, all meaning."

The switch in worlds is unequivocally abrupt, so devastating that I am breaking up into pixels, stretched across oceans, unable to reconcile being here and being there. I tell the truth: I say things that an anthropologist, a traveller, a dreamer, a refugee or immigrant might understand. But these are doctors, not travellers. This is psychiatry, not poetry. I am mentally ill, not heartbroken and disoriented. *Last week I was a bridesmaid. This week I am crazy.*

Three hundred people are crammed into a domed shrine to celebrate the miracles of the patron saint of the city of Harar. We are awake and buzzing; drumming, clapping and chanting our way through a monotonous series of religious verses into the wee hours of the morning. We are fuelled by *qat*—green leaves that when chewed have the effect of a mild narcotic—cut earlier in the day from squat bushes on the farms surrounding the city. We have masticated leaves stuck between our teeth, green film accumulating at the corners of our mouths; we have reached the state of *mirqana*. We are high.

The men drip with sweat as they beat drums, and some of the women, who dance together on the other side of the room, have reached a state of near-ecstasy—hissing through their front teeth, their eyes rolling backwards, they spin circles, lose balance, fall into the crowd, which gently pushes them upright and back into the circle so they can continue.

As high as I am, I'm taking notes. I am an anthropologist, and this is my job. I'm studying the religious practices of members of a community known for feeding hyenas and worshipping saints. I am veiled, abstinent, conversant in Arabic, and increasingly in Harari, the local language. I'm an aberration, the only foreigner for miles with the exception of a scattering of Somali refugees.

Fatima, my "mother," localizes me by giving me a name: Aziza Mohammed. The girls my age laugh and tell me it is very old-fashioned. They have trendy names like Orit and Titune. I've been adopted into Fatima's cluster of twelve children. She and her sisters and all their female children eat, sleep and pray together in one room; her husband, Mohammed, and their sons in another. There is little interaction between these two rooms; the world is cleaved in half. I am a girl by definition because I am unmarried. I must observe a curfew, I must wear a veil outside the household compound, I must not be alone with a man.

Somewhere though, somewhere under this veil, there is a woman who used to be me. The one who lives with her boyfriend in England, struggles with sanity, drinks too many pints at the pub and wears short skirts and steel-toed boots. They don't want her here, and I certainly don't want her here. Several months into this and I've all but forgotten her and the place she comes from. The one reminder that she is still here somewhere is the 1,200 milligrams of lithium I have to remember to feed her every day. The essence of *her* is captured in these white pills.

I am not at all depressed here, but I am, like most people who live in the city, chronically ill. There is the brown, intermittent supply of water that the neighbourhood shares. We drink it, we cook with it, we wash dishes in it, we bathe in it and then we throw it out into the street where it trickles downhill and seeps into the ground. We throw waste into the street as well, including animal remains, trusting that the hyenas roaming the city at night will have licked the pavement clean by morning.

We eat stew that has been made with the brown water. Four or eight or ten of us break pieces with our right hands from a large, unleavened bitter pancake—*injera*—over which the stew has been poured. We scoop it up with pieces of *injera*, pop these morsels into our mouths. Breakfast, lunch and dinner—three times a day, every day except Friday when we honour the Prophet and, thanks to a brief Italian occupation of Ethiopia in the 1940s, eat spaghetti (with our hands) for lunch.

There is the square patch of dirt behind the storage shed in our compound where we go to the bathroom, tiptoeing in flip-flops around the fly-covered excrement of our kin. There are flying cockroaches. There is leprosy, TB, hepatitis, HIV. We all have bloated, gaseous bellies and severe diarrhea courtesy of intestinal parasites. We routinely kill the parasites by taking pink pills that are sold singly alongside pieces of chewing gum and individual cigarettes in the makeshift stalls that line the main street.

I get better at interpreting the early signs of parasitic invasion, but I don't always catch it in time. When I fail to, I get dizzy and my vision begins to blur. I assume this happens to everyone, except that on the worst of these occasions, I'm suffering differently. My hands have begun to tremble just like they did in the early days of taking lithium. Lithium is toxic in high doses, and I'm pretty sure the dehydration that results from chronic diarrhea has increased the drug's concentration in my blood. I'm showing all the signs of being poisoned and now I'm scared.

I go to the local hospital in the hope that some form of testing might be possible. I pay the mandatory hospital fee and wait for hours before meeting the doctor—Dr. Abdulhassan Adem, a gentle twenty-four-year-old with an incredible command of English. He has had only one training session in psychiatric illness and no clinical practice in the subject, but he compensates for this with his bedside manner.

He can offer no means of testing my lithium levels, but he listens and empathizes as I reveal a deeply incriminating secret: a mental illness in a country where the crazy are those who sit alongside the lepers and beg on the streets. I am telling him something about the woman I left behind, the woman who has no place here, the woman under this veil.

His kindness is enough to make me feel calmer, and feeling calmer, I realize the only option is to simply stop taking lithium for a while. Bring on the depression—I'd rather take that risk than die here from blood poisoning.

Abdulhassan. Exceedingly handsome, six foot two, as black as black can be, with a soft voice that contradicts his size. He wears a grey suit under his white coat, and proper laced-up shoes as opposed to the flip-flops I wear and think of as national dress. *Abdulhassan.* Back in his hometown after four years of medical training at Addis Ababa university. A local boy done good. He dreams of doing specialized training in pediatrics in the United States. He's preparing for exams he's going to take in

Nuria and Sara.

39

Cairo in a year's time, the final stage in a scholarship competition for African doctors. He's made it this far; he thinks he stands a chance.

I am sick for a week and a half as the lithium leaves my blood. I want to lie in the dark with a sheet over my head, sleep in silence, daydream about Abdulhassan, but this is not the Harari way. No, to be alone is to invite evil spirits, so the women in the neighbourhood keep me company, sit around my prostrate body, sing songs together, weave baskets, burn incense, sort through grains. A tiny girl from the neighbourhood, whom they call Biscutti, crawls over me, tickles me, hides under the sheet.

Fatima tells me the reason I am sick is because when I first arrived I did not wear trousers under my skirts. Someone must have resented my bare skin and cursed me with the evil eye. Tariqa, her sister, tells me the reason I am sick is because I am not Muslim enough. She throws a prayer rug down and points in the direction of Mecca. "But I'm not Muslim at all," I protest weakly. "When then?" they shout. "You're sick! What more proof do you need?"

Finally I feel better, and much to my relief, my mood hasn't plummeted. I am eager to get back to work. I'm interviewing local midwives now, trying to gain some understanding of whether they consider the female circumcision they perform to be part of Muslim practice.

I start by interviewing the one midwife I know: Biscutti's grandmother. Biscutti and her mother are supported by the grandmother's paltry income and the three of them are desperately poor. They love Biscutti, but she is clearly suffering from malnutrition. I often find her sitting alone in the road during the day eating dirt. She must be about two and a half years old but she hasn't started speaking yet, she doesn't play with other children, she still breast-feeds and has open wounds on her face that refuse to heal.

She's taken to spending a couple of hours with me nearly every day. I give her crayons, fill buckets with hot water that I've warmed over the fire so she can bathe. She's aggressive, a wordless holy terror, eating crayons, splashing water and tearing up my notebooks when I'm not looking. She leaves for home when she realizes that no amount of tugging on my breast is going to yield the milk she needs.

The sores on her face get worse, not better. It's been two months since I've seen

Dr. Abdulhassan, but I decide to take Biscutti to him. He gives me some antibiotic ointment to apply twice a day, and while I hold her, he paints her face with purple anaesthetic. We have this baby between us and I cannot help but think: *Abdulhassan. If you and I had a baby would she be as beautiful as this?*

He invites me to a *bercha'a* on the weekend, a *qat* party, where people recline on pillows, drink tea, tell stories and chew their way into *mirqana*.

I think about him for the rest of the week. *What if we married? Would I become a real Harari? What if we adopted Biscutti and went back to my home country, Canada, and you could be a doctor there?*

The *bercha'a* at his house is a sultry affair. It is conducted in a hidden room because the company is mixed sex, young men and women, highly charged. It is conducted in the dark because Abdulhassan has something very rare: a television

I AM SICK FOR A WEEK AND A HALF AS THE LITHIUM LEAVES MY BLOOD. I WANT TO LIE IN THE DARK WITH A SHEET OVER MY HEAD, SLEEP IN SILENCE, DAYDREAM ABOUT ABDULHASSAN, BUT THIS IS NOT THE HARARI WAY.

and a VCR. We watch an American thriller, the name of which I forget because all I am conscious of is Abdulhassan, cross-legged and breathing beside me in the dark.

When the lights come on, we talk about my work with midwives. Abdulhassan does not believe in female circumcision. He believes it only causes harm and that it has no basis in Islam. He believes, as I believe, that the answer lies not in preaching or prohibiting it, but in educating women so that they have ways to achieve status other than through being wives and mothers. He offers to accompany me on visits to the midwives I have not been able to interview because they speak Oromo, a neighbouring language, which Abdulhassan speaks.

We do interviews together every Saturday after that, and at the house of the last Oromo midwife I interview, I marvel at Abdulhassan's tenderness as he strokes the foreheads of two girls who have just undergone the operation. Their legs are tied together to prevent them from moving and to promote the formation of scar tissue. Their requests for water are denied because it's best if they urinate as little as possible. Each has had her clitoris and labia minora removed with a razor blade, her labia majora scraped out and sewn together with a row of thorns. There is a matchstick held in place between her labia, so there will at least be a small hole out of which her urine, and eventually her menstrual blood can flow. On her wedding night, her husband will force himself through this barrier that has kept his bride a virgin. Abdulhassan tells the two girls they are brave and I feed them honey by the spoonful.

At his *bercha'a* the next day, he finds my hand in the dark. His hand is large and warm. He writes a note: *I love you.* I write back: *I love you too.* We cannot speak. In fact, we will not ever speak because we are not simply in love, we are in love with things far more complicated than each other.

And I am leaving soon. I'm taking lithium again, preparing for re-entry. Preparing to become my English self again. I'm snapping photos of people, wanting to take them with me. Many of them actually ask me to, say, "Take me with you. Sponsor me. Get me a visa." I try not to make promises I cannot keep. Some people treat me as if I have already left; Biscutti, for instance, has stopped coming to visit. Her mother, Tulu, says it's because she knows I'm leaving. *But how can she know?*

"Because you're taking her photograph," Tulu says. "Don't leave her. Take her to England with you."

When I tell Tulu that I can't take her daughter from her, she responds with an accusation. "You don't really love her," she says.

"She's being realistic," Abdulhassan says later. "She wants a better life for her child. And you could give her that."

Realistic? The only way I can imagine this reality is if we married and adopted Biscutti together. We could be black and white, Harari, African, Muslim, English, Canadian. Hybrids, hyphenated, our disparate worlds joined. I can think of no other way of holding all this together, containing Biscutti and you and me—both the veiled and unveiled—in one place.

In reality, the Canadian embassy says, "Not a chance. She has parents, both alive." I lamely defer to government in order to sanction my relief, though my guilt will never be assuaged. I go home and sink into a swamp, perhaps in lieu of having to feel fractured and sad and nowhere while I wait in the vain hope that my heart and my happiness will follow me from Africa. What I am left with are these hands, hennaed for a wedding where I was a bridesmaid a week before returning home.

Biscutti remains a fixed image of sad eyes, and Abdulhassan never leaves Ethiopia. He doesn't get the scholarship to study medicine in the United States. What he gets instead is very religious and very married. We continue to write, signing our letters with love, because there is no better word in either of our languages. It is as simple as that, and as complicated.

Camilla Gibb has lived in England, Canada, Egypt and Ethiopia, and has a Ph.D. in social anthropology from the University of Oxford. Her first novel, Mouthing the Words, *has been published in fourteen countries and was the winner of the 2000 City of Toronto Book Award. Her second novel,* The Petty Details of So-and-so's Life, *was published in September 2002. She lives in Toronto and is currently at work on a novel set in North Africa.*

ON THE ROAD TO SAN ROCCO A PILLI
Michael Redhill

In the springtime of 1998, we were pregnant with our first child. Anne was in her second trimester, big but not giant, always hungry but an enemy of all foods shiny, flaky or smelly. Still, this wasn't enough of a threat to make us hesitate about going to Italy, a country we'd romanticized for years, our imaginings hung with crusty bread, golden oil, old ladies in black dresses who waved sadly to us from stone windows, cookies so hard they could snap your front teeth. We had friends in Florence who were on an art exchange, and we met them there, hung out at their haunts with their worldly friends and ate their newly learned cuisine (ah, *panna*, I hardly knew ye). And in a tiny rented car, we all headed out for the Tuscan countryside for a week of exploring.

Tuscany trumped our imaginings: our fantasies of old-world charm crumbled before its reality. It was sun-soaked, redolent of fruit and fields, and we wandered through it, struck numb with pleasure. Our friends indulged themselves in rock climbing and painting; we went for rambling walks in olive groves. We'd come up the incline of one such grove only to see the vista ahead of us: more hillside groves. More olives than there are stars in the heavens. We stayed at an *agriturismo* that had on

45

its grounds a little customs house where Michelangelo once spent a night. Inside there were fading frescoes on stone walls, art no one would ever catalogue or preserve. And three parrots at large flying around the high walls.

We'd all read about Cortona, a hill town with two disconnected town squares that rose high above the Tuscan plain, and we headed out there early one morning and ended up spending most of the day wandering its alleys and cobblestone streets. An ancient, half-crumbling wall surrounded the town, a grey Etruscan wall meant to keep out the Romans. As we walked higher, into thinner air, the valley below receded into a landscape of churches and stone buildings, views that hadn't changed very much since the Etruscans had taken them in. To be walking in that history, the clonking of cowbells below the ancient walls, put us all in a reverie. A man who looked older than the four of us put together walked past us at a clip and with a warm smile said something to the two women; a typical gesture of Italian *amichev-olezza*. We wanted to wish him a good day as well, and asked our friend's husband to say something to that effect in Italian, but since the old man had actually told the women they had great legs, our friend held his tongue.

Being together, under the bright spring sun, supping in hole-in-the-wall restaurants and drinking unlabelled wine: it couldn't get much better than this.

Unfortunately, it was to end prematurely. Our friends, both felled by the flu, decided they'd better head home. We sadly bid them goodbye at the nearest train station and struck out for San Rocco a Pilli, where we'd stay and continue to tour the area. As we pulled away, the pathetic fallacy swooped in: the skies darkened and followed us west.

I'm remembering this now, so don't quote me, although I can quote myself: "We started on our epic adventure to find San Rocco a Pilli—ten kilometres from Siena, but it might as well have been on the moon." This is our diary—my physician-like handwriting alternating with Anne's crisp, light script. There is no mention of how long we spent that afternoon trying to find San Rocco, nor is there even a word of the sight we came upon while lost on those Italian roads, a sight that now remains in my mind as one of the most beautiful I've ever encountered. After the word "moon," Anne takes over: "We managed to avoid a fight by visiting the local co-op in god-knows-where for some fruit and mortadella, then we drove through a rain-soaked porch-green landscape."

It had begun to rain, and what looked like just a few miles on the map opened out into a long drive through territory that didn't agree with what the map showed. We drove, stubbornly, unwilling to believe we could get lost in such a minimalist landscape. The longer we drove, the steamier the car got. An incipient hunger was threatening to turn into a sugar crash for Anne: she couldn't go long between meals because of the baby's seeming ravenousness.

She'd finished off the last of the blood oranges (tiny fruits streaked with gory red that looked like they'd taste of grapefruit but were like honey on the tongue) and the hunger was building quickly. Rain pounded the little car. We began to fight: we were lost in the countryside under weather neither of us wanted to stop in, with a disaster in the making. For some reason the gods were angry at us. I dug in, "knowing" San

MORE OLIVES THAN THERE ARE STARS IN HEAVEN. WE STAYED AT AN *AGRITURISMO* THAT HAD ON ITS GROUNDS A LITTLE CUSTOMS HOUSE WHERE MICHELANGELO ONCE SPENT A NIGHT.

Rocco was close by. She kept her eyes to the grey weather. Another ten minutes crept by. Finally, a little country town appeared off the road—Radi—the first we'd seen in quite some time. It squatted there amongst the fields like a mirage, dotted with playgrounds and laid out in black streets. A little mall with a grocery store. We got out and dashed inside, mingling with the wet-coated strangers there, the scent of dank wool and muddy boots filling the place. We grabbed bread and meat and more fruit. Our day was so different than the one everyone else there was having: in from the fields, breaking from work or bringing the kids home for lunch, this was just one stop (one made probably every day) in a set ritual of activities, like anywhere else in the world. Its familiarity was as comforting as it was odd. Yes, this was Italy, but it was also a place where people lived with no mind to the uniqueness of the place. Why this struck me I don't know. At base it was probably a sentimental wonderment, a gee-whiz moment, but it made the place seem peculiarly layered. That it could be exotic to me but just home to others. We paid for our groceries. When we stepped outside, the rain had lifted, although the air was cool with it: mountain air. We got back into the car, rolled down the windows and left the parking lot without asking a soul where we could find San Rocco a Pilli.

We had the good sense to feel silly for getting so worked up over nothing, although it's always *nothing* with its barbs and poisons that threatens us. Anne speedily built a sandwich of fresh bread and mortadella and bolted it down to the baby and then settled back against the seat, sated and relieved. I continued to drive as if I knew where I was going. We had figured out, at least, that we had allowed a vaguely slanting road to mislead us west rather than north. We traced this road back to the fatal turnoff, reversing the mood mercifully back to square one. We then took the other vaguely slanting road, the one I'd confidently rejected, and immediately saw the signs for San Rocco a Pilli. Still ten kilometres. To the east and west, the last of the Tuscan hillsides were giving way to flatter topography, opening into long vistas.

The rain and the after-rain light had turned the fields an almost unnatural green. Stretching away from the road were rows of watercress the colour of childhood's unmown grass, a green that would smell of chlorophyll even if you were only looking at a picture of it. We'd seen fields like this before, of course; both of us had been to Ireland in the height of summer. But it was the context of these fields, their peacefulness after the storm, how the deluge had been nourishment, not a threat. And then, at a distance, but not so far away that it was swallowed up in the landscape, we saw a lone tree. Decidedly deciduous, vegetal as perfectly cooked broccoli, the trunk slightly tilted, a moment of lush imperfection in the midst of all this green order, and the sky above it suddenly harrowed like the fields below, light pouring down. Why the appearance of a single tree should have riveted us the way this did, I don't think I'll ever be able to explain. But after driving past it, we stopped the car, did a three-pointer and, in silent agreement, drove back.

What it takes us to stop and actually see something is made of circumstances we cannot prepare in advance. Perhaps it's the moments that stand out of the welter of official history and landscape that become totemic. This tree was in no book, there had been no signs that pointed us to it. If any one of those shoppers back in Radi had driven along that road at that moment, it quite possibly would have meant something to them: a clear memory of home or childhood or harvest. For myself, I think it was simply its quiet resonance: this riot of life with the archetype of its beauty and power growing in the midst of it. And us in the car, in the middle of a place we didn't belong to no matter how much we admired it, with the unnamed future unfolding in Anne's body. Somehow, this unadorned tableau expressed the connection between all these things for me. But only in that moment. Only after our sick friends had to go home, only after a rainstorm and an argument, only after a narrow escape from dangerous hunger. At any other moment, it would have just been a tree in a field.

We stood outside of the car in the rain-cooled air and stared at it. I still don't know what kind of tree it was. When we finally got back in and continued driving, it took us only ten more minutes to reach San Rocco a Pilli. It was where it had always been. That night, we drifted off to the sounds of the village bells. They floated out over the fields and joined the carillons in other towns, in Siena, in Radi, in Cortona, these peals presiding over the whole countryside, linking the three of us to everyone else in their soundings.

Michael Redhill is a poet, playwright and novelist. His first novel, Martin Sloane, *was published in 2001 and won the Commonwealth Writers' Prize for Best First Book (Canada/Caribbean). His collection of short stories,* Fidelity, *will be published in spring 2003. He lives in Toronto with his partner and two sons.*

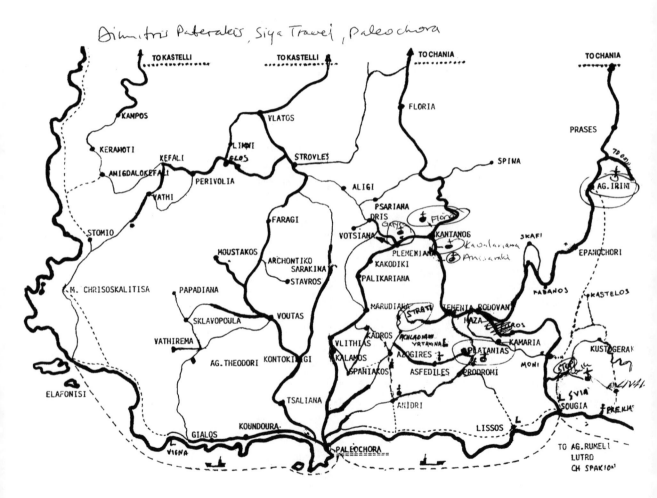

LOOKING FOR DEMETRIUS
Myrna Kostash

Chania, Crete

I sit in the quiet little bar of the Kriti Hotel, sipping an *ouzo*, baptizing this trip. Up in my room, my travelling icon sits propped up against an east wall. When I commissioned it from the iconographer in Edmonton, she laid out her art books in her studio, showing several different versions of St. Demetrius, and instructed me to choose one. What did I know? I liked the one where he didn't seem so much of a soldier and looked more like a saint, sweet-faced and mild of gesture.

On my icon, he is young and pretty, beardless, with thick hair tucked behind his ears. He wears the tunic and cloak of a Byzantine army officer and holds a round shield and long-armed cross. He died young, speared through his right breast, in the basement of the Roman baths in the northern Greek city of Thessalonica, for the crime of preaching the Gospel of Jesus Christ. This was in the year 304, and he was going to become one of the most powerful saints in all of Christendom.

I found him in a book. I was reading about Byzantium, the civilization that radiated

The symbol for a church—the cross-on-ball.

51

for a thousand years from its home in Constantinople throughout the eastern Mediterranean world, including God-guarded Thessalonica, the glory of the northern Aegean.

In Thessalonica, Demetrius was martyred and hastily buried in the red earth of the baths. Gradually the little shrine marking the spot fell into ruin, the relics disappeared and, after a time, the details of his life and death vanished from living

memory. In the early seventh century, Greece was invaded by wave upon wave of barbarians, mainly Slavs, who didn't stop until they got all the way to the Peloponnese. But there was one prize they never did take: the city of Thessalonica. They besieged and assaulted its walls and gates to no avail.

The city was impregnable: the Great Martyr and Holy Warrior Demetrius had come back, riding his red horse on the ramparts, his green cloak billowing in a heavenly breeze, to perform the miracle of the defence of the city. They say he is still there, at rest in a magnificent silver casket, in the nave of a grand basilica on one of the busiest avenues of the city, still performing his miracles for the faithful.

I was moved by the story, even aroused. In the 1980s I travelled repeatedly in eastern and central Europe, locating within those still-Communist countries heartbreaking stories of dissident artists and political rebels, mainly young men, whose desperate defiance of brute authority evoked in me a swooning kind of solidarity with their struggle. Communism, and their sacrifices, passed out of history. But now here was another of their beautiful and doomed company, a saint of the Orthodox Church.

As a third-generation Ukrainian Canadian in Alberta, I spent an entire childhood and youth in and out of St. John's Ukrainian Orthodox church in Edmonton. Now, in my travels, wherever there is an Orthodox church in the remnants of Byzantine Europe—Greece, Bulgaria, Macedonia, Serbia—I find myself in it, taking a kind of

This way to the Archangel.

rest in the homely peace that settles over me as I sniff the phantom whiffs of incense and beeswax, gazing at the icons who gaze back at me, and mumbling the few lines of text I know from the hymns and prayers of the liturgy.

So if Demetrius is a saint venerated by Orthodox Christians, he is a saint for me too. In November 2000, I decided to look for him in his homeland among the Greeks.

I began in Chania, wondering if Demetrius could possibly be a forerunner of these Greeks, of these Cretans, of the mustachioed men smoking furiously at the baggage carousel, of the travellers inserting phone cards—"Sofia! I am at the airport!"—of the policeman blowing his whistle regularly and inconsequentially at the airport traffic, of the worker painting "impressions of Knossos" on panels in the hotel lobby, tuning into Harry Belafonte on the hotel radio.

They once were Byzantines, these Cretans, and some of their towns and villages, Lissos, Souya, Anopoli, Leutro, Hora Sfakion, Kantanos, are sites of ecclesiastical and archaeological treasures from the spread of Christianity. This much I learn at the Byzantine museum into which I have slipped on a somnolent Sunday. There are bits and pieces of frescoes rescued from disintegrating churches, and on one panel I can make out two military figures in chain-mail vests, blue cloaks clipped at the throat. St. Theodore, holding a spear in his right hand, is the better preserved; all that is visible of St. Demetrius is his bare head, his brown hair curling at the neck, framed by the golden halo of his distinction. I am relieved that his small, well-formed ears are intact: the ears—or at least the earlobes—of saints on icons must always be showing, Marianna, the iconographer, had told me. "The whole purpose is for the saints to hear our prayers and take them to heaven."

Paleochora, Crete

November 8, St. Demetrius's day on the old calendar.

It's because I've seen the fresco in the Chania museum and learned it comes from a church of St. George near Kantanos that I seek the help of the only travel agent who is still operating this time of year. She has no idea how I might find this particular church; I need a guide and they are all off, now that it is November. I should come back in May. Between lazy puffs on a cigarette, she is posting the exchange rates on a kind of tablet. May? Who knows where I'm going to be in May?

I loiter in the little office, examining brochures. Under a pane of glass on the counter, I examine a map of the district around Paleochora, noting the symbol for a church—the cross-on-ball—all over the countryside hereabouts. The agent sends me down the street to the photo shop. The shopkeeper, she says, is selling a book about the area's Byzantine monuments. I rush over. The book, outsize and richly illustrated, a project of a historical preservation society in Kantanos, costs me almost forty dollars. I carry it back excitedly to the travel agent. She is no longer there, but her husband is, and he writes out for me a text in Greek: "I want to visit the church of St. George. How do I get there?" I am to show this at the *kafenion* in Floria, just north of Kantanos.

Kantanos, Crete

The bus from Paleochora to Floria was packed with the faithful going to the church of St. Michael the Archangel, today being his day, I guess. I sit in the sun that has sprung up from behind the hill across from this no-name café where I have disembarked, sipping my *metrio*, feeling pleased that I have made myself understood to the proprietor: *Tha ithela na pao sto Ayios Yiorgos. Apo pou?* I can see the church, blazingly white in the dun fields.

I walk over and step inside. There are no windows, only crude holes carved through the thick stone in the east wall and in the apse. So pushing open the creaky, narrow wooden doors has the effect of turning on a flashlight in a cave. It is a small vaulted room furnished with iconostasis, lectern, a cross-stitched icon of St. George—"the gift of Dimitra Lionaki, this year." The glory of this little space is the much-abused frescoes, cemented over in spots, gouged and pitted and scoured by time or design, with here and there the ochre of a cape, a horse's flank, the gilt of a crown and halo, the piercing gaze, all that is left of a prophet, the soft mouth and moustache, all that is left of a king, showing through the ravages. I can make out Demetrius's cherubic mouth upturned in a little smile, and the coiffure of curls framing his face, but the eyes have been torn out.

Back at the café, I learn, just in the nick of time, that it is not possible to return to Kantanos by taxi, only by bus—yikes, here it comes!—and my host makes a gallant flying leap into the bus's path to make it stop for me.

On a country road near Kantanos, I almost walk by the crudely lettered little sign tilted on a fence gate that tells me "this way to the Archangel." I creep down a stony path, ducking under the netting strung out to catch the ripening olives, and into the pristine courtyard of St. Michael's. The local worshippers have been and gone—I smell the dissipating wafts of incense even as I open the door. The interior is as clean as the parish ladies could make it, with fresh newspaper under the glass jars of fading yellow chrysanthemums that line the window sill, and a newly ironed, pure white altar cloth embroidered with the Byzantine motif of the double-headed eagle. (Ah, but they missed the little bit of cobweb dangling in a corner of the window.)

Even though the walls are heavy with the darkened pigment of the Middle Ages, all is lightness here, as if the Angel found the celebration in this modest church among the farms so much to his liking that he has decided to stay awhile. I can make out the frescoed figures easily. Although my poor Demetrius has had his face half gouged out of the plaster and thrown away (Turks? Iconoclasts?), his shoulders still bear an exhilarating amount of drapery blowing in the breath of wind. "Who are you?" I ask in a kind of prayer. "Where are you leading me? Show me a miracle." I feel a tenderness, standing as I am within the merciful gaze of a young man who had once been a fellow human being and to whom whole villages and cities prayerfully entrust the miracle of their salvation. He rides his red horse on their ramparts, defending their faith.

And so it goes, all day long, an itinerary of Byzantine chapels. I rest at each one, staring at images of St. Demetrius, or what is left of him, in profound silence except for the occasional faraway bleat of sheep and goats that reaches me from behind the splutter of beeswax tapers, which are always alight in these chapels. I step outside: birds and the wild blooming of geranium, and the soft breeze up from the valley. I sniff the end-of-season roses as I walk along pathways shaded by olive trees. I cannot be farther away from the rest of my life.

Temenia, Crete

From Elena, the forbearing travel agent in Paleochora, who is doing a bit of freelance research of her own, I have learned of other Demetrius churches in another direction altogether. And so I march over to the town's only taxi office and hire a driver, young Yiorgo, for a day's outing. He of the little spoken English and I of the less Greek do manage to communicate. "*To Ayios Dimitrios church in Moni, parakalo!*" And off we go, a bottle of water and bag of pistachio nuts on the seat between us.

We fail utterly to find the church in the valley between Moni and Livada, despite Elena's annotated map showing us where to look. "In the olive grove at the end of the road," turns out to be unhelpful. Yiorgo is sure he knows exactly where it is, and where we first stop looks promising: a well-kept, shaded grove, a rocky pathway marked by a bit of a grotto, and then nothing. We walk around peering through branches, squatting for another perspective, standing on boulders to see farther. No telltale flash of white church plaster to be seen. And yet when we climb up from the river bottom to the very apex of the neighbouring mountain, we see several splotches of white down in the valley from which we have just ascended. Damn.

The drive has taken us way up to an elevation alongside the magisterial White Mountains of the Cretan interior. We make our way over stony roads, winding around mountainsides of boulders, that link the villages. Bits of precious earth, ground up between the rocks, clutch the exhausted roots of spiny bushes and dying trees. Then down we go, hurtling seaward—it glints metallically from every direction—until we hit hardtop again.

As we climb into the town of Temenia, coming the other way in a battered green car is the priest of the St. Demetrius church of Moni himself, Father Panayiotis. We stop in the middle of the road so that he and Yiorgo can have a chat, hanging out the car windows, while traffic piles up behind us. Yiorgo explains that we have not found his church but that this Canadian in the car is hoping to speak with him about it. I push my face forward over Yiorgo's shoulder so Father Panayiotis can have a good look at my earnest expression. It is decided that we will pull off the road and convene in the nearest café, a charmless establishment of unpainted cement floors and a scattering of chairs pushed up against the scabby walls. A young man sits at a window, watching us with bemusement; another arrives to pick up his newspaper and winks at us.

As I set up the tape recorder, I become aware of the hum of the ice cream cooler, but I cannot prevail on Father Panayiotis to sit with Yiorgo and me at our table. He has leaned up definitively against the opposite wall, tilting back in the chair, as though to be at the farthest possible reach from me and my microphone, which I now stick out into the several metres of space between us, hoping for the best. He's wearing baggy soldier's pants and army boots under his worn-out dark-blue cassock. His hands are stubby and calloused, and I wonder just how reverential I am expected to be. He can't be more than thirty.

I have enlisted Yiorgo as co-interviewer and supplied him with the basic questions I can manage in my pidgin Greek. *Who was St. Demetrius? How do you celebrate St. Demetrius's feast day around here?* He's scribbled them out for himself on a small piece of paper, which he grips with a kind of terror. Father Panayiotis's thick hands chop the air around him as he speaks rapidly, loudly, non-stop. I am at the other end of the microphone, oblivious.

This is what he is saying: "St. Demetrius and the Romans struggled with each other. He was in the Roman army but refused to collaborate with the Romans in their persecution of the Christians. He was very young when he was brought to trial and executed. He was tortured, which is why he is a martyr. He died for his beliefs. That is why Thessalonica has him as its protector. He helped Constantinople in its times of trouble too. In Salonica's times of trouble, the people saw the saint as a horseman [mumbling]. That's all I know. If you want to know more—how he lived, where he grew up and studied—you have to do research.

"[mumbling] The reason the people go to the church is that they believe, not just to please their parents or the priest or their neighbours. [He keeps repeating:] They go for the saint."

Sweet martyr Dimitri, whose bones, they say, exude an aromatic oil that has healed the sick and dying, body and soul. Later in the afternoon, when Yiorgo and I are driving back through Temenia, we see Father Panayiotis again, priest of Livada, Souya, Kostogeraki and Moni, cutting up wood with a chainsaw by the side of the road, tossing logs around like bowling pins.

When I pack up, ready to leave Paleochora, I leave my icon to the last, as though it is important that St. Demetrius supervise every one of my gestures, reciprocating the contemplative hours I've spent looking at him. He's a presence: not in the paint on the wood or on the plaster walls but *behind* the image, an intense energy that is merely using the exquisite lines and hues of the picture to send his sweetness out to me.

1) Γιατί η εκκλησία ονομάστηκε Άγιος Δημήτριος

2) Ποιος ήταν ο Άγιος Δημήτριος (την ιστορία του).

3) Πώς γιορτάζουν την γιορτή του.

4) Ποιος Άγιος Δημήτριος είναι και γιατί έγινε Άγιος

5) ΠΟΟΟΟ ΚΑΙΡΟ ΕΧΕΤΕ ... ΓΙΟΡΤΗ ΤΟΥ ΔΗΜΙΤΡΙΟΥ - ΤΙ ΧΛΕΝΕ ΕΧΕΙΣ; - ΤΙ ΑΝΘΡΩΠΗ ΕΧΕΙΣ ΤΟΥ ΕΚΛΗΟΙΑΣ ΠΟΟ ΕΝΟΟΙΘΗΣ ΟΗΜΕΡΑ ΧΡΗΟΤΙΑΝΟΙ ΟΤΟ ΧΟΡΙΟ

Mirna Kostash
Kanada, Ortodoks, writer

Yiorgo's scribbled questions.

Weeks later in Thessalonica, I am in a *taverna*, tapping my foot to music from Greek films. Niko, the proprietor, is a particular fan of Melina Mercouri. While he cooks my supper—lamb chops and garlic cloves sizzle in the pan—he circles my table, pouring the house *retsina* into my small glass tumbler. He seems about twenty-five years old, but on a small shelf by the door, he has arranged an old oil lamp, an ancient water pipe, and a bleached cloth as though he has laid out a shrine to the irretrievable past.

I tell Niko what I'm doing here: haunting the Basilica of St. Demetrius and prowling through religious bookstores. For a break, I visited the Museum of Byzantine Civilization, I tell him, and chatted with the young security guard. In front of a case of silver reliquaries in which pilgrims bore away with them the *lythron*, the soil mixed with the holy blood from the tomb of St. Demetrius, the guard told me shyly that once, and only once, when he was praying in the basilica, he smelled the sweetest smell, as though he were standing inside a rose bush, and he knew he was in the presence of the saint.

Niko leans against the door frame of the kitchen. He's not surprised, he says. While paying their respects in the crypt of the basilica, both his grandfather and father heard the clangorous hoof-beats of St. Demetrius's horse clattering over the stones as he descended from the city walls. He has been riding there forever.

Full-time writer Myrna Kostash lives in Edmonton but is a persistent traveller to eastern and southeastern Europe. She has followed St. Demetrius around Bulgaria, Macedonia, Serbia and Istanbul as well as Greece.

BUS RIDE TO BIG JESUS
Rick Maddocks

Standing on the baking tarmac of the bus station outside Guanajuato, Mexico, I'm sure I can see the blurred shape of Christ looming on the mountaintop to the west. "Erected in 1950," she reads from our guidebook. "They say it's situated smack dab in the exact geographical centre of Mexico." We've been waiting a half hour for the bus to Cristo Rey. Sickness clings like damp clothes to our bodies; we're both hot and irritable, but mostly tired. (In Guanajuato the caged birds start singing at daybreak, and that's just a prelude for the church bells.) She's annoyed at my lack of excitement. It's she who wants to go to Cristo Rey today, though I've been the one compulsively drawn to churches and cathedrals, I who haven't stepped foot in a church back home for nearly twenty years, save for weddings and funerals. Before we left for Mexico, my father wrote to say, "I hope you find what you're searching for." I'm not sure what it is by name, but I have always been drawn here, by Mexico's real and fictional past and its brooding, religious rituals and icons. My companion grew up Catholic; until now she hadn't been so interested.

Cristo Rey.

61

Mexicans are interested in her; they're not used to seeing someone of Chinese extraction. An Asian woman with a white man is an even more exotic sight. Alone I hardly get any attention, gringo that I am. She says the crowds part like the Red Sea when they see her coming. Small children clutch their older sister's or mother's arm as they pass her. Young girls lean toward each other and giggle. Boys nudge elbows, hiss, "*Chinita*," perhaps to impress each other more than get her attention. Men

The Wild Bunch.

study her with dark curiosity, look her up and down. Whole families stop their squabbling to stare. We buy drinks at the concession stand—*agua purificada* for her, Coke for me—to get away from the attention, but even there the girl behind the counter can't stop giggling at us.

Finally it arrives: a royal blue school bus with a large crucifix fastened above the windshield. At the main stop in town, the Americans get on the bus. Nick, Sally and Leo from Portland. They're on their way to the Valenciana silver mines. They wear their moneybelts outside their clothes. We met them when we arrived in Guanajuato three days ago, and we keep bumping into them everywhere. They're middle-aged folks who are as bright and kind and interesting as they are bossy and opinionated. Generous too. Last night they took us out for dinner to a place definitely outside our price range. As soon as we walked in the place, Nick demanded that the music be turned off. The portly middle-aged waiter unhooked the nearest speaker, tottering dangerously on a wicker chair. "No, no, señor," said Nick, pointing around at all the speakers. "*Todos.*" The waiter gave him a long stare, then went and turned off the stereo.

The Americans flaunt a practised, serene enthusiasm over everything. "Will-to-happiness," D.H. Lawrence called it in *The Plumed Serpent*. At dinner they confessed about failed marriages and attempts at celibacy and laughed over some sexual innuendo between Leo and Nick. Life as talk show. Meanwhile, she and I, the consummate Canadians, made the odd agreeable remark and silently analyzed their conversation and characters. When asked to take a side on one of many seemingly contentious issues, I said, "You're both right." They got a kick out of that. The waiters, their dignity untainted, brought paella and enchiladas verdes and bottles of Negra Modelo.

Next the Americans joked about the religious superstition of the Mexicans, and everybody else come to think of it, and then, catching their breath, said, "You guys aren't religious, are you?" We smiled and shook our heads, saying nothing about how I spent my entire day searching the town's *antiguedades* shops for a religious icon, the Virgin of Guadalupe, painted on a square of tin. After dinner Sally joked that they had bored us to death. "No, no," we protested. "Thank you, it was a great dinner." The Americans did pay our way after all.

The Cristo Rey bus leaves Guanajuato behind. We rumble past worn-down buildings and rubble and wrought-iron fences, tiled courtyards. Faded yellows and pinks and greens. We pass over a valley miraculously flooded, a ruined church half-submerged in water, vegetation luminous and dripping from bleached stone. Like something out of a Tarkovsky film. At the Valenciana mines our American friends alight from the bus. "Enjoy the big Jesus," says Leo.

"*Vaya con Dios,*" shouts Nick from the sidewalk as we pull away.

My heart sinks at these words, "Go with God," their wistful scent of mortality. I've always had the premonition that I would die in Mexico. A flash of lying broken in a sweating motel room, staring up at a ceiling fan, a big black cross whirring to a stop above me. But now I'm certain it's going to happen on this ride. The road is already steep, and we keep climbing higher and higher through narrow zigzagging roads. Below the crucifix and the stickers of the Sacred Heart and the Virgin in the front windshield, there's a No Fear sticker. The driver is a burly guy with big-lidded eyes, who likes to wave at people. Maniac. He takes big wide turns, almost runs one truck off the road. He and the conductor—a thin kid with a wiry moustache and an unerringly good memory for who's paid the two-peso fare—have a good laugh as the bus skitters around a gravel bend.

I think how, despite their chaotic history and legacy of violence, their suffering under the gluttonous weight of North America, Mexicans on the street seem to be such a calm people, unfazed by anything, sitting in a town's cobblestone square for quiet hours full of dark serenity among friends and birds and shoeshiners, seeming to live each august minute as a slow-moving thought in the mind of God. Yet get them behind a wheel and everything changes. I'm ghost-white and shivering with sweat, fists clenched on the seat in front of me.

Worse, my Coke has shown itself as the pure bottled evil it is; I have to pee bad. It occurs to me that for all the people on the bus, this trip is probably a daily occurrence, and here I sit, a thin pale gringo who's romanticized Mexico for years, visions of Sam Peckinpah's *The Wild Bunch* and Sergio Leone flicks and Cormac McCarthy's Border Trilogy now crumbling like weathered stone in my mind, nearly pissing my pants and thinking I'm going to fall to my death in a careening school bus. She's serene beside me, taking it all in and sipping primly from her water, looking like a pretty nurse's aide in her blue gingham dress. She hasn't been stared at once on this ride. I look around at the passengers, their oblivious faces. Doomed, I think, all of us, but you don't know it! So this is where my fantasy of Mexico has led me.

We climb higher through spaghetti-western countryside: arid hills, scrub. Dead cacti turn brown then black, charred in the sun. We stop to pick up school kids, drop

others off, see them run away amid a flurry of chickens and dogs. People waving from their shiny swept porches. The bus windows don't open, or at least no one else wants to open them on account of the dust. I don't know if my full bladder is taking my attention away from the road, or if it causes me to be more petrified than I'd otherwise be. Then suddenly the trees fall away and we find ourselves high up on a sheer cliff face, hairpin turns. Tiny mountain villages with pigs running through yards, and cattle on the already treacherous road. Every once in a while I can catch a peek of Cristo Rey rising above the mountains, and I swear it's getting farther away. Crosses loom amid cacti at each and every turn.

My life flashes, a ribbon of flawed dreams, before my eyes, all its sins and small humiliations. Starting with kindergarten, when I stole Martin Price's toy van, and my teacher asked me to help him look for it, and reeling toward the present. But it's Mexico that has burned itself into my immediate memory: The baby sleeping among the mangoes in an Old Mazatlán market stall. The groups of people that congregated when my companion and I had problems with the language. A wasteland of volcanic

"Vaya con Dios."

rock fifty miles or so outside Zacatecas. Seeing a small child attacked by a dog, in the neck or ear, and then the mother and child screaming, the street frozen, only to watch the dog scamper away down an alley. An army checkpoint with small fires in the middle of the road. A flatbed truck full of young *policía* waving rifles in the air like tennis racquets. Hundreds and hundreds of poor families lined up alongside the highway into Guadalajara, camped outside the many *maquiladoras*, (foreign-owned manufacturing plants). Mobil, Kenwood, IBM. A huge stone carving of an angel being hoisted, unsuccessfully, onto a truck.

A tight spiral of cobbled road corkscrews up to the summit. There are radio transmitters everywhere. Garbage strewn over the ground. Stalls of poor families selling tortillas, candy, corn slathered with coconut and mayo. An old man, one eye blasted white, gets on the bus, leaning on a gnarled walking stick. He looks back, studying us, then exchanges quiet words with the driver. I'm sure I hear the word *"chinita."* I say nothing. If I talk, release my muscles even for a second, that's all she wrote.

At the top, Jesus has to wait. I run up the last stretch of cobblestone, wheezing at the first person I see: *"Donde está el baño?"* The washroom attendant is absent, just ranchero music crackling from a radio, so I don't bother paying the two pesos. (Meanwhile my companion has to put up with a little girl pulling her eyes *chinita* tight while her mother laughs, looking on. A guy decides he wants to record her on his video camera, follows her around for a while until his friends tell him to stop. "How does it feel to be travelling your first time in Mexico with a freak?" she will ask me and laugh, frustrated and a little shaken.)

Checking my fly twice, I step back out into the thin and perfect air. Everything is unreal here, exaggerated. People walk about, empty vessels infused with light. The land around us is hazed by height and distance, the vegetation up here so green it seems as if each leaf has been painted. And looming above us stands the resurrected Christ. Some forty feet high, though He seems much taller, and fashioned from black polished stone. A solitary white cloud in the blue above His head. Two stone cherubs play at His feet, one holding aloft a crown of thorns, the other a crown of gold. The folds of His robe cascade down from His outstretched arms, as if He embraces all Mexico.

We stand there, for what seems like forever, at the threshold of the round chapel beneath Cristo Rey. Holding our breath, we will step inside, and above us we'll behold a magnificent, palpable crown of thorns that circles the entire ceiling. Two hours from now we will see the Americans again on the bus, and they will show the semi-precious stones they bought from the Valenciana mines. "They've only got these little trinkets left," Sally will smirk, "for us travellers." Nick's will-to-happiness will still be going strong. "See the intricacy, the veins?" he will say, twirling a pendant in his hand. "See how it catches the light?"

And we will nod politely and say yes, but my companion will be self-conscious on account of a new, staring batch of passengers, and I will be thinking already of going back into town and searching for an icon of the Virgin. I will imagine returning to Vancouver and perhaps going to church for the first time in almost twenty years, which I won't do, and I will later begin to wonder if the illusions and expectations I've brought home are just the oxidized flip side of the coin I took to this country. An unreal movie spinning in tandem with the unfathomable day-to-day. I will see how, like a holy image crudely painted on tin, everything is an illusion once you try to make sense of it. But now, here in the centre of Mexico, we walk inside the suffering head of Christ and look above.

After Rick Maddocks wrote his first book, Sputnik Diner, *he went AWOL in Thailand, where he saw an elephant with a tail light playing the harmonica. He didn't see as many foreign-owned assembly plants there as in Mexico.*

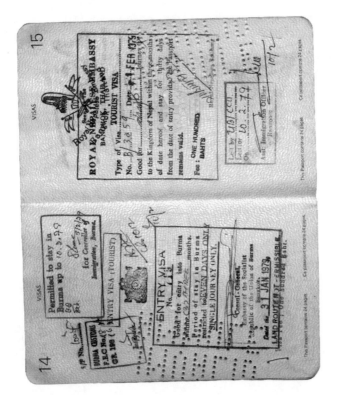

VISAS

Royal Service of the
ROYAL NEPALESE EMBASSY
BANGKOK, THAILAND
TOURIST VISA

Type of Visa ....
No. B/3859   Date F 1 FEB 1979

Good for .... journey to
to the Kingdom of Nepal within three months
of date hereof and stay for thirty days
from the date of entry provided the Passport
remains valid.

Fee : ONE HUNDRED
BAHTS

Left by ....
Entered On 10.2.79
Asst. Immigration Officer
Remarks:

The Passport contains 24 pages   Ce passeport contient 24 pages

---

VISAS

Permitted to stay in
Burma up to 10.3.79

for Controller of
Immigration, Burma.

/P No. ....
BURMA CUSTOMS
F.E.C No..................
Gr. 199 ( ) ENTRY VISA (TOURIST)

ENTRY VISA
No. ....

Good for entry into Burma
within .... months.
Period of stay in Burma
restricted to SEVEN DAYS ONLY
SINGLE JOURNEY ONLY.

Consul - General,
Embassy of the Socialist
Republic of the Union of Burma
Bangkok.
Dated the 31 JAN 1979

LAND ROUTE NOT PERMISSIBLE

This Passport contains 24 pages   Ce passeport contient 24 pages

EXIT PERMIT
Grant Buday

Her name was Sheila, and she was home from nursing school in Delhi. She was nineteen, had black hair loose to her hips, and an accent so elegant it made me whimper. I thought: Marry her. Live here amid the tea plantations, with Kanchenjunga—third highest peak on earth—right there on the horizon. Life could only be good.

We met in Darjeeling's central market.

"You're bumming about?"

I corrected her. "Travelling."

She elevated her chin and considered this distinction as if not quite convinced. But there was a smile at the corners of her mouth. We wandered past silver jewellery, bricks of tea, orchids, ginger, and coriander from Kalimpong. We sipped tea and watched a man pass, carrying a bundle of goat legs under his arm.

Sheila was a Christian. "RC," she said.

When I told her I was raised a Catholic, she appeared skeptical. She frowned at my beard and faded jeans and road-worn runners. I didn't look like an altar boy any more. Fortunately I hadn't worn my Frank Zappa T-shirt featuring him seated on the toilet.

Sheila switched the subject. With splendid composure she asked me about North American culture. "Of course I have seen the idiot box," she said, meaning television, rare in India in 1979. "But it's all such bunk, don't you think?"

I thought: She's your ticket to a superior life. Win her. Do anything, say anything, but win her.

We agreed to meet the next day at noon in the botanical gardens. I was too busy fantasizing to sleep that night. Our children would be striking. My friends back home would envy me. Life in Darjeeling would be healthy. At seven thousand feet, breathing that alpine air, I'd have the lungs of a twenty-year-old when I was eighty. My fantasies did not include what I'd do for work, though I felt certain my prospects would be better than they were back home in Vancouver, where construction jobs and factory labour awaited me, or if I returned to school, discussions about whether the table in the middle of the room really existed—objectively speaking, that is.

I arrived early. While I waited I looked at the orchids, roses and rhododendrons. By one, Sheila hadn't arrived. By two, she still hadn't shown.

I tried to read my copy of Joyce's *Ulysses* but couldn't concentrate. At three o'clock I left, bewildered, recalling our parting handshake. When she'd disappeared into the crowd, with her went another life I might have lived. I now realize she was not all that exotic or mysterious; she was pragmatic and maybe even dull. But that didn't matter. I saw only what I wanted.

My plans were to see Kathmandu and find a Buddhist monastery where I'd learn to meditate. After that I'd be so calm, so centred, so glowingly enlightened that work and money wouldn't matter and the women would flock to me.

I was seeking alternatives and falling in love. In Thailand with an elementary school teacher named Willawan. In Hong Kong with a woman who waitressed in a won ton house. And in Calcutta with Mrs. Sydhwa. Her house had twenty-foot ceilings, old copies of *Punch* and novels by Marie Corelli. I guiltlessly dozed away entire afternoons there. She was seventy and had cataracts but she was beautiful, and I was never happier than when sipping afternoon tea with her and spreading her guava jam on toast, listening to her talk of old Calcutta.

In Burma there was the girl in the Maymyo market with white patterns decorating her lovely face.

"What are they for?"

"For the skin."

She sold herbs. I fancied a life there in the market, sitting amid the incense and cool fruit, smoking cheroots and idling my afternoons away, bantering with the man to the left selling canaries and with the lady to the right selling sugar cane drinks.

Everywhere I went, from Tokyo to Darjeeling, Kathmandu to Colombo, I was smitten with a woman and by the life she represented, the identity I could occupy, the culture I imagined I could join.

"That's wonderful. That's marvellous." The Reverend Raymond Butcher had just learned that our taxi driver was not a Buddhist or Hindu or a Muslim, but a Protestant studying for the ministry. The driver was a Gurkha named Deobahadur Rawat, Deo for short.

The taxi was an old '65 Mercedes with burnt-out dashboard lights and collapsed seat springs. It smelled of hair oil and bodies and the portly Reverend's aftershave.

He, his wife, April, and I were en route to the India–Nepal border to catch a bus to Kathmandu. It was four in the morning, and the gears of the Mercedes groaned as we descended from Darjeeling's heights.

Deo concentrated on the road. The quarter moon was just bright enough to reveal plunging valleys.

Raymond told me, "Our son is here with the Peace Corps."

"He loves it here," said April proudly.

I nodded to her in the dark. Had their son found a girl? Three days had passed since Sheila had failed to meet me. I'd walked from one end of Darjeeling to the other but never caught a glimpse of her, though I did see a lot of entrancing girls.

When I'd given up and gone to the bus station, the ticket seller told me of an American couple going to the Nepali border by taxi. They'd leave early enough to meet the bus to Kathmandu, and we'd make the two-day trip in one for the same cost.

"He's a civil engineer," said Raymond. "Pretty much writes his own ticket. What did you study?"

That was an awkward question. I'd dropped out of university after a year of C minuses. "I was working," I said.

He nodded deeply as if to say work was a good thing. "What field?"

That was another awkward question. I was in the field of working in sawmills and

71

on construction sites, never longer than three weeks before I quit or was fired. "Construction."

"John's constructing irrigation systems," said Raymond.

"He has all kinds of people under him," said April.

"Great." I began to wish I'd taken the bus.

Raymond shifted so he could get a good look at me. "So what are you doing way over here in this neck of the woods?"

The car continued its descent as I sought an appropriate response.

"Tourist."

"Uh-huh." He waited for me to go on, but I didn't. "And what will you do when you go home?"

Trapped and exposed, I heard myself say, "Go to university. Philosophy."

"Philosophy. Well, I'm a bit of a philosopher too."

Seated in that car, fearful of hearing the Reverend Butcher's undoubtedly elevating philosophy, I decided I'd do anything to avoid becoming like the Butchers. I was not a Christian but a Buddhist. And I didn't want all kinds of people under me— I wanted to be one with the people. I'd much rather be the Darjeeling night watchman, for example.

I'd met him earlier that morning while waiting for the taxi. He was about fifty, gaunt-faced, dark-skinned, wrapped in scarves and sweaters, and sat cross-legged before a fire of oil-soaked rags, smoking a bidi. I squatted there too, despite the ache in my knees, wearing all my clothes—faded blue jeans, the Frank Zappa T-shirt, the "Relax for Survival" T-shirt, the grey pullover—my bath towel wrapped around my shoulders. The cold hurt like a needle injecting my bones with ice. The watchman's bidi stood upright between his fingers while he sucked the smoke through his fist. I was tempted to take up smoking myself to have some hot air heating my chest. The burning rags hissed and whispered in the mountain silence. And what a silence. No dogs, radios or traffic, just the fire, and beyond that an immense black sky. When I closed my eyes, the fire remained visible. Flames were probably burned permanently into the watchman's retinas. I imagined him here each night and decided he must dream of fire: bonfires, forest fires, cities ablaze. I imagined that everything he looked at would be fringed in flame . . .

The landscape changed as the taxi descended, cedars and firs giving way to palms and bamboo.

By half past seven that morning we were rattling along at a fair clip between rice paddies. I watched a man work a post-and-beam water pump, irrigating a field. A man passed with a hoe over his shoulder, his hands three sizes too big for him. A boy passed, prodding a bullock in the anus with a bamboo stick. Three women in saris balanced brass jugs on their heads. Their bare feet were large and their splayed toes gripped the ground. I caught the scent of their coconut-oiled hair and heard the tinkle of their

THE COLD HURT LIKE A NEEDLE INJECTING MY BONES WITH ICE. THE WATCHMAN'S BIDI STOOD UPRIGHT BETWEEN HIS FINGERS WHILE HE SUCKED THE SMOKE THROUGH HIS FIST.

anklets. Of course I married one of them on the spot, and in my mind I unwound the endless length of her sari while cicadas hissed through the night. At dawn she heated milk for chai over a dung fire while the smoky sunlight stirred the mist . . .

The border consisted of a man in a crate-wood booth. He wore a deep-blue uniform and a David Niven moustache, and he tapped his silver pen ominously. Judging by his expression, he'd recently been demoted. On the boards of his booth were the stencilled letters of shipping labels.

The customs official's frown deepened as he paged back and forth through Raymond's and April's passports. "Eggzit parmit?" He turned his hand palm upward in an accusing gesture. "Where is?"

Though it was only eight a.m., discs of sweat darkened the Reverend's under-arms. He brought his formidable focus to bear on the issue. "Exit permit? I don't, they didn't . . ." He looked to Deo, who took a step back. "They never said anything in Calcutta about an exit permit."

The customs official slapped their passports down and dismissed them. "Go back."

"Back?"

The man signalled me forward, found my exit permit, stamped it and waved me on.

"Look here, we were not told—"

Voice sharp as a split stick, he said, "Eggzit parmit!"

Deo regained his fortitude and negotiated with the man while Raymond paced.

"I fought in the war for you people. I stayed with the American ambassador in Delhi."

The official pursed his lips as if enjoying the sweet scent of his own moustache and the even sweeter taste of power. I imagined that later, over a glass of cashew fenni—the local firewater—he'd tell his friends how he'd dealt with those who think themselves above rules and regulations.

April hurled herself onto the hood of the car in despair. "No wonder our son hates this country!"

At Nepali customs a smiling man ambled out from a card game in a shed, stamped my passport and ambled back in. Across a field stood the bus, exhaust rolling from the tailpipe as the driver gunned the motor.

The bus smelled alternately of dust, coconut oil, and betel nut. At times the mountain slopes were forested with immense rhododendrons thirty metres high, and at others with fir and cedar. We passed stone mounds flying flags of bright paper. The higher we climbed, the more the sky took on a blue-black colour. We passed a family hiking a steep stretch of road. They leaned hard into the hill, father, mother, three kids, all barefoot and carrying conical baskets held to their backs by woven straps that looped across their foreheads. There I was with them, basket on my back, feet calloused, thighs mighty.

The trip to Kathmandu took fourteen hours, plenty of time to feel bad for Raymond and April Butcher. And I did. They were admirably intrepid in their way. But now I was free of them and the reminder of the arid culture I was so desperate to escape. And anyway there was Adhe in the next seat, whom I promptly fell in love with. She had been visiting the Tibetan refugee camp in Darjeeling. Her red T-shirt and black suit coat gave her a curiously urbane look that contrasted with the copper mask of her face, her Buddha eyes, her brilliant teeth. We shared oranges and admired the mountains. As the bus bumped and turned, our bodies swayed and knees touched. She said in her slow but solid English, "I was born in Kathmandu . . ."

Grant Buday's fiction includes the novel White Lung, *shortlisted for the City of Vancouver Book Award and co-winner of the British Columbia 2000 Millennium Book Award. A chapter from the novel won the fiction category of the 1997 Western Magazine Awards.* White Lung *has also been optioned for a feature film. His travel writing includes a memoir of India called* Golden Goa *and his latest novel,* A Sack Of Teeth, *was published in 2002.*

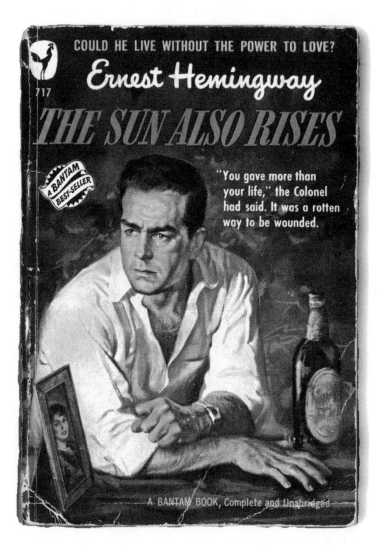

COULD HE LIVE WITHOUT THE POWER TO LOVE?

Ernest Hemingway

717

THE SUN ALSO RISES

A BANTAM BEST-SELLER

"You gave more than your life," the Colonel had said. It was a rotten way to be wounded.

A BANTAM BOOK, Complete and Unabridged

PENETRATING EUROPE-LAND
Mark Anthony Jarman

1981—the year of the coup in Madrid. The Irish virgin and I are under a foreign mountain, we're retreating. What drives us from Spain? Nothing really. *De nada*. The Moorish man flicks his lighter in the long dark railroad tunnel. Molly, the Irish woman, has it out. The Moor's smile wilts. What are these infidels doing? *Goats and monkeys!* It's not what it looks like. Well, maybe it is.

What draws me to Spain? Let's blame Hemingway. The bull and the running of the bulls, anarchists, Orwell, Koestler, John Dos Passos at the Hotel Florida, trout streams falling down the hills, toreador pants on a certain someone, Guernica's Heinkel bombers, a bull's horn pushed in the horse's stomach, Franco and the gory civil war, the Russians executing Dos Passos's translator, the Russians executing

Let's blame Hemingway.

77

everyone, men falling in Canada's MacKenzie-Papineau Battalion, the fifth column, fascist shells smashing the roof tiles, a siege, oh Madrid, my Madrid, *la movida*, the action, the all-night clubs, wild dancers, wild nights now that Franco is dead, the witch is dead.

Down down down, travelling with Molly from Dublin, down from Paris and Bordeaux and Biarritz where the doomed U-boats slid and hid and the German troops swam and drowned in the big surf. Now goofy-foot surfers flying down a wave's glass lip, flipping over the bodies and rising beds of weeds past the topless beach.

Down Europe's body: slip down into Basque territory, ETA (*Basque Homeland and Freedom*) bombs going off, smoke curling in the car park, wheat holding up the sky, mayors assassinated, et cetera, et cetera. Europe-Land slightly off the rails.

Pass through the frontier into Spain and change trains at Irun, a portal of dank steps, dark and sombre, reminding you of refugees fleeing firing squads and bombers and machine guns. Don't they know mildew can cause depression? I am reminded of crossing into Mexico, but this is more serious, harder, more violence is implied (*Badges? We don't need no stinking badges*).

Earlier this year an attempted military coup, people edgy, dark eyes in steep treed valleys: Which side are you on, boys? The guards with the Mickey Mouse tricorne hats, and machine guns they pass to each other like women's purses with long straps.

I must consult my phrase book. How do you say, *Señor, don't pop a cap in my ass, por favor.*

In France, we couldn't get out of the City of Light, we were prisoners, me a sweating madman galloping down train aisles, looking desperately for two open seats. So fucking hot. Bank holiday, all trains sold out in advance. Everyone knows this but us. Paris eating into my travellers' cheques, eating into my brain. Must leave and can't get out—a strange feeling. Will die here (*must see Paris before I die*). No one tells you of these scenes when they say how GREAT their trip to Europe was.

Maybe they do and I don't hear (I'm no more bitter than your average bitter person). All trains full, nearly midnight and life is the slowest ever pie in my face.

Moments when I can't believe I chose this, paid big bucks to come to this grief. No one tells you.

A train to Bordeaux, two seats, we will take it, life is possible. From there we can move on to Madrid, Portugal, later Italy, perhaps cooler Switzerland, look up that Swiss woman I met months before in Hampstead. Perhaps Greece, far cheaper than the City of Light. O to move, O the optimism of a Eurail pass, O the young traveller on a first trip to Fortress Europe.

Molly saves our seats in a sweltering compartment, and I sprint back to our locker before the train pulls out without me, yank both our big packs from said locker and run and run as fast as I can up stairs and down the platforms with the double weight, bashing through overheated holiday crowds, rich sweat falling from me like money.

Our arrangement: we left Dublin to travel illicitly to the continent, boarding the same DART at different train stops to travel down to the Irish port of Rosslare. I met Molly through a cousin in Dublin. No one must know we are together.

Molly told her parents she is travelling with a group of female friends. Molly has been seeing a policeman or guard or peeler and she is saving herself for marriage. This is over two decades ago; the old order still has some power in Ireland. The big white boat crossing the channel, shaking itself like a dog, the two of us necking and drinking on the deck at night, aware of engines and screws announcing that she can't go all the way. A calm sea for the crossing, lights of boats strung in a blue evening, pieces moved on a flat board game, an industry serving us, a new Operation Overlord serving me oysters, all the old battles here, all the ghost voyages, Conrad to Africa, the Spanish Armada on its way to wreckage, to a laundromat in Galway.

Bordeaux: something very heady in its mix of summer air and salt water surf, and French wine and cafés—craving congress constantly, rooster madness, blood up, nothing will satisfy me here (*nothing will come of nothing*).

Molly the virgin tries to help, does what she can. In a French bed she rolls on her stomach. I gather I am allowed to move against her, move over her like a tourist, but not in her. Why can't we just talk about this subject? We can't. Her nipples glisten where I linger. We come to our solution, we improvise like jazz musicians and I can't stop, necessity the mute mother of invention amid the terrible fear of motherhood, fear of pregnancy, yet neither of us is really getting laid, though we do our best *(isn't it pretty to think so)*. It just has to be near, she says, and it's near her all the time, and she soon convinces me that she may be or likely will be pregnant, even though we're not even doing anything.

Perhaps this is similar to a kind of surface travel: skim like a bug, there but not there, moving across a country but not allowed to penetrate *(only connect)*, can see but not let in, learn and not learn a thing, sleep with her and don't sleep with her.

I remember the story of my sublime old buddy F. Scott Fitzgerald taking a saw to the roof of his rental car in France so he could have a convertible. I want to saw the roof off something. Continental breakfast my ass: a roll that'd break a window if I threw it.

And everything stolen from me while we sleep on a night train between San Sebastián and Madrid. I squeezed Molly's backpack up on the crowded overhead rack. No room for mine. I am being chivalrous, careless, leave my pack on the floor just outside our compartment. During the night someone climbs off the train with my pack. Many stops in the night. I am a careless person.

How often I joked: I wish someone would steal this damn thing. Like a mother I carried it every day for months, grew to hate it. As your mother warns you, be careful what you wish. Your mother should know.

Molly shaking me awake, we check washrooms, running up and down the confined train. All my rolls of film from London, Holyhead, Dublin, Dingle, Galway, the Aran Islands, Le Havre, Cherbourg, Paris, Arcachon, San Sebastián, my film blistering in the desert plateau, my handwritten journals gone with the newspaper clippings and pub coasters, and my favourite Ramones T-shirt. Who wears that T-shirt now?

My psychobilly forty-fives—hours poring through used record racks in London and Dublin—and coil journals tossed to rot in the blank Spanish sun. What I value so highly is worthless to those who steal from me.

On a bed in Madrid, heat an affront, a weapon aimed at you, sapped by heat, the old Moorish city *Mayrit* makes it known you're close to North Africa, cruel blinding sunlight and dark hallways, a giant ant colony, an ancient hotel shelled during the Spanish Civil War, home now to my immutable irritability.

I hit the wall, fell in the apples, succumbed to Weary Blues—on the road for months. Now I just want to stop the bloody carnival. My middle-class failings, my guilt: I *have* to enjoy travel, it's my duty, I must love Madrid's secret *tabernas* and *alcazars*, must keep up with the Joneses and Lady Brett, but I have to stop moving. I'm failing the legacy, letting down the side.

A hubcap rolls downhill from a small car. I chase the hubcap on its wobbly wanderings and carry it like an errant baby back to the *castizo* owner coming down the hill on foot.

Gracias, he says.

De nada, I mutter shyly, secretly thrilled to be able to say something, however inexpertly, in this beautiful language.

God is in the details, the stunning details, the palace gardens, the Gran Via, the Museo del Prado, the statues and horses, the tapestries and Toledo marble, the debris and bric-a-brac at the centre of an empire of gold and silver, all this moving sunlight, gold from the Incas, and two Madrileno guitarists on the cobbled street, gypsy fingers flailing on gut-strings, a haunting foreign voice travelling dark roads, dark chords, frenetic strumming in an alien lane.

El Corte Ingles department store, Molly with me as I buy T-shirts and one pair of pants to replace those stolen.

Why is one item a pair?

Molly and I travel room to room, drink to drink, Raphael to Rubens to Goya, insane art and traffic, the strange history of this country, churches and thieves, Old World women in black shawls looking on new sin, the new young skin everywhere in the streets that have always been there.

I can't look. Bourbon buildings so perfect, Hapsburg, art deco, soaring Moorish arches—these all sound so beautiful, but I have lost my eyes, my curiosity; it was exhausted, stolen like a backpack.

The mandarin in the police building with such beautiful writing. Is he alive now? He takes down the details. The backpack, the train. It's cooler inside this office on the Puerta del Sol. More machine guns and the beautiful handwriting. Colonel Tejero of the Guardia Civil held the parliament at gunpoint while on camera, trying to trigger a coup on television. The revolution will be televised. I'm reporting the crime. We all know it's futile. *This wouldn't have happened when Franco was alive.*

The mandarin writes and I find myself thinking back fondly to Bordeaux and a nearby beach town. Lie on a topless beach, French women stretching on all sides, lovely breakfasts at the Lion d'Or hotel, cold golden beer in afternoons under umbrellas, jump in the sea anytime, drink anytime, morning or night. Men playing bocce above the sea. A simple easy life—just want to stop somewhere for a while, get to know something of a place and not be uprooted each day.

Molly is agreeable; we like each other and we hate each other, our crush, our civil war, our puppy love transmuting into something more complicated and fine, for travel makes for strange bedfellows. We decide: back to the Lion d'Or, our clean well-lighted place.

I will return, come back, make amends to Madrid, take a hacksaw to my Hertz, join the First of October Antifascist Resistance Group, partake in stunning stinking sheep cheeses and bandilleras and spicy chorizo, yell hi to Dos Passos and Papa Hemingway at the next iron table. I'll have more energy when I'm old and in the way. Right now I'm young and I just want to sit around and do nothing.

The train rocking in the long tunnel, our train completely dark, under the Pyrenees, a mole pushing through a mountain, the River Ebro crossed, leaving sunny Spain, travelling north in the dark, her lithe white Irish hand travelling south.

Her hand opens a zipper on newly purchased Spanish *pantalones*, she is game despite her vow of chastity, she likes to pay attention to it, it's hers, she has it in hand, going north, up, going up the country, she is Molly Bloom at *la frontera*, yes, up, moving up the map, Molly's bloom opening with honey inside her lightless tunnel *(wish you were here)*.

We are in the dark and then the Moorish man lights his etched czarist lighter and we are illuminated, we see the light and cover up as best we can and pretend nothing is amiss, just Cassio and Desdemona caught in the act, just your average North American shrinking-violet bozo and the Irish woman he should be nicer to and will never see again (she cries at the station in London, but she never answers his letters), just your average retreat from Moscow.

Mark Anthony Jarman is the author of Ireland's Eye; 19 Knives; New Orleans Is Sinking; Salvage King, Ya!; Dancing Nightly in the Tavern; *and a poetry collection,* Killing the Swan. *Jarman has won the MacLean-Hunter Endowment Award for Literary Non-Fiction, a National Magazine Award, and the ReLit Short Fiction Award. His stories and essays have been shortlisted for the Journey Prize, the Pushcart Prize, Best American Essays, and the O. Henry Award. He teaches at the University of New Brunswick.*

LE BATEAU IVRE /
THE DRUNKEN BOAT
Stanzas 12-14 15

Whitehorse
March 3
2002

Westmark
HOTELS~
ALASKA/YUKON

Unruly hair later
imitated by Emile
Nelligan

← General facial
expression seemingly
inherited by
Ken Babstock
(see author
photo in
Mean)

Rimbaud, around
1869-70

(stanza
12)
"J'ai heurté, savez-vous, d'incroyables Florides
Mêlant aux fleurs des yeux de panthères à peaux
D'hommes! Des arcs-en-ciel tendus comme des brides
Sous l'horizon des mers, à de glauques troupeaux!"

[I ran aground on]

12
I've run aground on Floridas, incredible
coasts whose foliage concealed panther-eyed men;
where rainbows stretched as taut as any bridle
mixed with glaucous flocks beneath the horizon.

[stretched out taut as

? traps? le mot est "nasse"

13
I've seen immense marshes festering and weirs nets
where Leviathan rotted among reeds; the sea's
calm face gaping like a crevasse, and vistas
fanning off into far, cataracting bays.

[but: rhyme on "nets"/"vistas"]

"vers les gouffres cataractant"

silver
14
Glaciers, silver suns, pearly waves, embering
skies, groundings at the head of murky lagoons
where enormous serpents, beset by vermin,
flop from twisted trees in whiffs of black perfume.

⇒ [or "fall
but th
loses the
sense
"flop"

? would have
liked children
to see" 15
the...

I would have liked to show children the [sea-bream
                                          dorados
in the blue combers, those golden fishes singing...
Blown seaward I was cradled by spindrift flowers
while winds [indescribable] winged me. Tiring ← [Tired]?

"martyr lassé"

?

18 Hotels in 11 Locations
For Central Reservations Call
Inside Alaska (800) 478-1111
Outside Alaska (800) 544-0970
In Canada   ZENITH 06003

THE DRUNKEN BOAT
Steven Heighton

Steven Heighton is the author of seven books, including the story collection Flight Paths of the Emperor *and a novel,* The Shadow Boxer, *which was a bestseller in Canada, and in the U.S. was a* Publishers Weekly *Book of the Year for 2002. His work has been nominated for the Governor General's Literary Award, the Trillium Award, the Journey Prize, a Pushcart Prize, and Britain's WH Smith Award (best book of the year). He has received the Gerald Lampert Memorial Award, a gold medal for fiction in the National Magazine Awards, the Air Canada Award and the 2002 Petra Kenney Prize (UK).*

Writer at work in a Yukon hotel.

A LESSON IN DANCE
Gillian Meiklem

Theresa is a gossiping gypsy who sells cakes up on main street. She possesses the kind of beauty that seems to better itself with each passing year. She is ten years older than I am and ten times as notable. I count each turn she makes on my fingers as I watch her dance. If she were an ugly woman, all that prancing might look tasteless—lifting her skirt while she twists to the floor, teasing some imagined spirit into chasing her to all four corners, until he succumbs to her and lays her breathless. But Theresa is bringing the dead back to life, making the coy girls feel plain and making me get unbearably high to keep up. Theresa and her tiny nephew Leo live beside my *pousada* in a town built on sand. At low tide it's possible to walk fifteen minutes out to sea without getting your hair wet. By way of laziness and practicality I've learned to swim in two feet of water, with Leo beside me, diving into the shallows in a flail of crazed laughter that gets lost in the wind.

It is said that this same wind will carry away the two-hundred-foot dune that shields the oasis and governs the town of Jericoacóara in less than five years. It makes me feel sentimental to shake it out of my pant cuffs onto the floor and sweep it outside to the fence I share with Theresa. Leo is usually there, pushing a toilet paper roll on the end of a metal rod over dumps of shit and through the laundry of the yelling woman who hosts the cockfights. She's an intimidating figure and much more captivating to watch than those tortured roosters. For the past six weeks that I've stayed here, her yard has become my Sunday matinee. We've never spoken to one another, but I've studied her for hours—her black-soled feet, the slip she wears as a dress, the way she shifts her weight and sneers to harangue both the winners and losers. Eventually the men wave for me to join the betting, and jest with great grins that Leo is my son. I've never been certain if they're making fun of Leo or me or whether the whole notion of me as a mother is hilarious. It's particularly hurtful on the days I'm practising to be one. When I finally asked Theresa where Leo's mother was, she simply said she had gone away.

Early each evening, when Theresa has combed her hair and Leo has agreed to play with other kids, she and I amble through streets, ankle-high in sand, toward the beach. By then the night's *capoeira* has reached a frenzy, outlined by a trio of torches, a half-lit moon and a gallery of admirers. There are congregations like this all over northern Brazil. *Capoeira* is a sport as popular here as soccer is in Spain or how we like to think hockey is back home. It is an ancient dance and a martial art—a great spectacle of warriors set to ballet. One pair at a time enters the circle, the victor staying until he's outshone. The rest of the athletes wait their turn. To get in the ring, one must also make music: anthems and rhythms and beautiful chaos pounds from voices and drums. I have seen these same men in the honesty of day and noted that they are five feet tall and as mortal as I, as earthbound and predictable as any other, but here in the hour after dusk they soar. I envy them so much my chest hurts and I lose feeling in my feet.

Theresa is tall enough to take a position in the back of the crowd, but on this night as in most, she grabs me by the elbow and drags me to the front. I hate the first row. I have been landed on twice, tripped, kicked and asked to play the cymbal. How this happens to me, inches from Theresa while she sambas untouched, is a perpetual mystery. She has vowed to protect me tonight and watch for the little man who refuses to be appeased. She points him out across the crowd. "There's your boyfriend," she teases. The truth is that this man wants to get me in the ring.

I had met him on my first night in town. I was with Stacey, an American girl who wanted to listen to un-American music, a depressingly difficult request. Out of the dozen bars in town we were left with only two to choose from; she picked the quieter one, intent on learning how to dance to *forro* with the smallest number of people looking on. *Forro* is a traditional, popular music meant for couples. If the pair is experienced

WHILE WOMEN MAY INDEED OUTNUMBER MEN IN THE REST OF THE WORLD, IN THIS LITTLE TOWN THE RATIOS ARE REVERSED, AND IN THIS PARTICULAR BAR THE NUMBERS WERE APPALLING. AMONG THE THIRTY OR SO PATRONS, THERE WERE FOUR WOMEN, INCLUDING THE GIRL SERVING DRINKS AND AN UNCONSCIOUS LADY, BOTH OF WHOM WERE EXCUSED FROM DANCING. STACEY AND I WERE VERY POPULAR.

it can be a very sensual thing; if not it's little more than a dirty polka. Now, while women may indeed outnumber men in the rest of the world, in this little town the ratios are reversed, and in this particular bar the numbers were appalling. Among the thirty or so patrons, there were four women, including the girl serving drinks and an unconscious lady, both of whom were excused from dancing. Stacey and I were very popular.

The first two men to approach us were the little man and a lanky fellow named Tomas. The little man was a good foot shorter than his friend but much thicker. He had a boxer's build and strutted like a champion, crowned in a silk cap and wearing a matching vest. I have since learned the little man's name but because it also doubles as a term of endearment and because we've become sworn enemies, I refuse to say it. But on that first night, six weeks ago, the little man was trying to court me. He asked me to dance. We had been talking for an hour or two and he seemed jovial enough. He understood my patchwork Portuguese and had taken it upon himself to get us rather drunk. I ordered one more to get up the nerve to dance.

I didn't want him to know I was uncomfortable; insecurity is often misread as snobbery. It wasn't the dancing nor the partner so much as his height that made me feel ungainly. It was a gruelling embrace, holding him there, chest-high to me. We danced six songs in a row until he conceded that nature was against us. Stacey, to my chagrin, was a natural, leaving my companion and me to drink alone. The spectacle of us had sobered me, and I abandoned beer altogether. The little man drank four more tall bottles before Stacey joined us with her latest partner, an immaculate-looking man who had fallen in love with her in the hour or two that I hadn't been watching.

It was nearly five a.m. when I asked for our bill. The little man excused himself to go to the bathroom and never came back. I asked around the bar for "the little man in the hat." No one knew where to find him, but they did caution that the little man was a *capoeira* master, an adulterer and a cocaine dealer on the lam. When he skipped up next to me on the walk home to ask me over for a drink, I forgot all about the warnings given and demanded he pay me his share of the bill. He called me cheap. I said he was a thief.

"I want to take you home," he countered.

"I want to kill your dog," I said. It was a pitiful rebuttal from a forty word vocabulary, and it stunned us both.

"What?" he asked.

"Dog. You. The same. You're not my friend." He took a minute to size me up, pivoted on his sandals and sashayed into the dawn. Given the drunken circumstances, I considered the drama we shared rather insignificant.

It has taken four altercations since that night, with numerous pokes to the chest and six cigarette burns to my hammock, for me to realize that the little man saw the entire evening much differently. A poke may seem like a juvenile assault, but a poke into a bony bit hurts and an angry poke can bruise for weeks. This silly poking business has become a pattern between us. There are variations to the routine but the conclusion remains the same. He will poke, push or mock me and then ask for a kiss. It's now a tradition. The bar scarcely comes to gawk anymore. Without the crowd, his threats have lost their theatrics and become rather sullen. "You're in my town," he stated the last night we met, "and you're not wanted." The barman reminded him that he wasn't from here but a city six hours away, with a wife and son awaiting his return, now six months overdue.

Theresa points again across the crowd. "There won't be any fighting tonight." We often make wagers on these fits of his. I tried for the longest time to avoid him, but in a town as small as this there aren't many places to hide. I've come to rely on luck. Theresa taps me on the shoulder and says we should go before the gathering thins and leaves us exposed. She invites me to her shop, to cut a piece of cake and watch me eat it. We sit in shared gratitude: a lover of strays and a lover of sweets. We drink red wine with our chocolate and she goes to great lengths to set the table for three. For in a town as small as this, she tells me, one has to rely on hope.

The room is tiny and cluttered and filled with her scent. It's the smell that perfume emulates—the primal glory of spices in the heat. It's the kitchen of someone else's mother that makes you hungry, brings water to your mouth and eyes. It's something that you want without knowing what it is.

We part ways for a nap, meet again for some wine, and by two a.m. Theresa wants to dance. The bars in this town leak onto the street; the outside often more festive than the party within. Tonight it has taken us twenty minutes to get inside the door. We're waved over to a table full of familiar faces that Theresa kisses two to three times, cheek to cheek as if choreographed. I kiss indiscriminately, grazing the neck occasionally, the forehead, the neglected temple or on the lips when my confusion infects the crowd. I've worked in this bar in exchange for sandwiches and drinks since the first week I arrived. With four bosses the odds are rather secure that I'll be in favour with at least one of them on any given night. Tonight they tell me to join the dancers, and during slow songs they fill me with drinks. The little man finds me in the hour when I stop keeping count. He says he wants to kill me. There is a sadness to him. He gives the impression that we have indeed reached our end.

"Do what you want," I answer. "But tell me why." I hadn't thought to ask him that before, to treat him as if he was sane. "You don't have a reason, do you?"

"I do," he says.

"Then what is it?" The sight of us conversing has attracted a crowd. He takes a step toward me, close enough for me to make out each word, close enough for the group behind me to hear.

I KISS INDISCRIMINATELY, GRAZING THE NECK OCCASIONALLY, THE FOREHEAD, THE NEGLECTED TEMPLE OR ON THE LIPS WHEN MY CONFUSION INFECTS THE CROWD.

"Because you save to travel," he spits, then pauses, "and we save to eat."

I wish he had poked me. I wish he had thrown me to the ground only to ask for a kiss. This minute is much too long for me. The bar is waiting for my redemption, and my brain sits there, between us, looking up at me from the floor. I'm touched, saved, brought to my senses by the white sleeve of Theresa. Theresa who doesn't believe in hate, who swears to all who will listen that spiteful words are merely those of unrequited love.

"Save to eat?" she breathes his words. She waits, there on the pedestal I built for her, and stays the execution. "Then let us eat well."

She takes my man by the hand and leads him onto the floor. I don't see either one of them again. It has been two days and I've decided to move on. I've found a ride to the big city six hours away. I pass by Theresa's shop to give thanks and kiss her goodbye, but I'm stopped at her door by two voices coming from inside. I place a note on her flowerpot and leave the little town in the middle of the night. We drive past my *pousada*, past the bars and the barmen taking down chairs and preparing for the night, past the beaches and the dune. The *capoeira* boys will be taking their showers now, Leo will be swimming in his dreams, and Theresa will be telling a story over chocolate cake at a table set for three.

Unable to shake the mantra of "better there than here," Gillian Meiklem is as much a wilful transient at home in BC and Alberta as she is travelling the continents.

LOCAL RULES
Brad Smith

The Writer is always the first up. The Steelmaker will argue this point but he will be wrong. The Writer is always the first up. There are a number of pat reasons that can be applied to this: perhaps the Writer simply requires less sleep than the others, or maybe he doesn't sleep well in a strange bed.

In reality, it is suspected that the others sleep the deep sleep of the clear of conscience while the Writer, for reasons which will certainly not be addressed here, enjoys no such luxury.

Besides, a day here on Lake Nipissing is a remarkable thing, and getting up at dawn is a part of that.

The group, a ragtag assortment of occasional sportsmen in their thirties and forties, spends a week annually at this camp. Lake Nipissing is a perfect little lake, positioned in what is known as Ontario's "near north," a third of the way between the pretense of Toronto and the polar bears of James Bay. The group has been coming here for two decades now. They return because they must, it seems. Unlike Papa's Paris, Nipissing's feast is not moveable in the least.

Upon rising, the Writer drinks coffee and watches the surface of the lake out the window as he waits for the others to awaken, not yet thinking of food. His stomach sleeps longer than his head.

One has to wonder how the fish keep abreast of the latest fads.

The Auto Worker is usually next up, rousing himself from the nest he has fashioned out of blankets and underwear and fishing tackle in the corner of the west bedroom, leaving the double bed to the long-slumbering Hockey Player. The Auto Worker is thick and muscular, with a large balding head and heavy wire-rimmed spectacles. He has a habit of walking around the cottage stark naked; his body is completely covered with a bristly blond-ish fur, which gives him the look of a large koala bear. Eucalyptus trees being damn near extinct in northern Ontario, the Auto Worker usually breakfasts on pickerel fillets, fried in bacon grease.

The Writer will walk down to the dock while the naked Auto Worker sizzles and sears, will move down the hill, past the main house, a few auxiliary buildings, and the canoes leaning up against the pines on the hill. Most days he will find the camp dog, a golden retriever of considerable years, on the dock, watching in the water for

LAKE NIPISSING IS A PERFECT LITTLE LAKE, POSITIONED IN WHAT IS KNOWN AS ONTARIO'S "NEAR NORTH," A THIRD OF THE WAY BETWEEN THE PRETENSE OF TORONTO AND THE POLAR BEARS OF JAMES BAY.

signs of the smallmouth bass who nest on the pebbly lake bottom around and beneath the docks. The bass are fat and sassy and they hover over their hatching grounds like gilled mother hens. The retriever, when spotting one, is fairly beside herself in her desire to leap in after the fish. She is all nervous energy, raised up on her toes, her entire body quivering in anticipation as she does everything short of diving in. But she never does. Year after year, the Writer has watched her watching the bass, driving herself to distraction and yet never making her move—it's as if she agreed a long time ago that this is a matter of turf, and she has resigned herself to the honouring of that agreement. Perhaps in her most satisfying of sleeps, she

dreams of a morning when she wanders down to see the smallmouth actually loung-
ing on top of the dock and then, by God, all bets are off.

By the time the Writer wanders back up the hill to the cabin, the Steelmaker will
be up and he will have encouraged the Auto Worker to cover up. The Steelmaker is
a take-charge guy and he soon has the kitchen humming. He is the smartest one in
the cabin. He is twice as smart as everyone else but only half as smart as he thinks.
It's a combination that seems to work. While cooking breakfast, he will periodically
poke his head into the bedroom and shout at the Hockey Player to get up.

Which eventually the Hockey Player does. The Hockey Player is a voracious and
slow eater. The rest of the group sits and watches the feeding process, impatient to
get on with the first half of the day's activity, which is golf.

Clear Springs Golf Course is located south of Astorville, on a gravel road in the back-
woods, a little eighteen-hole gem of a course cut precisely into the heart of the
Canadian Shield. Porcupines are as common as birdies on this track, and the
unsuspecting hacker who arrives without bug spray will soon become acquainted
with a particularly bloodthirsty strain of black fly, whose bite would put your average
pit bull to shame.

The course is run by a French Canadian family, the distaff side including the
three lovely daughters usually featured in farmer's-daughters jokes. But these
women are nobody's punchlines. As hard as the Precambrian rock on which they
were weaned, they are more than a match for a hungover crew of misfits from the
south of the province. (It is quite likely that the women suspect anyone hailing from
south of Weber's hamburger joint on Highway 11 of being a little on the soft side anyway.)

Heading for the first tee, the group watches cautiously for telltale signs of
Dwayne. On their first visit to the course, several years earlier, they were teeing off
as a threesome, when the pines suddenly parted and Dwayne strolled out onto the
teebox, like Meriwether Lewis just returned from the West. Dwayne announced that
he was looking for a game, although where exactly he'd been looking was question-
able, the area he'd just emerged from being one inhabited by bears, skunks, porcupines and raccoons. The group, courteous to a fault, welcomed him along.

Dwayne is long on information pertaining to his expertise in golf and short on any other aspects of his life. He reveals that he is from the nearby town of Callander and not currently employed, as he is working on his "thesis," the subject of which remains a mystery. There is somewhat less mystery surrounding his skill on the links. Teeing off on the second hole, Dwayne launches a screaming hook that flies so long and high and left that it sails over the road that borders the course and lands, presumably, somewhere just north of Lake Ontario. Dwayne tees another ball, hacks it down the fairway and then announces to the group that due to a "local rule" there is no penalty assessed for his first shot. Over the course of the day, several such "local rules" crop up, basically every time Dwayne loses a ball or hits a clunker out of bounds. It is quickly assumed that Dwayne's thesis is not on ethics.

It is Dwayne who introduces the group to the actual spring that lends the course its name. After unleashing a slice off number eight tee that would make Jack the Ripper blush, Dwayne watches the ball soar far to the right, his head cocked, listening the way a cocker spaniel listens for the can opener. When he hears the splash, he turns to the group.

"Come on," says he. "And bring your canteens."

Alas, the group has forgotten its canteens, along with its Winchesters, lariats and spurs, but it follows along. Dwayne leads the group through a grove of scrub oak to the edge of a large pond. The pond is fed by a two-inch steel pipe, which has been tapped into the underground spring. Dwayne is kneeling beside the pipe, and yes, he is holding a canteen.

"This is the best water in the north," he announces. "And as cold as ice. It must be a hundred degrees."

Presumably, Dwayne's thesis is not on weights and measures, either.

After playing the front nine, the group stops at the clubhouse for lunch. The featured item on the menu is the Hound Dog, which consists of a large wiener on a bun, the wiener butterflied flat and filled with ham and melted cheese, and the whole thing grilled to a gooey state of what Dagwood Bumstead would surely call perfection. The proper way to order a Hound Dog, the Steelmaker has decided, is to howl like a lovesick coyote at the top of one's lungs. The management has grudgingly come to accept this method of placing an order, and when the whole group opts for the special, the result is a cacophony as blood-curdling as anything Céline Dion has ever recorded.

The group arrives back at camp at around four o'clock, having stopped in Callander for bait, liquor, newspapers, beer, bread, lottery tickets and ice, and begins to prepare for the night fish. Coolers and bait and tackle are loaded into the boats. Coveralls and jackets for the cool nights. Rain gear. Whatever miracle fish-catching gizmo the Hockey Player has purchased at the bait shop.

There is considerable talk all the week long about the most efficient colours to use in the angling process, whether one is using jigs or lures, spinners or harness. In this, there seems to be a bizarre connection to the world of fashion. Several years ago, it was accepted as fact that hungry pickerel were enamoured of anything chartreuse. As a result, men who until that point in their lives would have actually questioned the sexual orientation of anyone using the word "chartreuse," were now tossing the word around like a Frisbee. Since then, the chartreuse phase seems to have faded—each year another colour is the rage. One has to wonder how the fish manage to keep abreast of the latest fads, especially when the lack of sunlight at the depth of sixty or seventy feet pretty much makes one colour indiscernible from another anyway.

For the record, the Writer is convinced that fish, like most of God's creatures, will, when presented with food, eat when they're hungry, fast when they're not, and not give a damn whether the food is red, yellow, green or plaid. The Writer further

MEN WHO UNTIL THAT POINT IN THEIR LIVES WOULD HAVE ACTUALLY QUESTIONED THE SEXUAL ORIENTATION OF ANYONE USING THE WORD "CHARTREUSE," WERE NOW TOSSING THE WORD AROUND LIKE A FRISBEE.

believes that men who are already jigging, rigging, quaffing, listening to the Jays game on the radio, and talking philosophy are just a tad busy to be fretting over the sartorial condition of their bait.

A Lake Nipissing pickerel is not the lunker fish found in the Bay of Quinte or Lake Erie. Most weigh in at between two and three pounds, and they provide a beautiful example of their species, varying in hue from a pale to brilliant yellow. In a frying pan, they have no equal—their bigger kin from the south are as tough and as tasteless as your average work boot, due in part, one suspects, to sustained marination in polluted waters.

The best time of the day is dusk, with just the right chop and a few fish on the stringer, and two or three old and genuine friends in the boat, talking a lot about nothing or talking a little about everything and not caring, finally, if the fish are biting or not. Late at night there exists on the lake something liberating, something which suggests that the usual rules don't apply here, that this is neutral ground and that all that matters is the company and the conversation and the brilliant sky to the west.

Upon the demise of a clear day on the lake, the anglers are treated to as beautiful a sunset as is found on the planet. The sun hangs suspended over the water, sinking slowly from the western sky into the western shore as if being extinguished in the lake. As it sets, there appears a shimmering corridor of red light across the water, wide as a prairie field. The corridor recedes and narrows as the sun dips farther into the horizon until it disappears altogether, like an eyelid descending over an eye.

As if God has decided that he will end this glorious day not with a nod.

But a wink.

In his twenties, Brad Smith travelled around Canada, the southern States and in Africa, searching for the spirits of Jack Kerouac, Jack London and Jack Daniel's and working as a farmhand, bartender, truck driver, teacher and railroad signalman. His second novel, One-Eyed Jacks, *was nominated for the Dashiell Hammett Award and Arthur Ellis Award and was optioned for film; his third novel,* All Hat, *will be published in the United States and Canada in the spring of 2003. He works as a carpenter and a writer in Dunnville, Ontario.*

A BRAZILIAN NOTEBOOK
Andrew Pyper

February 8
São Paulo

Smashed bottle of raspberry-like juice (they call it *guarana*) on the marble floor of the airport looks like spilled blood.

The city seems to have been built overnight in 1960 with no changes made since, except perhaps for the newsagent stands selling hardcore porn on every corner (newspapers are a sideshow). Even the clothing the women wear is perfectly uniform, as though they are on their way to jobs involving the *making* of porn: supertight white pants, heels, push-up bras and tank tops.

Tired, and the city isn't made for sitting but moving. Everything is fast food: the cafés, the bars, the restaurants. Where is everyone going? Why do they need to get there so quickly? I'm just shy. I'd like to be flowing along with the others to fixed destinations—offices, meetings, lovers' apartments—if I knew them, or could see this city as home, as they do.

Piranha's jaw necklace.

What was I expecting of this place? Not quite as exhausted-looking, perhaps. More direct North American rip-offs (the sports bar with Bud signs in the window, the sit-down greasy spoon). A more "tropical" look (neon, indoor palms, references to "beach"). But there *is* the private helicopter taking off from the roof of the Bank of Boston building, and the odd Mercedes limo to show that there's money here looking to "develop" more money. And look: a too-loud American bore at the bar of the Hilton.

Note: Brazilians don't provide change. The onus lies with the customer to pay the exact amount. A curious and irritating way of doing business. If you have even close to the right bill in your wallet, the waiter will shrug and look at you as if to say, "Well, what are you gonna do?" As a consequence, I end up involuntarily leaving large tips.

However, the manioc with eggs (crunchy farina dust studded with scrambled yellow chunks) is better than you'd guess.

February 9
São Paulo

A.M. Off and on rain, the morning spent looking for stamps—and then a mailbox— to send letters home. Have idea for a short story, "Postcards," as a result of thinking of ridiculous time lag ("I'll be home by the time you get this . . ."). A guy in Canada keeps receiving these postcards from his girlfriend whom he already knows has died down here. It's like he's hearing her voice from "beyond," these dispatches hanging in the purgatory of snail mail, captured in canvas sacks sitting in the airport warehouses of Manaus, São Paulo, Atlanta, Mississauga, etc.

P.M. Really raining now. If it keeps up, I'll be forced to eat in the discouraging hotel restaurant (although I like the bar, in a 1975-golf-club-lounge sort of way). Must mention the hot-dog smell of the streets here. Partly because there are hot dogs for sale on every street, but the meat-composite theme seems to have been taken up in a more general way. Not unpleasant. Unlike, say, the gusts of concrete moistened by last night's piss. But it sounds like I'm complaining.

It can rain suddenly here! Heading to dinner around the corner from the hotel, then WHAM!, the heaviest rainfall I've ever been caught in. Waiting under eaves with people smiling sympathetically and saying things I can't understand. And what can I say? So far, nothing but "yes," "beer," "thank you"—and "Antarctica" (a type of beer), which doesn't count.

February 11
Manaus

The craziness begins here. The jungle (the *jungle!*) is visible on the airplane's approach, which from ten thousand feet up appears as a field of broccoli that spreads out farther and farther until the earth gets tired of it and drops away.

And heat. Like I've never fucking been slapped with before. One step out of the lobby of the Ana Cassia and I thought I was a goner. Improvements after a cold Coke bought on the street and a new ball cap (the Toronto one with the nylon flap in back from Urban Outfitters is too, too ridiculous).

Much stimulus on walk through the market: slabs of meat and fish offering unusual perfumes, the clustered riverboats, the Rio Negro itself, broad as a lake. Reminds me of a documentary of the kind shown in Social Studies classrooms when I was a kid. Something lens-distanced, containable, tidily anthropological about it all. Yet I know that this impression is only a mental defence mechanism, a way of seeing that calms the anxiety of being so far away from home.

No shit: black vultures fly over town. They eat fish guts and human filth, I'm told, and likely not humans themselves. Two just landed outside my window and are looking in at me hungrily nevertheless . . .

P.M. At night, a haunting image. Down a street away from the centre, one of the old French-style townhouses stands empty and cracked, full of bats, wrapped in vines. I stop and look at it, transfixed. A woman (a girl?) standing there assumes I want her attention and starts calling to me from across the street: something in Portuguese, then in English, "My friend! My friend! Come *here*, my friend!" I take off at a trot.

I love the weirdness of this town: a stucco pimple growing out of the middle of the jungle, a rubber fortune built on the backs of slaves, a sudden economic crash, empty shells. Yes, it's sad. And spooky. But mostly, I find it thrilling.

A drinking friend after dinner, an American who's just spent six weeks with a

National Geographic photographer in the jungle. Forty-five, a teacher in Maine. Fat (from a parasite, he says). Good stories. One involves Tetunka, the German-Indian son of a rape victim who acts as a guide and kills a good number of his guests for revenge, for the hell of it. Another is about the Brazilian government encouraging Indians into towns on the river to be "slaves" in lumber, but they end up sitting around watching TV most of the time. (Which is worse?)

Behind us, two barely teenaged prostitutes throw bits of napkin at my back to get our attention. My friend looks like a walrus. We exchange e-mail addresses that both of us know we will never use, lumber back to our hotels past the haunted house.

February 14
Valentine's Day in the Amazon: Will you be mine?

A.M. Trip to Indian village, which involved a long, Marlow-esque trip in a motorized canoe, which scratches some cinematic itch of the imagination. The forest slouching past, the water holding the boat to an even world. A fresh, moist breeze, the clouds a textbook selection of the flat, the explosive, the braided and the wispy. The planet, despite our very best efforts, continues to be beautiful.

In the village, a marriage of old and new (the handmade canoes, the one-shack school, the Tweety and Britney Spears T-shirts). We are watched from hut windows like uninvited soldiers.

Being far away and alone produces in me the side effect of having random snapshots of home come to mind with extraordinary vividness: the backyard of 571 Dovercourt, the view from my father's old office in Stratford. This is the strange way memory sharpens the world, so that the recollection becomes more tangible than the thing itself.

I felt, for an absurd moment, that I could live here.

Now a giant, translucent, grasshopper-like thing on my shoulder.

And now, a tall, stork-like bird—a *juburu*—lifts into the air, its legs dangling like cut ropes behind it. The few clouds pull back to throw laser beams down upon the canopy on either side of us. Only a moment ago the air was a mustard haze. Now it's instantly burned away. And we can see how close we are to the jungle, crowding in on us, standing atop fifty-foot stilts. So high and uninterrupted, our voices bounce back and forth in millisecond delay within the rib-cage of trees.

February 15

The Rio Negro is not black. It's a shadow. Deep and untouched by the sun except for a skin of purple scales on the surface. Look down from straight above, and there is nothing but oily shade, licking and curling upon itself. The narrow line of our wake bubbles up like agitated Pepsi.

People wonder about a man travelling alone: "What's wrong with him?" Yet this wondering lends him greater mystery than he likely deserves. Most of the people on these tours and in town are South American—exceptions are three or four German backpackers and a Japanese couple on the boat. The fixed tours booked in North America must protect the Midwestern hobblers from general public view.

Just had first mosquito bite.

Asked the guide about the dangers of travel in Colombia (abductions, tortures, ransoms), and he denied them. "The media," the guide said. I don't believe him.

February 18

A walk in the jungle this morning, learning all about how gum, Pepto-Bismol and tonic water come from trees.

In *Huck Finn*, the river was life, an almost innocent discovery, flowing outward through to the "discovery" of America. In *Heart of Darkness*, it's the inward path to the soul. What does it feel like to me? I'd say it's the path to the real, that which lies beyond the virtual, the programmable. The river has a way of peeling away our trained affectations and responses, the layers of protective irony. It takes manners out of us and replaces them with what, in time, might turn into simple madness.

Missed the afternoon's excursion as I fell asleep in a hammock by the river. Don't regret this. The American guy with the equestrian wife got on my nerves a little, though his condom in a cashew trick was very impressive.

February 25
Manaus

Bugs falling on the page.

Back in Manaus temporarily, waiting for the next boat to take me upriver. Walked by the harbour bars tonight: two fluorescent rooms side by side opening onto the street. Across from them, a bingo hall and a narrow entrance with a turnstile and, upstairs, a grim strip club. From an abandoned building with walls blasted out, the powerful stench of shit and garbage and piss all wound up by humidity and months of equatorial heat. I find all the decay and depravity kind of exciting. That is, it frightens me.

March 1

Aboard the *Clipper*, chugging north toward São Gabriel. Saw a beautiful green comet from the upper deck and made a wish. The stars are different here. The Southern Cross (a perfect, absurdly geometrical square) above instead of the Big Dipper.

Out of the bush comes a bug sound like some electronica backbeat: echoing, multi-layered, symphonic.

March 3

Jungle walk at dawn. Rougher. Had to machete through. Got bite on my face from something and now one side of my mouth has swollen up like a baseball. Realized how easy it is to get lost in forest this thick: the American couple took a wrong turn and for a minute, there was only their voices calling out, "Marcos! Marcos!" (the guide).

Ants literally in my pants. And my pack. Long lines of them hiking from one sock to their anthill. Their organization calms me.

A beautiful name for a butterfly I saw: Blue Morpho.

Note to self: Change your socks. These ones feel bad.

March 4

Up at 6:20 A.M. for breakfast. Inflamed throat and sinuses from now obviously ill-advised swim in the Negro yesterday. I gave the cook my Urban Outfitters cap in trade for her fried banana recipe (fry sliced banana in vegetable oil, sprinkle with cinnamon). People here smile a lot.

Saw meeting of the waters, where the tea-coloured Negro meets the *caffe latte*–coloured Amazon and then forms two ribbons that run side by side for several miles before mixing together and heading out to the Atlantic. After this, we made our way past Manaus to the Tropical Hotel. There's a mini-zoo, where there's monkeys in the cages, who, when you unzip your bag or put your hands in your pocket, stop everything and gather against the fence, hoping for food—as they do in every zoo, everywhere.

March 12
São Paulo

Hanging out at São Paulo airport, waiting for transfer flight to Toronto. Outside, the beautiful planes landing in impossible suspension in the Brazilian night. No, not "Brazilian." Any night, in any airport lounge, raising my head from the page and being happy to be here, nowhere in particular, carrying a head cold and my knapsack, going home.

Andrew Pyper is the author of Kiss Me, *a collection of stories, and* Lost Girls, *a novel selected as a Notable Book of the Year by the* Globe and Mail *and the* New York Times. *His second novel,* The Trade Mission *(researched in part by the journey described in "A Brazilian Notebook"), was published in the fall of 2002. Mostly he lives in Toronto.*

UP THE HOLY MOUNTAIN (AND DOWN BY CABLE CAR)
David Manicom

This is a Canadian brain—one of the youngest brains on the planet—looking at a Chinese thing. It is also the away-from-work brain, trying during a long-weekend outing to tear out some of the corporate synapses that train and constrain it, find some Web-free space and maybe a little startling beauty. It is a modern brain. While respectful of humanism's traditional urge to link up all with all, its first-things-first, survive-the-stress motto is "only disconnect." And now it is looking.

One of the particular beauties of Tai Shan, most holy and rootedly Chinese of China's sanctified peaks, is cypress. Living antiques, wind-grey, age-sprained like free-range bonsai, yet green still, supporting verdure after so many centuries of blood and thunder and ceremonial tea. The textured foliage is cut-papercraft complicated. Look at them all, says the Canadian brain, lining the unscrolling ceremonial path up the mountain, filtering the sunlight into lace handkerchiefs, each with a goddamned tin strip nailed into its venerable flesh. Number tags, naturally. Inventoried cypress. A calculated forest. You could doubtlessly load the thing into a database and run some stats.

Probably planted in the Ming dynasty, pruned in the Qing, and not quite chopped down during the Cultural Revolution.

A sound idea, presumably, counting your trees, logging them in a ledger for the annual tree report and maybe a five-year tree plan with the word "conservation" in the title. We've flown down from Beijing where we live, where there are ten thousand red taxis with "Green Beijing" bumper stickers, and decals in their windows chanting "Build New Beijing Hold Great Olympics." Amid an ideology of demolition, the rhetoric of conservation thrives.

But the gleaming backdrop for cypress grey and green, that sky, new every day, beyond the tenacious counted trees, lifts my spirit toward beauty. I have the kind of Canadian brain now, at forty-one and in its eighth year abroad in societies old as coal, that says things like that to itself. And then notices it said it. It's a gorgeous autumn day, and I'm on a holy Chinese mountain, moving steadily along its elegant narrative spine up a set of 6,600 broad stone steps (laid by the Ming, spruced up by the Qing, and too sturdy for the Red Guards to scar). I'm walking it with my wife and children and thousands of holidaying Han Chinese. We're a ten-thousand-segment snake with its head on the bald crown of heaven and its tail down at the Red Gate with the taxis and souvenir stands. The gate is the official launching point of the climb, and pretty new by local standards. It was built around Shakespeare's day by the Ming, refurbished by the Qing a few centuries later, and is flanked by one Taoist and one Buddhist temple in honour, respectively, of the Princess of the Rosy Clouds and the Amitabha Buddha. Hedging your bets is, in general, the Chinese approach to stairways to heaven.

The Chinese are chatting, grinning, plodding, eating as regularly as Hobbits and having a whale of a time. I figure they'd be having an even better time if their numbers were doubled. I've been in Beijing supermarkets where the fruit and vegetable section felt like a mosh pit—just as crushing and just as buzzing with good vibes. It's not badly crowded here. There's a lot of mountain to spread out on, six hours foot-to-peak at our pace. Just a steady flow, half ascending, half (having overnighted on the peak to watch the sunrise) marching down.

Except I'm not marching anywhere at the moment. I've sat down in the diffuse autumn sunlight to take notes about one of the lovelier temples and to breathe a little air.

Tai Shan has been sacred through Communist, Qing, Ming, Song, Tang, Han, Confucian, Buddhist and Taoist dynasties, ideologies and faiths, back to the earliest cults. This, combined with the emperors' habit of climbing the "Honourable Mountain," has led to a Central Way littered with temples, stelae and relics galore amid the enumerated groves. The Five Taoist and imperial holy mountains (there is also an agreed-upon set of nine Buddhist holy peaks) have held their special status since before the Han dynasty; they were already ancient in renown to the great Han historian Sima Qian in the second century BC. In the Tang, a mere 1,300 years ago, this mountain was given the title *Tian Qi Wang*, "King Equal to the Sky." We're a quarter of the way to the sky.

Across from me is a gracious small Taoist temple with red-brown walls. It has a modest paved plaza with a view over the gardened rooftops of a small village and on into cypress and pine. The Goddess Doumei temple has sat here since ancient times. An inscription suggests a Ming bureaucrat-abbot guarded it just the day before yesterday, in the 1500s, when the Spaniards were bumping into America. A cool courtyard within is of swept earth, centred by a small pond for luck, getting the wind and water on your side. The grey-tile Ming eaves fold down like half-enclosing wings. It is dim in the inner sanctum, incense and candlelight and gold. A vendor's shrill speaker back down the path scrapes my eardrum like a fork on a plate, but for a moment here and there, you can screen it out and catch a bit of birdsong.

The breeze is cool, but each sunlit stone is warm as fresh bread. The others have gone on ahead. I'm trying to focus on the geometry of sensation in this courtyard, soil and grey eaves, and coins in the pool under dusty cypress beneath high-voltage sky. But my multi-tasking modern mind is remembering a note in my Blue

Guide that says the actual tip of the mountain is now enclosed within a building. This seems like moving Mount Kilimanjaro to Vegas or wrapping a pool with a swim-up bar around the source of the Nile; but a colleague will later remind me that the hushed titanic cathedrals of Europe were, in their heyday, hubbubs of market and pilgrim trinkets and sweat.

So I try to stop thinking, and I look up from my nib's inky trail. A ring of Chinese tourists has formed three feet away. They smile pleasantly, eyes open and direct. If there is any social taboo against staring in China, it doesn't apply to *laowai*. They are murmuring and pointing, gaga at my spectacular gymnastic feat of carving out English letters with my left hand. I lift my pen and shrug, to their enjoyment. Behind me, a sign hammered onto an outcropping reads, "The Vocks Are Dangerous, No Staying Place."

There are no staying places. Time looks after that. We've come down from Beijing two weeks after the World Trade Centre massacre. The nearest airport to Tai Shan is at Jinan, where it was unseasonably cold, damp with drizzle. At the door of the plane, coal smoke stung our eyes; a damp mist that was part nature, part burnt sulphur followed us through a barren terminal to an under-lit exit and a disinterested club of taxi drivers hawking phlegm and slapping cards. All the way into town, factories and brick kilns funnelled burnt earth into the air. Jinan, like all Chinese cities worthy of a dot on the map, has millions of people, but few were out. The noxious cloud was suffocating the street lights. At ten on a Saturday night, Jinan had the feel of a town that turns in early.

The arrival of twenty-first-century Asia à la Hong Kong, Singapore and Shanghai is still spotty in the Chinese provinces, where a city of two million is small potatoes and barely noticed on the org charts. The old government-run three-stars still clock in with one-star service, though the smiling desk clerks with one hundred words of English are trying to try. The marble and tinsel lobbies are spic and span. Little else is. The rooms are bleak and musty, the beds rocky. Coffee may or may not be had; the cable package has fourteen local channels and Star Sports Spanish League football. The cheerful lady who sets up the extra cot for our six-year-old proceeds to neatly dress it with a damp sheet. Doesn't she notice? Doesn't she care? Over our bed, someone has hung a photo of a couple embracing in Hawaii-sunset silhouette, one female nipple outlined against the sky as clearly as a holy mountain. A stab at sophistication gone askew: apparently scissored from a magazine, it has been glued on at least ten degrees off square. Didn't they notice?

But morning dawned clear and washed, breakfast was decent, and our car zipped toward Tai'an, the town in the shadow of the mountain, down a freshly built toll expressway through a lush autumn harvest. The road looked as though it had been dumped rudely on the landscape yesterday, a bit crooked. It didn't seem to touch the Shandong plain, but we were cheered by the sky and the smooth ride. Cornstalks were tied in grey-green stooks; rooftops and farmyards and the tarmac at gas stations glowed ripely with the old-gold burnish of nubbly seas of spread corn drying on the cob. We passed a man under a peasant hat and shoulder yoke, trundling the expressway shoulder, walking in two different eras. The Ming emperors

THE ARRIVAL OF TWENTY-FIRST-CENTURY ASIA À LA HONG KONG, SINGAPORE AND SHANGHAI IS STILL SPOTTY IN THE CHINESE PROVINCES, WHERE A CITY OF TWO MILLION IS SMALL POTATOES AND BARELY NOTICED ON THE ORG CHARTS.

may have seen the same image. Is China full of history or empty of time? The roadside stands were laden with two mellow fruits: plastic Confucius tourist baubles (the sage's birthplace at Qufu is nearby) and bins of stupendous red apples. Above Tai'an, the mountain reclined like a lazy green panther as we pulled in.

Poorer than Beijing, the city has more the air of South Asia due to a plenitude of belching buses and whining scooters bearing entire families. Dusty, it is also well-treed and, in many districts, freshly painted. In the middle of town, a broad street exits straight uphill to meet the god. In the opposite direction, the boulevard's lower reaches are a perpetual bazaar, vending a herbology of plants from sprouts to trees via the scout-knot contortions of bonsai, and an accompanying cordillera of pots, from thimbles to planters the size of pickup trucks. Lower still, a bird market. In China, birds, for mysterious reasons, are the companions of old men—never children, never workers, never retired women.

At the very bottom of the inverted T, whose tip is the holy peak, broods the massive Dai Miao temple, one of the greatest and saddest of Chinese relics, constructed for the rites of visiting emperors as far back as the Han, rebuilt in splendour during the Chinese cultural zeniths of the Tang and Song, supplemented during the Ming and Qing, and crudely patched over in recent decades, with a few dusty exhibits of painfully poor quality. The central hall of the Imperial and Taoist cult is again in full operation, with photo-snapping tourists burning incense and buying prayer sheets. This cult has the official thumbs up. Yet somewhere far off, there is a fine filigree crack in the globe. A small whine of dental drill, or a water droplet falling, or a *tock* like a woodpecker's assault on the spine: a devotee of the wrong cult, a Falun Gong follower is being tortured.

Hiking the trail up Tai Shan, like all wondrous journeys, has pace and rhythm, and a great narrative hook. The hook comes at the halfway mark of Zhongtianmen, the gate of Middle Heaven. We have been climbing the steps for three hours. The shoulder of the mountain and the thick cypress groves have permitted no vistas forward. We are refreshed by a simple lunch of thin pancake, egg and shallot fried on a barrel-top charcoal burner and folded—a sort of Chinese fajita. This is a nice hike, we say. As we see the first signs of the midway station, we know we will make the top. Another couple of hours of strolling. The three kids will be fine. Adrian, the youngest, has only needed to be carried a few times.

Twenty minutes later, our thighs are numbing on an unusually steep flight of steps without landings; but, gasping, we emerge as if from a basement staircase onto a busy piazza, amid milling crowds. Flexing our knees, catching air, we wander forward. We are stopped short by a dynamic and deflating panorama. We have cleared a ridge, and now, across a broad depression, a span of mountain lap, we can see the top. The kids weren't prepared. "Wow. No way." Not a jagged crag, but, impossibly far off (given we are walking with the expectation of actually *going* there), a blunt stone forehead against a stray cloud and, at the edge of sight, a thin line scratched vertically to a notch at the top: a human ladder carved in stone. The steps.

We won't walk it all at once, I announce, trying to quell rebellion. We will climb it a bit at a time. There's no hurry. Now I am under the power of the place. A wisp of worshipfulness slips through my work-a-day cortex. The worshipfulness, like love, joins me to something, connects me to histories and cultures whether I wish it or not. We refuel, visit appalling toilets, head down into the pines and then, slowly, the mountain rearing and steepening and then standing up straight, we put one foot in front of the other, step after step after step, all afternoon.

Hours devolve into minutes, minutes into seconds, the mass into the moment, the here and now of the next step up. We thirst for the flat, the brief landing, the pause in the vertical. Adrian now clings to my back. As we haul forward, upward, I can balance him using a walking stick as the third leg of a tripod. Those passing us on the way down nod approvingly and give me a thumbs-up. I am being absorbed into their communal project, and that's okay by me. The trees thin out, uncounted. The treads grow narrower, half a foot deep, and the risers grow higher. The staircase narrows. Entrepreneurs appear, wiry veterans, offering rides on their shoulders for a fee. I have a momentary madcap hallucination of me astride a bony neck, Adrian still on mine, a jerky giraffe scaling the holy heights. The notch in the sky creeps toward us.

During the final ascent, there are no more landings, no spots broad enough on the steep flights to trust my trembling arms to lift Adrian off my slack shoulders, so he stays put in spite of my fatigue. On these last few hundred steps of the 6,600, we are above shade, silhouetted on the mountain's face. It is so steep that Caitlin, fourteen, can face only forward due to vertigo. Twisting around to look at where we've been on this journey is dizzying and menacing, Eurydice's path turned inside out and exposed. We realize that going down the way we came up would be lunatic. The cable car we had sniffed at (how can you do a pilgrimage, see the "real China," cruising up Tai Shan in a cable car?) will have to ferry us down.

We're there. We stagger to a benison of the horizontal and sit down. The crown reached, Shandong province far below reposes dustily in all directions. Crowds beat a hasty path to a summit street jammed with karaoke and postcards, and loudspeakers playing the light pop that China adores; Britney doing it again, Backstreet being back. The view is gorgeous; it's as holy as Wal-Mart.

But we are almost immune. We are high with our own perseverance and the glorious millennia-rich pathway we've trodden. Maybe our Chinese co-walkers are immune too, inoculated with their labour. Of course they haven't walked encumbered with Canadian brains. But I've gradually come to conclude that the only thing more dangerous than indulging in ethnocultural generalizations is ignoring them, intricate and evolving and elusive as they are. The Chinese think without thinking that they've always been here and always will be. China has various anxieties, but the reality of their link to this vast lobe of Asia isn't one of them. They're well-connected. The Communist Party, currently playing P. T. Barnum and John D. Rockefeller by turns, may be as identity-conscious as a teen with bad skin, but the populace they deign to protect and torture exhibit less cultural anxiety than any on the planet. I envy them this from time to time, I think as we go dutifully to the gleaming new Swiss-built cable car and swing out into green air.

But if I didn't have this particular brain, outgrowth on the edge of an assortment of empires, I would have no envy to meditate on, to eventually dismiss. I belong to enough networks. It may be arrogance to believe we have a more Heisenbergian angle on things than the Ptolemaic imperiums, more sapling flex than countries older than coal, but we permit ourselves few other boasts, so what the hell.

On the plane back to Beijing and toward Monday morning and the office and budgets and personnel plans and embassy committees and the diplomatic formulae of tough business with this compelling, inferiority-complex-ridden, polite bully of a newly emerging ancient nation, I realize what's nagging the back of my head, what's different about this flight. The TV screens are illuminated, the music channel is on, then the news. But there are no headphones. An alternative voice is not an option. Silence is not to be thought of. We sit in our schoolroom rows with traces of the holy mountain of cypress and dove-grey temple roofs and stone gates and the endless unfolding fan of the steps as an autumn liqueur in our veins: all of us listening to the same damned thing, tin strips being hammered in. In China you need a thousand images just to begin the poem. One down.

David Manicom has published three collections of poetry, an award-winning volume of short fiction, and Progeny of Ghosts: Travels in Russia and the Old Empire, which won the Quebec Writers' Federation Mavis Gallant Prize for Non-Fiction and was shortlisted for the Writers' Development Trust Award for Non-Fiction. A Canadian Foreign Service officer, he currently lives with his family in Beijing. His next book of poetry, The Burning Eaves, will be published in 2003.

OFF-SEASON IN PUERTO VALLARTA
Warren Dunford

Directly beneath the balcony of my hotel room is the main beach of Puerto Vallarta. In February, the scene will be wall-to-wall towels, but now, in September, the golden sand is almost bare. Palm trees gently sway. The sound of the surf is loud enough to create a constant hypnotic spell. It's the epitome of tropical splendour.

I am determined to ignore it.

My goal for the week is to hide in my room and not speak to a single soul. I am here to write, and off-season—the hottest, most humid time of year—provides the perfect conditions for self-discipline.

How could I sunbathe when merely removing my hat for ten seconds feels as if someone has splashed hot oil on my bald spot? And the undercurrent on Playa Los Muertos—Beach of the Dead—is so strong that tourists frequently drown or break ankles or at least dislocate shoulders.

So I'm better off staying inside, sequestered in my minimalist white room, cooled by the ceiling fan and focused on writing ten pages a day.

Culturally distinctive but practical souvenirs.

My only torment is the maid.

I know she's not intentionally trying to provoke me, but it annoys me that she doesn't clean my room at the same time each day. Her inconsistency profoundly affects my concentration.

Will I have fifteen more minutes to be prolific? Or two hours? I like to know this, so I can pace myself.

Each morning at nine, I silently, surreptitiously, open the door to the hallway and look for the maid's cart. It's not there. So I go back to work. I lie stomach-down on the bed and scribble longhand in a school notebook, while the rough cotton sheets give me elbow burn.

Was that a sound in the hall? I sneak open the door and spy on a family of German tourists as they head off to the beach. I wonder if they'd let me go with them.

But no, back to work. I check again five minutes later. And five minutes after that.

After two hours, the maid's cart suddenly appears beside a room at the far end of the hall. Now I must guess her exact time of arrival, based on the cart's proximity, so I can put on my sandals and be ready to evacuate at a moment's notice.

The problem is I don't speak Spanish. Despite my frequent visits to Mexico, I know little beyond *por favor* and *gracias*. The one phrase I really should learn is "When will you be cleaning my room?" Or better still: "Would you please clean my room NOW?" It would be so simple. I could look it up in any Spanish phrase book.

But my whole reason for going to Puerto Vallarta is to stop communicating, and as a writer, frankly, I'm sick of knowing so many words. I find it refreshing to go to a place where I don't understand any of them.

So I wait—writing, or more likely, reading a trashy paperback—and finally the maid knocks on my door. She wears a fitted white uniform. She's in her forties and she has tired eyes but a lovely, warm smile. I smile back, mumble, wave my hands, gesturing obliquely to the tip beside the bed, and scurry off down the hall.

Outside the hotel, the cobblestone streets are lined with white-washed condos

From the origami-laden bathroom.

and tiny red-tile-roofed houses. Families lounge on lawn chairs on the sidewalk, and home cooking thickens the air with a spicy, smoky aroma that's almost intoxicating.

This neighbourhood is known as the Zoña Romantica—though romance is not on my personal agenda.

I go to the convenience store.

On my first visit to Mexico, I was thrown into a gringo panic attack: I was ravenously hungry, yet terrified that whatever I ate would induce immediate vomiting and diarrhea. Feeling weak, I found a small grocery shop and purchased the only items that seemed safe and familiar: tequila and baby cookies. The cookies—just a few pesos a roll—are called Marias, and they're like arrowroot biscuits, only slightly more lemony. Their sweetness is perfectly cut by a tequila chaser.

THE PROBLEM IS I DON'T SPEAK SPANISH. THE ONE PHRASE I REALLY SHOULD LEARN IS "WHEN WILL YOU BE CLEANING MY ROOM?" OR BETTER STILL: "WOULD YOU PLEASE CLEAN MY ROOM *NOW?*"

Over the years, these items have become staples in my Mexican diet. I stock up with a fresh bottle of Cuervo Gold and a few packages of Marias.

When I get back from the convenience store, the maid's cart has been abandoned. She hasn't even started my room.

I think about all the brilliant writing I would definitely be doing right now, and I head back to the street. In the midday swelter, I walk several blocks and discover the hyper-air-conditioned Farmaçia Guadalajara—the perfect place to cool down.

I scour the aisles, searching for culturally distinctive yet practical souvenirs for friends back home. I find a brand of toothpaste called Lucky Star—the ideal gift for Madonna fans. I know several people who'll appreciate an underarm deodorant called Mum for Men. And I become infatuated with a box of women's hairpins that must have time-travelled to the shelf from the 1930s. The olive-green woman on the package resembles Gloria Swanson in *Sunset Boulevard*.

As I walk back to the hotel, I stop by the beach and stare out at the water. The bay extends in a massive sapphire-blue circle, defined by matching mountain slopes that remind me of two curving arms, with the old town right in the heart of the embrace.

When I get up to my room, the maid is nearly done. She's mopping the red-tile floor, and she doesn't notice me, so I tiptoe down the hall and sit on the staircase. Hiding there, I open a package of cookies and wonder if I'll ever be able to recover my concentration enough to write.

Then, suddenly, there's the maid standing in front of me, watching me knock back a mouthful of tequila. She motions to my room, smiles shyly, and we both say, "*Gracias.*"

In the bathroom, I find that she's left me with intricate towel and toilet paper origami—delicate sculptures resembling sailboats, swans and tuxedo shirts—so lovely they're like those gifts you can't bear to open. But by now I'm so hot and drenched in sweat that I desperately need a shower . . .

In the evening, after I've finished work and taken myself out for dinner, I sit on the balcony and watch the rain. That's what I love most about September in Puerto Vallarta. Every night there's a thunderstorm of a magnitude that I might have to wait for all summer at home. In the darkness, lightning forks down viciously into the bay. But sheltered here, behind a veil of pelting raindrops, the night feels blissfully calm.

After seven days of this identical routine, I can't write or read another word. The solitude, the repetitiveness and the tequila slow me down to a numb, zombie-like lethargy.

But I've come to see boredom as healing. My mind achieves a stillness and quiet that other people might find

124

through yoga or meditation—renewing my patience, lengthening my attention span and increasing my appreciation for just about anything. I actually start to miss my hectic lifestyle back home. And that's the sure sign that I'm ready to end my off-season and turn myself back on.

Warren Dunford is the author of two novels, Soon To Be a Major Motion Picture *and* Making a Killing, *both of which were partially written in Puerto Vallarta. He lives in Toronto.*

CLOSE ENCOUNTERS OF THE EURO-TRASH KIND
Deirdre Kelly

Gabriel lived in a noisy section of Saint Germain, upstairs from a Greek restaurant and around the corner from an outdoor market hawking fruit and fish, oxtails and onions. A well-travelled acquaintance had given me his number when she found out I would be spending a few weeks in Paris that summer. "He's fun," she had said in a smoky Toronto bar. "He'll show you around."

I called a few days into my trip, out of boredom. "*Ah, je suis une amie d'Astrid,*" I said with eyes closed over the telephone, hoping he wouldn't hear me blushing. He told me to meet him the next night, at his apartment in the Latin Quarter. He would take me to dinner. And to the famous nightclub Castel, where he was working as a kind of disco manager.

I was staying with a high school friend, Danielle, who had been living in Paris since taking a business degree at Fontainebleau, and her prim virginal ways were chewing on my nerves. She had taken up photography, and everywhere we walked, through the Marais, the Place des Vosges, Montmartre, she held a Canon camera protectively against one eye. She took pictures of monuments only, not people.

Since escaping the ivory tower of university I was looking for more flesh-and-blood action. I had been a nun consecrated to books during all of my undergraduate years. I was now full of sexual yearning. I took to reading a worn copy of André Gide that I had found in an English bookstore—*The Fruits of the Earth*—and one night actually started to weep because his words made me realize that I was missing out on life somehow, by refusing to savour its sensual riches. I resolved then and there to do something reckless. Like have an adventure. For all that might involve.

But as my guide to hedonism, Gabriel was more than I had bargained for.

He answered the door wearing a thigh-high black kimono, his blond mane of curls sliding off the satin at the shoulders. He asked if I wanted a *coupe de champagne*. I heard it as *coup*, and thought at first he was offering me a slap. I sipped self-consciously while sitting on a chocolate-brown sofa strewn with animal-print cushions and throws, while he got ready for dinner.

It was the summer of Michael Jackson's *Thriller*. I can still remember the thrusting pulse of "Billie Jean" as it blared as we entered the restaurant. It was one of those insider places where the owner behind the bar nods silently at you as at an old friend. I was deeply impressed. It was also the summer of Yannick Noah, the dreadlocked, drop-dead gorgeous tennis star. And he was right there at a table, with an entourage of fabulously good-looking people, celebrating his victory at the French Open that day. Gabriel called it the "Roland Garros," like I and everyone else in the world knew what that meant.

The more I drank the more fluently I could speak French. Gabriel was clearly bemused by me. He looked at me, his eyes crinkling at the corners, probably thinking, "Astrid owes me a favour."

After dinner, we moved on to the celebrated nightclub where he worked, party palace to lubricious European princes and their leggy model girlfriends. But it was early when we arrived, ten o'clock. The dance floor in the bowels of the discotheque was empty. Gabriel slipped off into the darkness, leaving me in the care of a burly Lebanese bodyguard named Fifi. We chatted amiably about his job: limousined thuggery, or so I thought he said. Castel was dark and labyrinthine, with a narrow spiralling staircase and dark wood panelling, and corners where blow jobs were given, coke was snorted, and deals were whispered through thick clouds of burning Gitane cigarettes. It was difficult to hear anything over the pounding music: Duran Duran, Bowie, raspy-voiced Italian pop. After a few more drinks, it started to sound pretty good. I gently excused myself from Fifi.

The dance floor was now awash in Gucci shoes, Ferragamo neckties, real diamonds, fake tans, and eyeliner. Sometimes I clued in that someone was trying to dance with me. But I didn't want to connect. I ignored all with the exception of a dark older man whom I met while ordering another drink. He asked, in dignified French, where I was from, and when I said, "Canada," he leaned in and said he was a good friend of my prime minister, Pierre Trudeau. Talk about an icebreaker. He said he was a minister in the government of Morocco. Had I ever been to Morocco? "Ah then, you must come to Morocco. I will buy you gorgeous clothes. Take you to all the best nightclubs."

At dawn, I left with Gabriel instead. He had occasionally come to check on me throughout the night with a "*Ça va?*" and a good-natured squeeze of the shoulders. He was likeable. At the end of the night, when I felt I had had enough, I found him upstairs in an inner chamber, sipping Scotch and playing cards with Duc de So-and-so and his titled *confrères*, their ties pulled from their collars in full playboy fashion. I hadn't planned on being seduced by Gabriel. But when he asked if I wanted another *coupe*, I thought: You want experience.

I went upstairs, and with lightning speed, off went my bra and the black silk wide-leg pants that my mother had bought me, hoping I would have a swellegant time in a city she had only ever dreamed about. I was wearing a G-string, which Gabriel also tore off with a swift swipe of the paw. "You like gay?" he asked. "I am gay." I didn't know what shocked me more: his first words of English or this startling admission. The person who had given me his number was 100 per cent woman. I was still grappling with the meaning of it all, when Oh! Ouch! Stop! So that is what he meant.

After my night in the jungle of Saint Germain, I felt lonely. And loneliness in a foreign city can drive you to do things you wouldn't normally do. It makes you desperate to connect. Which is why the next day I called the Moroccan with the beautifully tailored suit and avuncular manner: I wanted to be adored.

I wanted security—the kind only someone in the full narcissistic bloom of youth could convince herself comes from an older and rich man wanting to shower her with compliments and gifts. I called him at his Paris hotel, and he was thoroughly delighted and cute on the phone, calling me "*chérie*" and saying, "*je t'embrasse.*" Because he was just about to fly back to Morocco, he would leave all the arrangements for my visit in the hands of his female associate, who was staying behind in Paris. It seemed so effortless and easy. I thought: If this is the continental way, I'll just go with the flow. I relaxed.

Off I went the next morning to meet his female associate for café au lait on the Champs Élysées. The woman with the large sad eyes called him Doo Doo, but I couldn't laugh because her manner was solemn. Morocco, she told me, was a land of beaches and late-night parties. My understanding was that Doo Doo was a busy man and likely had a wife, and would be joining up with me only occasionally, when he could. Again, the emphasis was on gorgeous new clothes, and, in addition, there would be a house on the beach; it was in Marrakesh and I would go there after first landing in Casablanca. The woman had first-class airline tickets in her purse, which she stuffed heatedly in my hand.

But first I was to meet the family. Why, I wondered? To show me off? A custom of some sort? I didn't question it, however, and followed her meekly like a pup through the busy, winding streets of Paris's first arrondissement. She led me to an apartment where her Arab sisterhood lay waiting. The shutters were closed, the lights dimmed. In a corner sat the matriarch, a square block of black robes, fanning herself with a worn copy of *Oh la!* magazine and staring menacingly. Other women burst through the door, armed with shopping bags filled with designer clothes. They wiggled their ample figures in and out of garments at least two sizes too small, grunting and sweating and invoking Princess Caroline, patron saint of the Euro-trash community. They stared, envious of my twenty-three-year-old figure, then cooed that I was so lucky to be going to Morocco with cousin Doo Doo because he was VERY gentle.

When I heard those words I realized the general expectation was that I was going to be having sex with this guy. I had been a bit staggered by the suggested transfer of wealth my way. Of course there had been fleeting moments of concern, but I was a student with an opportunistic streak, and arrogantly, I did think I'd pull it off. I thought this was about a free trip with a little hand-holding to a city that Humphrey Bogart had made glamorous. I had assessed Doo Doo to be gentlemanly and devoted, and I thought I would somehow just slip out of the noose at the last minute. But I suddenly saw myself in an over-decorated apartment, clutching the embroidered arm of a faux Louis XV chair, about to sell my soul for a night in Casablanca. And just in time, a voice in my head screamed, "HELL NO!"

Miserable in the streets of Paris that afternoon, I worried about how I would escape this fine mess and come out wearing my own baggy clothes.

I confessed all to Danielle. Flabbergasted, she dropped her croissant and grabbed me by the arm, hailing a taxi. I was sheepish standing beside her as she banged on the wrought-iron door of the apartment. In strident French she declared that I was NOT going to Morocco, there was a mistake, excuse us, but here is the ticket.

The woman stared dumbfounded. She asked what the problem was.

Danielle, bless her simple Canadian soul, said, "Doo Doo is married, right?"

Miss Sad Eyes sharply sucked in her breath. She ran after us into the street. "*Mais tout le monde le fait.*" Everyone does it.

Well not me, I finally whispered in response. "*Pas moi.*"

A staff writer for the Globe and Mail, *Deirdre Kelly has over two thousand stories to her credit, from ballet criticism to investigative reporting on the world of international art. Now the paper's fashion reporter, covering the runway shows in Paris, Milan and New York, she travels frequently for business and pleasure.*

WE TURNED SOME SHARP CORNERS: A Marriage Proposal in Durango
Nick Massey-Garrison

No sooner had I proposed marriage than I began to have misgivings.

We were standing in the *plaza major* in Durango, our knees already weak from hours spent reeling through the Sierra Madres on a stretch of treacherous highway known as the Espinazo del Diablo. We were wearing creaking motorcycle leathers and clutching a bottle of tequila. And the bells of the cathedral were booming away in the empty square to welcome in the new year. The arcades were lit up with strings of lights, the hulking sixteenth-century basilica bottom-lit and lemon yellow against a black sky. Drunken singing came from a distant café. We were intoxicatingly alone, untold miles from friends back home who would be toasting and kissing.

We were truants from that familiar world, untethered under the whirl of unfamiliar stars and privy to the mystery hinted at by whatever we call sacrament—that the everyday world is not where the important things are happening. Travelling on a motorcycle through Mexico induces this feeling regularly. We had encountered other tourists only once in two weeks. We had crossed featureless purple deserts and shrieked recklessly down mile after scrubby mile of dusk-bordered nothingness scattered with lonely oil rigs, telephone poles with their sagging wires loping along beside us, silhouettes leaning irregularly into the flat sky. Of course, we couldn't talk on the bike, so we just held hands, squeezing every once in a while to draw attention to something interesting or to let each other know that we were happy.

We had stopped for gas in tumbleweed towns with rusty old pumps, and breakfasted on burritos and bitter coffee in roadside cantinas. We had dodged chickens in dusty villages with bloated fly-blown corpses of dogs strewn on the side of the road. Christmas night was spent drinking imprudently in Cuatrocienegas with a seedy mariachi band and a cowboy named Nacho. And each night we curled up in a lumpy bed in an unlikely hotel and reminded each other of how lucky we were to be there, far from everything familiar except each other.

We rode and rode. Crossing cold deserts on a motorcycle is a lot like drudgery, and eating burritos of indifferent quality day after day quickly loses its appeal. But we romanticized as we went along, quickened at every turn by the recurring realization: *This is us; we are here.* We were nothing like the swashbuckling adventurers we felt we were. But that didn't really matter.

I had heard, of course, of the fruity coolers and the SUVs that share the name, but I had never heard of the city of Durango before we saw the name on a map spread out on a table in a cantina somewhere in the Coahuila desert. It turned out to be a city of over a million people, a provincial capital, and when we emerged from the desert, we found it shimmering in the orange plains at the foot of the Sierra Madres.

We had stumbled upon a city of ambiguous charm. Durango is a prosthesis of the Old World, built by people looking for gold, a place where the Inquisition was administered. From the plaza, all arcades and mosaic, you can see the spires of half a dozen brooding churches, each sheltering a mournful Madonna and a grotesquely lifelike

Christ, some with human hair and painted rosy cheeks and dolorous blue eyes, his head mutilated by thorns the size of switchblades, dark blood dripping from his hands and feet. We marvelled at the dates on buildings—A.D. 1887, 1744, 1625—stupidly astonished that we could have gotten on a motorcycle and ridden to, well, this.

Durango reminded me of some of the great cities of eastern Europe, like Belgrade; fashioned by carpenters and stonemasons and sculptors and architects of an unknowable past, then allowed to lapse into decay. The bottoms of intricately carved doors rotted away where centuries of rain had splashed, hinges rusting off. Sidewalks cracked and heaved. Friezes obscured by soot. Walls blackened by the centuries of bodies brushing by, hurrying somewhere.

But this is not squalor or decrepitude, or not quite. It has all the haunting love-liness of ruins, which stand as testaments to their own lost mode of being, to uses to which they are no longer put, to the unforeseen nature of their desuetude. Ruins jut out of the irrevocable into the mundane, where tourists like me stumble over them and consider them minor epiphanies. No one builds things to fall down.

Now battered, wretched cars lurch and jangle through the narrow cobbled streets where, presumably, the coaches of imperial functionaries once clattered. No doubt there had been torrid affairs, thrilling swordplay and knots of swooning women with heaving bosoms and scented handkerchiefs. Their coats of arms are still carved in the lintels of their decaying houses.

A few days before New Year's we had walked through a market. The vendors' booths were arranged according to the objects they sold: one aisle of garish clothes, knock-offs and sweatshirts with the logos of faraway sports franchises and nonsense slogans ("OKAY Boy Is Here To Jazz It Up"); a florists' aisle; an aisle of dry foodstuffs; a butchers' aisle, reeking of generations of offal; an aisle of ceramic madonnas look-ing heavenward.

In the leather goods aisle, among the saddle- and shoe-makers, we met an old man with the long hair and wild eyes of a locust-eating prophet. He stared as we approached. I warned Ange not to look. A glance would have made avoiding an awkward conversation impossible. But as we passed he called to us in Spanish. We turned to shrug innocently and mumble "No hablo Español" when he asked,

smiling, earnest, "Are you married?" We conceded that we were not. "So young," he beamed. To Ange: "So beautiful! Why you're not married?!"

These were neither compliments we could return, nor questions we could answer. We stammered and looked at each other. "You have children?" We smiled uncomfortably. No. "So nice, so nice, so young." Shaking his head, but smiling. Then he pulled a yellowed photograph from the wall. He showed us a burly young man in a white shirt and a vest of indeterminate colour. The young man stares at the camera grimly, intently, as though trying to communicate something of grave import, like a euchre player trying to table-talk. His moustache is a push-broom and his hair is slicked back. One hand is on a hip.

"Is me," said the shoemaker proudly.

We've all seen pictures of our grandparents as hale youths, photos of our middle-aged parents as infants, irrefutable evidence that things have not always been what they are. Strange, then, our assurance that they will never change. We will always be young, we will always be happy.

We had left Mazatlan the morning of New Year's Eve, heading for Torreon. But we had dawdled a little. I stopped at a cathedral to buy a St. Christopher medal, only to be admonished by a baleful old woman in the mandatory black dress that the patron saint of travellers had been de-canonized. I settled for the protection of St. Michael. We spent hours stopped on the shoulder of the highway, tossing pebbles over the cliff. We stopped in Durango for dinner and decided halfway through that we would stay the night. We immediately ordered the beers we had been lusting after. The other patrons in the cantina were drinking heartily in anticipation of the night's festivities, and the man at the next table, who had earlier offered to share his salsa, invited us to a disco. We declined, asking him whether a crowd would gather in the plaza. He seemed to say yes.

We found a hotel room and set off through the narrow, exhaust-choked streets in search of a *liquoreria*. The city was abuzz, vendors selling peanuts and tamales. Street lamps cast cones of light through the haze of dust. We finally found a little shop, its iron grille almost shut, which sold only two brands of beer and two brands of tequila. We hurried back to our room through the gathering bustle to nap and have a quiet post-prandial, and smoked in the elevator, just because it was permitted.

As midnight approached, we ran, hand in hand, toward the plaza. The narrow streets were quiet and dark. A car would pass and throw our shadows onto the sidewalk and the pocked walls with their peeling posters. We laughed and the tequila burned.

But the square was empty. All the shops were closed. Little white lights outlined the contours of windows and arches. The cathedral leaned into the sky. We sat on benches in the little park and waited. The sound of drunken singing came from a distant window. We felt, once again, that we had discovered this remarkable place, that our intrepidity and boldness had brought us here.

There is a mode of happiness that is the promise of happiness. Contentment in the moment is something that can be foreclosed upon by the thought of the future: the drinker contemplating his hangover. But to be happy because you expect to be happy, that horizons await—this happiness is not so easily extinguished.

When the bell rang out, Ange and I stood there embracing. For a long time. The world spun while I weighed like pebbles in my mouth the question that had at that moment occurred to me to ask.

The idea of proposing marriage had arrived uninvited and I had no words rehearsed. I stammered and shuffled my feet. Finally, exasperated, she told me to spit it out.

I could manage nothing better than a mumble.

"Are you joking?" was her reply.

Hence my misgivings. They lay not in my choice of bride but in my means of securing her. I had offered no ring. I had not dropped to my knee to ask. I feared that in the hierarchy of moments this blunder would wield tyrannical dominion over the years to follow.

But the best reason to propose from one's knees is that so little discourse is conducted from that position. Kneeling is a signal that something extraordinary is happening, that the succession of everyday moments is about to be interrupted. And in our case it already had been. Ange and I had stepped out of our everyday lives weeks before when we set off for Mexico, and we did not need rings or gravitas to know that we had entered a new order of experience.

This sense that the concerns that regulate the banal procedures of daily life have fallen away, that the inveterate world is hushed and dimmed and may have paused altogether, is just what you need when you are asking someone to marry you. When Ange said yes, this moment of perfect freedom and promise slipped coolly into memory, invulnerable to the encroachments of time.

My misgivings did not last long.

Nick Massey-Garrison is a writer and editor. He lives in Toronto with his wife, Angela.

BROKEN HEAVEN, BROKEN EARTH
Karen Connelly

For months, the long earthen faces of the Buddhas of Pagan will return to me in dreams. Pagan, where the villagers call themselves the slaves of the temples. Sometimes written "Bagan"; the first *a* is short. I repeat the word to myself as I wander, slack-jawed, from holy place to river to holy place again. The entire immense heat-shimmering plain is scattered with pagodas, temples, toddy palms, goats. And boy and girl shepherds, whose wooden slippers clack on the stones. Sometimes even the coat of lime is gone, revealing the Buddha's countenance as deep red, the same colour as the bricks the people bake near the river's edge, but eight hundred, nine hundred, almost a thousand years old now, naked of the gold and gems that made them so famous.

Before I left Rangoon, Ko San Aung gave me an obscure little book that describes the magical history of this place, the lavish courts of King Anawratha, grand battles on the plains, fates decided by strange dreams and numbers, a crocodile called Rain Cloud, alchemic preparations. Pious noblemen and women, kings

"We are not waiting. We are working."

141

and queens built the extraordinary temples in their dedication to Theravada Buddhism, hoping to make merit for their next lives. This golden age lasted from 1044 to 1287, when King Narathihapte fled from the Mongol invaders. Time and wind have eaten away the palace and pagoda walls. The crumbling hands of the statues remind me of living people. The hot dust and hotter stone remind me, at every turn, of Greece.

I think of the poet Seferis: *These stones I have carried as long as I was able.* All the young women here with bricks on their heads make eighty cents a day. The children slide down the hill to a water hole, struggle up the hill with the buckets hanging off the ends of the thin poles. I pick up one of these buckets and gasp. The girls and boys are so young, eight, ten, twelve, and so sharp. One of them looks me up and down as if she has the street smarts of a kid from Brooklyn. The toddy palm– smarts of Pagan.

We come and go, the tourists, the well-wishers, the do-gooders. I have come and I will go, visiting, seeing, taking these stories, photographs of these places. The people who live here will remain. They drive their cattle and fill their tin water-buckets; they sell rice and fall in love. They write, they push through the labyrinth of silence, they wait. Daw Aung San Suu Kyi said, emphatically, rather insulted, "We are not waiting. We are working."

They do work, the hounded politicals, the people who believe in the possibility, the *inevitability*, of change. I have never met such dedicated, generous men and women. The children work hard, too. Their labour is ubiquitous all over the country. Every day, no matter where I am, I sit in a tea shop at a low wooden table and watch kids washing dishes, loading crates, mixing the great, steaming vats of tea. Children also build roads, mix cement and carry stones. Like most child-labourers, their relatives live far away and are very poor. The children are sent to work in the cities and towns.

Without words, they speak of the great generals. All children raised in a traumatic poverty communicate in a language filled with silences and omissions, as though their vocabulary were written with an eraser. What they do not have dictates who they are and who they can become. The lucky ones have attended school for three or four years; the unlucky ones have not and never will. Though I use the words *lucky* and *unlucky*, none of this happened by accident. The narrow lens of the children's existence can be turned to focus clearly on the corrupt wealth of their rulers.

This morning, I watch the smallest boy in a tea shop retinue; he perches on an overturned stool, scrubbing away at his pile of dishes. When he gets up to drag in another load of cups and plates, I notice he already has the gestures and jaunty swagger of the bigger boys. His suffering is understated, not yet embittered with anger or condemnation. But as he grows, he will understand more than he does now about why he has so few options, why he cannot read, why he is trapped this way and who has trapped him. He is only one of hundreds of thousands of poor children. Every morning, before I finish my tea, he teaches me a few words in his language.

Cup. Table. Sweet. Lizard. Child.

His name is Hla Win. He is nine years old. One morning, as I'm leaving, he calls out to me, with the spontaneity of a songbird, "Chit-day!"

I love you.

There is only one other person staying at the hotel above the river. She is an artist from Spain. On the evening before her departure, we dine together. She has a pressing need to explain herself.

"I'm an idealist like you. I really am. I grew up in Spain, you know. I remember what it was like, during Franco's time. My parents were always telling me not to get involved in the politics, it was very dangerous. Really, I am an idealist, and I think it's terrible that these people are so badly off."

"I don't think 'badly off' really explains it. They are poverty-stricken, malnourished. And oppressed. Hungry for many things."

"Do you really think they are? Really? Is it really possible to be hungry in the tropics? There is so much fruit everywhere. When I was in the north, there were two children sitting outside my restaurant with empty bowls, so of course I gave them some of my food. But someone else would have fed them if I hadn't. They wouldn't have gone to bed hungry."

I swallow a sip of my water, bottled water.

She continues, "A doctor I met up there said that he has never seen the infant mortality rate so high. I agree, that is really awful. But in a way, it's a natural form of birth control."

I want to ask this elegant, beautiful woman if she is on the pill. She was educated at one of the most expensive art schools in London. Has she ever had a baby, and watched her baby die, slowly, of diarrhea? Dysentery? Malaria? Food poisoning? Those are the common killers of babies born in Burma, ailments often complicated by malnutrition. I finish my glass of water. The food has come but my appetite has left me.

"And they are always smiling! I really don't believe they're so miserable. They're always so happy."

Surely she will hear the exasperation in my voice. "But that's part of being Buddhist. Many people, especially the poor, accept the conditions of their lives, and they revel in whatever life is around them. The Burmese are a deeply hospitable people, too—that's why they smile at us."

"They look so happy. There seemed to be a lot of people with bad eye diseases in the north, and even *they* laughed a lot."

Awkward pause. What can I say?

"I really am an idealist, but if democracy came all at once to Burma, this country would disintegrate! It can't come too quickly."

"But the people of Burma already voted in a democratic government. There were elections in 1990. The NLD, Aung San Suu Kyi's party, won by a landslide. The military refused to hand over power." Surely she must know these little details from her guidebook.

"Well, voting for freedom is one thing, but living with it is another. If it comes too quickly, Myanmar will disintegrate!"

How can she not see? She is a painter; her vocation is in her eyes. "But the country already is disintegrating. Nothing works here. The currency is a farce, corruption is rife, the military makes deals with drug lords, and the overwhelming majority of people cannot afford to live on what they make because inflation is so high. Even the electricity doesn't work. People die after operations because the hospitals cannot afford proper sterilization equipment!"

She looks at me squarely, condescendingly. "Journalists exaggerate the situation."

"I haven't been talking to journalists. I've been talking to Burmese people. Students, doctors, artists, market women."

But the doubt remains plain on her face, tightening her lips. "I know how bad it is. But if democracy comes too quickly . . ." Her voice trails off. She begins to eat. I move my food around with a fork.

Strange, the fork. Lately I've been eating Burmese-style, with my hands. There is something intensely pleasurable about touching the food one puts in one's mouth. Messy, but fun.

The Spanish artist looks up from her curried chicken with an alarming intensity and asks, "What are you trying to do for the Burmese people?"

This question takes me by surprise. I think for a moment but can't decide how to reply. I feel acute embarrassment. Flustered, I say, "Nothing."

"But you must be trying to do *something*."

I raise my eyebrows, searching. "Um. No. I'm not."

"Why did you come here then? You said you would never come here only as a tourist, so what are you doing here then, if not trying to accomplish something?"

"I'm just talking and listening."

"But aren't you trying to accomplish the freedom of these people?"

I laugh out loud; her statement is so lofty. I am embarrassed and uncomfortable that we are sitting at this table in Burma, talking about the Burmese, while the waiters stand at the dining-room doors like sleepy sentinels. They might understand every-thing we're saying. Or nothing, which is worse. I want to apologize to them. I want to flee. "I don't pretend anything like that. It's too presumptuous. It sounds silly. Only they can accomplish their own freedom. I am . . . hanging around."

"But you've been going on about how terrible the government is here, and how much all these people you've met have suffered, and how powerful this place is for you. Don't you want to do anything? You must be trying to do something. Why don't you just say it?"

"I just want to write about what I see here. That's all. That will do whatever it can do. All things considered, that will be very little."

Now it is her turn to sip water. Oh, let the meal be done, let this be over. In other circumstances—in a gallery in Madrid, for example, or drinking sangria in a bar in

Segovia—I know I would like her. It is foolish as well as fraudulent for me to stand on the moral high ground, though the natural birth control comment was appalling. But we all say appalling things sometimes. It's the nature of being white or powerful or simply human. I have Gorky to temper me: "By then I could see that all people are more or less guilty before the god of absolute truth, and that no one is as guilty before mankind as the self-righteous." The sharpening edge of defensiveness in her voice comes from a guilt that has nothing to do with me. I want to say, "It's unnecessary, please don't feel that way," but I just listen to what she says next with a small, pained smile on my face.

"I really feel that I have done a lot for them. I have tried to talk and smile as much as possible. You know, I've tried to let them know that foreigners are not threatening, not awful people. And it's absolute hell up in the north where there are no other tourists. The locals won't leave you alone for a second. It's hard work, to be up there, wandering around, trying to get to places they won't let you get to, and all the people are mobbed around you, and there's no other white people. I kept calm the whole time, never lost my temper, always just smiled as much as possible."

I smile myself. The news is coming on. Out of respect, or perhaps out of curiosity and to catch more fragments of our conversation, one of the dining-room attendants

Listen. Hear the sounds of the street. See.

turns down the volume. Conversation wanes in the presence of the silent news; we turn, along with the young Burmese waiters, to watch images of a fine mango crop onscreen, box after box of the small, sweet spheres lined up and glowing like orange gems. Surely it is impossible to be hungry in the land of a million mangoes.

Now come the obligatory scenes of a military leader inspecting a new factory. Then a whole troop of soldiers marching on some road somewhere in the jungle. Shot after shot of automatic weapons, belts heavy with ammunition. They are very serious, very thin young men, every jawbone a study in angles, clenched muscle. The Spanish woman turns away from the television and talks more about the difficulties of being a tourist. I nod slowly, suddenly tired. White-shirted waiters come, take away our plates. With great concern, the younger one asks, in Burmese, why I have eaten so little. "I am not hungry." He is aghast, despite my attempts to reassure him. When the table is cleared and the poor waiter becalmed, the Spanish artist and the Canadian writer stand up. "Perhaps we will meet again some day in Madrid." Perhaps. We exchange *buenas noches*.

"BY THEN I COULD SEE THAT ALL PEOPLE ARE MORE OR LESS GUILTY BEFORE THE GOD OF ABSOLUTE TRUTH, AND THAT NO ONE IS AS GUILTY BEFORE MANKIND AS THE SELF-RIGHTEOUS."

Oddly enough, as I get ready for bed, I think about the Basque country, Euskadi: northern Spain, but not Spain exactly. And so very far from Burma, another world, another lifetime. But every country shares history, just as every human being does. If I know one thing, it is the ultimate meaninglessness of borders. A decade ago, I lived with a woman, also a painter, who was still a child when the tyrant Franco was pronounced dead. As soon as this news came, the children of Euskadi were turned loose from school. The most vivid memory of Maru's childhood was made that day, when she ran through the village streets with her classmates, crying joy.

Returned to Mandalay, I listen to the sound of Burma waking: a man crushes ice on a rare piece of sidewalk, cars honk, bicycle bells ring, a woman's voice sings her wares. I pull the curtains and push my nose against the screen to see straight down. The singing woman is selling mangoes from an enormous plate balanced on her head. When she passes into the next street, I still hear her plaintive voice praising the sweetness of the fruit. Now the man is shovelling the crushed ice into two enormous rusted barrels, and two other men help him load the cargo into a very small truck. The trishaw drivers are lined up in a row in the shade of the corrugated tin wall, a wall that stands for no other reason than to give them shade. They each spit betel nut at regular intervals, even though four of the seven appear to be sleeping.

Betel nut juice. Dark red streaks of it everywhere on the ground, in the gutters, on the steps, on the lower walls, dribbling down or dried, crusted. One cannot help but think, obviously, of blood. I have wandered through the streets near Sule Pagoda, where many protestors were shot in 1988. The eighth day of the eighth month of 1988. August eighth: millions of people began a nationwide strike to protest military rule and demand a return to multi-party government. A few hours after darkness fell, the soldiers stationed in the streets opened fire. This happened in many different towns and cities during a period of several months. Bodies disappeared. Thousands of people were murdered during the 1988 demonstrations; as many were imprisoned. Thousands more left the country to become political dissidents and revolutionaries.

Many of the protestors were students. Students began the demonstrations, orchestrated the strike. One of them, who now lives on the Thai border and belongs to a small guerrilla army, told me that if you enter certain streets near Sule Pagoda after midnight in the month of August, you will hear the ghosts of the dead still screaming, voices rising from the ground where their bodies fell. I find myself here in the month of May. *Tant mieux*. I do not need to hear screams. Girls with *thanakha*

dabbed on their cheeks, girls still dressed in their school uniforms—white blouses and green sarongs—fell in crumpled heaps on the road. Bayonets killed people, bullets killed them. Also wooden clubs—it was not physically difficult for a soldier or a riot policeman to bash a hole through the fine flesh and bone of the face.

There are pictures of the bodies, in books. Sitting for many hours in Chiang Mai and Bangkok and Mae Sot, hands filled with uselessness, I stared at the photographs, I studied them. They taught me all I need to know about our common, ironic weakness, and that is the fragility of the human skull. Even the heavy, capable jawbone is easily shattered. The photographs speak and speak. They scream, like the ghosts in

I have come and I will go, visiting.

the roads around Sule, they cry. Yet they are completely silent. Their silence demands, furiously, a response. But you will not find a word of reply in any language. You will just weep.

Listen. Hear the sounds in the street. See. Feel it, too, but not easily. You who know so little, do not utter a single proclamation. How to just see and hear? The world we live in doesn't teach us to see and hear well. It teaches us all kinds of other things: labels, theories, expectations, vocabularies, opinions, judgments, the extended measure of our fine intelligence. But to shut up and see—next to impossible! It's like meditating. Breathe in, breathe out, follow the breath, draw the mind away from thinking. The formula is so simple, yet how difficult it is to quiet the ever-loving, ever-chattering brain. I've read too many books and know the truth. We think we are walking beside it, but in fact, the truth is a step ahead of us, or flying with a ragged wing somewhere above. I forget this, or become dishonest, secretly thinking: I am quite clever. Atrocious, how often I know what I'm talking about. Only a short while later, I remember what has come out of my mouth and I cringe, look for a rock, a bench will do, but there is nowhere to hide.

God, I think. Buddha. Jesus Christ. Even Allah lives in this city. At five o'clock—or was it four?—I awoke to the cries of the muezzin calling the faithful to worship. The darkness in my narrow room was like heavy blue water. Where on earth was I? I had no idea, just a heart beating very hard, legs tangled in starched sheets. A nightmare hovered in the ebb of the unconscious, but the muezzin washed it away. I lay there, rocked by the swell of voices; the sound was dream-laden, disturbing, verging on chaotic. Or grief-stricken.

Very slowly, I understood. *Oh, yes, here I am. Mandalay.* The mosque in the next street. Prayers as deep as ocean pouring out the doors. The men were chanting in Arabic.

But it is Burmese I am trying to learn now.

Broken heaven, broken earth. Broken country.

And, God, I learn so slowly.

Karen Connelly is the author of six books of poetry and non-fiction. She is presently working on a novel and a collection of essays about the revolutionary politics of Burma and the Thai–Burmese border. Her work has been honoured with the Governor General's Literary Award, the Pat Lowther Memorial Award, and the Air Canada Award. Her books are published in several countries and languages.

WITH MY LITTLE EYE
Tony Burgess

And the first thing to me was the smell. What you usually smell in airports, waiting in line with your boarding pass and carry-on, is carpets, I think. That's what you smell, and occasionally the insides of other people, something you get used to, the roaming valves of strangers warming your arms and face, eventually comforting you.

But now I smell something stranger. Four people are in front of me, three behind, Rachel beside me. Something prickly. I lean back, then forward; it's not me. I wave the bottom of my coat around Rachel's back; not her. But definitely sweat, acrid, a bit burning, not new sweat, not coat sweat, no: this has been on a body for a long, long time. Clothes have been changed deeply by it. I lean back again. It's there behind me somewhere, and I step forward, but this smell is ancient enough, evolved enough, to leave its host from time to time, to move away, rotate on its own, enjoy itself, I imagine, like all fiends in mid-air must. I don't think it's a man's smell, but that's just speculation. I furtively glance at faces. A bearded, balding man. Eyes like a scientist, he's dying to talk. Not him. A Goth couple. Actually, he looks like one of the Corrs. No, nothing cleaner than a Goth. A nun in front of him. Ditto.

We move onto the plane. Lots of hollow plastic, the familiar certainty of catastrophe. Then after that we sit, death maybe comes later, but I've dealt with it already, I passed on somewhere back there and now it's just a smooth flight—the funny suspicion I have as I look at the vapour below that I probably never existed anyway, not in the proper sense, not the way people think I did. Rachel sleeps and I pray for her because in all likelihood she does exist. I change while I nap, I am a kite or a bird or a ghost, but she cannot change, she is Rachel, in great peril, thousands of feet above the earth. What was I thinking?

You play with magazines, people smiling, jewels on wrists, half of Kevin Costner's face over the high bun of hair in front, the normal life you like—people in trousers, suits all reading together, mostly *Harry Potter*, shoes removed and placed under the seat ahead, maybe the little bombs that you've heard about—the fool with the plastic explosives disrupting a flight with requests for matches, cursing the pack he's been using, tossing itty-bitty deadheads on the floor. And now flying homeward over the Italian Alps, you trigger memories of Italian art, well, not quite proper memories, more like a richly chiaroscuroed mucous plug planted in the centre of your head, but in there, somewhere, are thousands of baroque masterpieces. Again, you become aware of a little snarl under your nose. That stench. That foul biting beak pecking upward at you. Then you realize what it is. Beside you. It is the *nun*. The nun. We must look closer.

Her habit is white with blue stripes, familiar-looking. The fringes are soiled, the sleeves are isobars of yellow and body grey. This nun is filthy.

Her little hands come up and waggle across her dinner, she mutters something to the sticky piece of chicken, lifts a cup of water to her lips.

She might be African, but quite light-skinned, large hooded eyes, very large like a big-eye painting in a motel room, or the catacomb painting of the Donna Velata, giant abstract hands bending up in a dark space. I turn away and try to reassess the smell, factoring in the source. If your father smells bad because he's dying it's different than if the big guy at Buns Master stinks as he pushes bread across the desk toward you. Same stink maybe, different set of reactions. Usually stink is bad. It means . . . what? Negligence. Physical or mental illness. Poor upbringing.

So here's this nun gesturing over the entree, waving the funk all up and down my face. And I think either she's poor or sick or something sickish, like neglect. Or is this stink a message-filled aura, the way a spouse wears a wedding ring, this radiant and anti-social emanation her I-married-Jesus effluent? This, I decide, as I pull my forked chicken toward me through her smell, is really all right. I turn to her when she's done whipping up the air and has settled into eating her bird and I wink, a kind of I-smell-ya-and-it-smells-good-to-me wink. She responds with a smile plump with chicken, her fingers and shoulders bunched around her, like a little girl. Mischief there. I lean closer, letting our elbows touch; she trusts this and I put more weight there, so does she.

Her head. I can see a crease around her mouth that wasn't there before. I can tell she's trying desperately to have something to say. I think that she has decided she likes me, all my sniffing and leaning and looking deserves something from her, conversation. She looks straight into my face, pauses, then wiggles her eyes nervously, her smile still big. I translate it this way: "Everything's crazy. Everything's good."

Her face shifts. If her mouth were a hand it would hold up a finger: "Wait a second. I have something for you."

Her arms leap over her tray as she dives her hands down in the tough pocket on the back of the seat in front of her. The yellow-grey sleeves soaking up mushroom sauce and tea. She holds up a card. Eyes sparkle. A little girl's muscle in her voice.

"Excuse me."

We both pause, sniff a bit, wondering if "excuse me" is right, then simultaneously shake, a little *anyway-whatever* tremor between us.

I say, "Yes?"

She holds the card at the corners with the thumb and forefinger of each hand.

"Do you have a landing card?" She's holding up a perfume sample from the *enRoute* magazine. I'm momentarily confused, then realize this is a symbol. I smile and nod, and start foraging in my seat pouch.

"Where did you get it? I mean, did you have it when you came on board or did . . . do I . . . ? I mean should I have one?"

I don't find it.

"People come from all over the world for these."

I say "shit" under my breath and she laughs. "You have to ask a stewardess . . . steward. Uh . . . they're not called that any more . . . what's the word?"

I am really upset that I can't remember. The only thing I can think to say is "shit," but I don't think it should be a running joke.

She knows what I mean, thanks me and leans into the aisle to attract one.

I feel self-conscious that I am waiting for the nun to return to the conversation. I push back in my seat, away from the half-eaten food on the tray. Rachel's reading. The plane is a long curtain pulled across her.

I feel the stinky nun's elbow again, this time she pushes, dropping my forearm out from under me. I turn and smile, exhaling lightly through my nostrils.

"I can't seem to get her attention."

"The flight attendant?"

That's the right word, and she flies past us, swinging a towel that touches every-body's shoulders up the aisle. I return my elbow and send it into the nun's ribs.

"Trip her."

She laughs suddenly, an emotion inside suddenly out, then turns to me. Not just turns, but seems to rotate in her tiny seat to face me.

Pause. There is a mighty excitement in her. In me a sudden Italian memory—a white bridge—and I realize it's a cliché from Andrew Cunanan's Florentine diary. Who is this stinking nun, really?

What follows is spoken with a single flash of feeling, manic and childlike. I have the sensation that her dirty little hands are touching my face.

"I am seeing my family for the first time in ten years. I'm only allowed one visit every ten years. I'm preparing the canonization of Mother Teresa in Rome and I have to do certain things. Some of them who are standing down there right now I have never met and most of them, my parents, my sisters, I will never see them again. I'm very nervous, I'm very afraid. One time I get, just this once and I don't know what to . . . you and your wife are my only travelling companions and I will pray for you every day and night for the rest of my life. It's something I have to do. I have brought special prayers for you and her. And I started them a while ago. I don't even think I need a landing card. They are down there. All of them."

Her eyes are huge and I can see yellow jelly holding on to the white.

"I'm sorry. I don't usually talk. I think you think . . ." She laughs, unable to finish or maybe she doesn't like the phrase "I think you think."

"The canonization of Mother Teresa." I kind of go "phew" and touch a wet carrot with my baby finger. "How do you get to do that?"

"I was in her order in Calcutta."

Full stop. Something unprotected, like pride.

"Wow."

Of course, the white and blue habit, that's where I'd seen it. She goes quiet. I turn to Rachel and try to whisper, putting my words carefully onto the page she's reading.

"We're getting prayed about over here . . ."

Rachel leans forward, smiles at the nun.

The nun looks as if someone famous has just acknowledged her.

She pulls up a small oily bag. And pours four little oval pendants into her palm.

"People come from all over the world for these. They were laid on her tomb and blessed by the order."

They look like bugs in her hand. Like little Dali ants.

"And these two are for my mother and father." She returns two to the small bag.

"And these two are for you."

She abruptly pushes them into my hand, almost dropping them in the transfer. Then straightens up frantically.

She looks afraid of Rachel and me now, because we don't know what to say.

Rachel reaches across and covers the nun's hand with her own.

I look down and roll my super religious icon end over end.

Rachel has a nice deep voice when she thanks her. The nun gives out a dreamy little *hmmmm* song to herself.

"They're down there right now."

Standing in a group. Looking at the red arrivals and the blue departures.

"I'll never see them again."

I close my eyes and sniff hard to collect her beneath my face, a march of nerves inside me. The smell is awful; burning and offensive. I feel angry and the memory I make is of a foolish woman, her head tilted like a dog, looking out the back window.

A shivering daughter with the heart of a slave. Does that sound bad? I'm so tired. It's been a long trip and I've spent so much money. It sounds like I don't even like her, but I do. I do. It's just that I can't remember a single painting, a single statue, nothing, just her, on my shirt on my pants on my hands.

Tony Burgess is a writer from Wasaga Beach. He has published several novels about life in small-town Ontario.

THE LAST HIPPIE
James Grainger

Every evening I played a game as I walked down to Commercial Drive. Across the Burrard Inlet the lights in the houses on the north shore and up Grouse Mountain were coming on. I had two minutes to think up a metaphor to describe the lights or I had to take a quarter out of my pocket and throw it down a sewer from a distance of three feet.

The first night the lights were votive candles on an altar. Later they became holes in the mountain letting out fairy light; then a blanket of stars; then a landing strip designed to confuse pilots. Tonight the air was hazy, and the lights became the torches of angry North Vancouverites climbing the mountain to finally murder the monster in Frankenstein's castle.

Gary, dragging a hockey bag and couple of suitcases—his worldly possessions pared down to a greatest-hits collection of books, clothes and cassettes—would be getting off the Greyhound bus from Toronto tomorrow. He would quote a line from *On the Road*, a book we'd outgrown years before but which still clung to us by threads of irony, and I would tell him about my new but still larval life in Vancouver, about this new man I'd become, a sober man who read in cafés and wrote apologetic letters to ex-lovers. And he would laugh and laugh.

Tonight I was looking for an old hippie named Danny, one of the few Vancouverites I'd met since arriving. The acquaintanceship was part of a new resolution to widen my social world beyond the cliques of expatriate Torontonians who crowded the Italian coffee bars along Commercial Drive. All conversations there led back to the favoured scapegoat, Toronto, inevitably described as shallow, greedy, grasping—a "city of rats" was my favourite. When pressed to describe their new home city, the exiles resorted to a hazier spectrum of cliché. Vancouver was integrated, laid-back, holistic—character traits that formed a composite sketch of the sandal-wearing person they all hoped to become. This was my Vancouver, then: a low-rent Edwardian sanitarium where the disillusioned intelligentsia came to take the cure and write fractured free verse. The hippies couldn't offer much worse, I figured.

I found Danny outside the food co-op, sitting at one of the wicker patio tables with a few younger hippies. Danny liked to play the part of elder statesman to folks passing through on their way to the Gulf Islands. But his alcohol-ruddied cheeks, the sour smell of the van he lived in and his open lust for very young women rendered him a kind of anti-prophet, his life story—especially the pivotal rejection of a career in academia for a three-year acid binge on Vancouver Island—a cautionary tale. The younger hippies weren't here to hang out with Danny. Like me, they were looking to score a ride down to an annual barter fair in Washington state.

Like many drug casualties, Danny's ability to detect condescension had expanded in direct proportion to the withering of his other mental functions; one wrong gesture or tone, and Gary and I would be out of a spot in the van.

"I got arrested for impaired driving this morning," he told me.

"I thought your licence was already suspended."

"I was just *sitting* in the goddamned van feeding my puppies and the fucking cops busted me!"

Everybody else was clearly drained of outrage. I feigned shock and gained Danny's full attention.

"I thought they were going to try and take my puppies away, so I said, 'I'd rather have six puppies than a hundred pigs!' They fucking beat the shit out of me!" He suddenly leaned toward the girl on his left, giving her the full blast of his breath. "They beat me in forced confinement." The memory of a 1970s feminist consciousness-raising session seemed to waft up in him. "I know what it's like to be raped. I know what it's like to be a woman!"

"Great, but are you going to be able to get across the border with that ID?" she asked.

He pulled back from the repelled bonding moment. "Oh yeah, I got it made in my brother's name. His record's clean. He's a Mormon." He pulled out a generic ID card.

"My name's Dave. That's my brother's name. Your buddy's gonna have to do a lot of driving."

Gary immediately assumed the role of long-suffering rationalist to Danny's drunken stoner in the sitcom episode that was our drive to the border. Gary was driving. Danny was in the passenger seat hoarding the map, drunk on a magnum of home-made wine. We'd gotten lost three times while driving out to the suburbs to drop off Danny's puppies at his Mormon brother's house. Whenever Gary suggested that I be given the map, Danny would sneer and say, "This isn't Toronto." After that, Gary started repeating the last few words of Danny's sentences:

"Okay, now turn left at that variety store."

"At that variety store, yup."

"There should be a laundromat up here, eh."

"A laundromat, sure."

As we neared the border, Danny stuffed himself with peanut butter sandwiches to take the smell of alcohol off his breath.

"And remember, my name's Dave."

"Can you tell me three more times so I can dream about it tonight?"

"And the name of the guy who owns the van is Russell Cop. Like 'police-cop.'"

"I thought it was your van."

"It is, but I never changed the papers. So Russell Cop is the owner of the van, right. He went tree planting and lent us his van."

"Everyone get ready for a cavity search!"

"Listen to the Toronto fucking comedian."

I eventually convinced Danny to let Charmagne drive across the border. She was a nineteen-year-old tree planter and had the kind of cherubic features that authority figures want to protect and/or molest. The guard never asked who owned the van.

There were yellow ribbons tied on the trees in America, though the Gulf War had ended months earlier. The ribbons were still bright and untattered, like roses that grow in winter in a fairy tale, or a saint's relics, impervious to rot. Flags as big as Buicks hung from poles carefully set at the same noble tilt as the raising of Old Glory at Iwo Jima.

But out on the interstate the road cut through the forests like a railway through wilderness, with only the odd turnoff sign to remind drivers of the American towns huddling behind the trees. At predictable intervals a combination gas station/liquor store would float by in a halogen bubble, briefly commanding our attention like a television set flicked on in a dark room.

ALL CONVERSATIONS THERE LED BACK TO THE FAVOURED SCAPEGOAT, TORONTO, INEVITABLY DESCRIBED AS SHALLOW, GREEDY, GRASPING—A "CITY OF RATS" WAS MY FAVOURITE.

Danny had passed out after finally relinquishing the map, and only Gary and I and a young hippie couple—Ken and Diane—were still awake, huddled in the front of the van, passing a joint back and forth. Back in Toronto, "Hacky Sack" and "patchouli" and any other words connected to hippies were as automatically laugh-inducing as speaking in an exaggerated German accent, but we were getting along with everyone but Danny. Ken asked Gary about the different punk bands that he'd roadied for and the two of them began trading traveller's stories. Gary's always featured an adversarial redneck or two and some unlikely saviour, maybe an old black cop who collected obscure jazz records.

Ken then explained the idea behind the barter fair, how people there were trying to "get off the money grid" by bartering what they made or grew.

"I see it like this," he said. "A bunch of people could get some land up around Alaska—it's practically free under the Homestead Act. We would put up cabins and waxworks and ironworks and stoneworks, so that all the North American gypsies like us would have a place to make their crafts in the winter."

When we were alone, Gary would mock Ken's idealism, but for now he was gracious and attentive, like a father listening to a child's plan for a go-kart with amphibious wheels and retractable wings.

The barter fair's campsite was set on a plateau against the side of a low, crumbling mountain. It was the only flat land in sight. The yellow grass and little herds of trees rolled off in uneven waves toward the mountains in the west and the prairies in the east, giving the place the lonely feel of a borderland. My first thought on stumbling out of the van was that the site was a pioneer homestead abandoned in impossibly tragic circumstances by the very family that broke their bodies clearing the trees and rocks.

Danny was already awake and talking to a muscular hippie in a porkpie hat named Sage.

"You know a guy named Ernie Low?" Sage asked.

"I know Ernie Wild."

"What about Free?"

"Where's he from?"

"All over."

"No. What about Tripper John?"

Sage's story: Sage is a sacred plant burned in Native American ceremonies. Sage wears a sprig of it in his hat. Sage is an ex-Marine who worked for three years as a bill collector for hospitals before a vision changed his life. In the vision, everyone around him was a walking corpse. "Was he living or was he dead?" he had to ask himself. Now he barters handmade hookahs.

Gary and I began to explore. A kind of oval roadway had been mowed through the grass, with cars and vans and buses tightly parked all around it. There didn't seem to be much organized bartering—no one had travelled by caravan to trade a season's harvest for bolts of cloth and spices and cooking pots. There was organic produce "For Sale or Barter," handcrafted pipes and drums and silver jewellery laid out on blankets, the odd keener standing behind a folding table displaying home-made soap or lumpy pottery. Massage tables were set up about every fifty feet, and a few professional flea market vendors sold a hundred things made out of plastic. The younger hippies strolled around like party-goers checking out the host's book-shelves and record collection, pausing to touch something they coveted but rarely asking how much it cost. Their bodies displayed patches of Lollapalooza paganism—piercings and vaguely Oriental tattoos—and they'd replaced 1960s tie-dye with Mayan and Incan peasant wear, but otherwise the young hippies were doing a cover version of another generation's anthem.

Within an hour Gary had divided the campers into three categories: weekenders, freaks and real people, the first category outnumbering the other two by a wide mar-gin. We retreated into our private world of nasty asides and withering comments.

Gary (standing before a canvas teepee with some kind of bird painted over the entrance): "You think there's any Indians in there?"

Me: "Jungians, maybe."

Me: "You can't find yourself when you're high all the time."

Gary: "You can't find your shoes when you're high all the time."

Gary had stopped to buy three cases of beer in the last town before the campsite, violating the No Alcohol or Firearms sign at the gate. The beer was in high demand, though. We traded beer for food, two thick undershirts and a set of coasters. After trading eight beers for two grams of mushrooms, we accepted just about anything—little wizards carved out of driftwood, packs of damp incense, a pack of nudie cards with a Queen of Hearts who looked like Gary's favourite high school teacher.

Eventually we shared the beer with the real people. A guy who lived in a trailer and made jewellery, upon hearing that we were Canadian, told tender stories of Neil Young's influence on his life. Around a communal campfire, two ex-therapists joked about their former clients. A woman and her husband explained a system they'd developed for getting their goats in faster at the end of the day. They all wore plain faded clothes over their faded skin and had home-cut hair; their arms were tightly wound rope and their midsections were shaped like feed bags. Something had been broken and remade in every one of them, and in the firelight you could catch their former identities asserting themselves in ghost gestures: a sudden hand movement acquired in boardroom deal-making sessions, a batting of the eyes that was once a signal for flirtation—the fading accents of pioneers abandoning their mother tongue. One of the ex-therapists would rest his chin in his right hand—the professional's pose of thoughtful introspection—but he'd shoo the affectation away by squeezing his jaw.

A GUY WHO LIVED IN A TRAILER AND MADE JEWELLERY, UPON HEARING THAT WE WERE CANADIAN, TOLD TENDER STORIES OF NEIL YOUNG'S INFLUENCE ON HIS LIFE.

Some people were just broken. A bearded man in a David Crosby hat wandered a tight circumference around his ex-wife's car, lamenting everything from their failed marriage to the death of the counterculture.

"My woman," he cooed, "she's still into that Tom Robbins rainbow bullshit because she can't accept the responsibilities of motherhood."

Both of them had been beautiful once, you could see it in their fairy-faced children. She had driven the kids to the fair from Seattle, and he had followed. She was hoping to sell enough of her belongings to make it to LA where some unspoken salvation waited for her. Her possessions were laid out in neat rows on a blanket in front of the car. There were scuffed beauty products and hair clips, broken toys, radios and mounds of clothing, all arranged in a series of seemingly patterned lines like a cyclical epic poem recorded in pictographs.

"You didn't even bring a tent," he said.

"You can't keep a fucking job," she said.

People were heading toward a dome of orange light and shadow flickering against a hill just beyond the campsite. A few bongo drums began shepherding the looser beats around a simple, mid-tempo heartbeat.

We were lying in the grass and Gary grabbed my arm. "It's a fucking *drum circle*. Can you believe people are still doing that shit?" We started to race toward the light. *When was the last time I'd actually raced anyone?* We were giggling and trying to trip each other, ruts and little rises nipping at our ankles, and when I got ahead, Gary tackled me from behind.

We sat on the hill and looked down. At least two hundred people were gathered around a bonfire. Some were dancing, the rest watched and swayed and clapped and played drums. Many were falling into self-willed trances, and they took off their shirts and described shapes in the air.

Gary was furious: the three personality types he had so meticulously classified had spontaneously come together, and the weekenders were, as always, calling the most attention to themselves. Even the firelight seemed to favour them, striping their young bodies with shadows that highlighted the women's ripe curves and the men's easy musculature.

Gary waved his hand at the scene and yelled, "You're all going back to fucking work on Monday!"

I wasn't so sure. The Neil Young fan was quietly smiling to himself. One of the ex-therapists was dancing naked before the fire and laughing, possibly at himself. And there was poor, red-faced Danny, blowing a huge joint and duck-walking around the edge of the circle. He handed the joint to someone and pulled a harmonica out of his back pocket and began to play.

James Grainger is an editor and writer in Toronto who doesn't leave the city as much as he should. His work has appeared in Quill & Quire *and the* Toronto Star.

एअर इंडिया
AIR-INDIA

विमानयात्री श्रेणी
Economy Class

बोर्डिंग पास
Boarding Pass

उड़ान नं. / तारीख
Flight No. / Date

185

नाम Name

167

BASu/ARjun

बोर्डिंग Boarding
समय Time

0530

गंतव्य स्थान Dest.

LON

गेट Gate

12

सीट Seat

20J

HOW I LEARNED TO LOVE SCOTCH
Arjun Basu

Even by the dusty standards of India, this is a dusty place. The air is thick with it. Street lights are rendered impotent. Dust coats the buildings, the sidewalks, the cars and taxis and auto rickshaws.

The bus pulls into an empty plaza and sighs. It's midnight. I've just come from Delhi. Eight hours. My bones ache.

The driver opens the door, and the dust rushes in. I stand and reach in the overhead bin for my backpack. I wait. The front half of the bus is crammed with families overburdened by a Korean factory's worth of home electronics purchased in the big city.

Whatever I came to find in India is not going to be found here. The town is unremarkable save for its botanical institute and an exclusive private school. The Gandhi boys went to school here. The locals are proud of that. I step off the bus, take in the surroundings and read my Lonely Planet. The town rates less than a page: Dehra Dun, gateway to the Himalayan foothills (though here, in the shadow of the "roof of the world," eight thousand feet will get you a foothill, if that).

I have come looking for answers to a question I am just starting to formulate.

Scrawny chickens are everywhere, pecking at the gravel on the dusty roads. The plaza is surrounded by small tin-shack restaurants advertising tandoori chicken, the smoke from the ovens a low-lying haze.

I make out a hotel sign down a side street. Behind a ratty-looking door is a flight of brightly lit stairs painted what I've taken to calling "Krishna blue." The distorted

sounds of a television fill the stairwell. All I ask of this hotel is basic cleanliness. And a lack of smells.

I could use a beer.

At the top of the stairs, a man with a round face and simple expression stares intently at the TV. An actress lip-synchs to a voice that is just this side of chipmunk. She dashes from tree to tree, coyly hiding from a flaccid-looking guy with a cheesy moustache. I have just described a scene from every Bollywood production that has enthralled this crazy, complicated nation. The actress has finished singing and now the actor gets overly emotive as he lip-synchs his lines. The innkeeper turns to me and smiles. A large, friendly smile.

"No more room," he says, his head doing that comical head-shake Indians do to affirm the negative.

I drop my backpack. "I'm tired." I say.

"No room." The innkeeper waves his hand in the general direction of my face. "And no English," he says.

"I just got off the bus and I need a bed. Anything you have. I'm tired. Please."

"Bed," he says. He points to a cot in the hallway behind me. "Light off. No problem." And with this he smiles some more, generally pleased to have offered me something.

The actress starts lip-synching again and I've lost him. "Ah hah hah," he says, closing his eyes rapturously. His head bobs to the tune like paper caught in a gentle breeze.

I walk to the cot and sit. "I'll take it," I say. The innkeeper is lost in his Bollywood

The innkeeper.

reverie. "I'll take it," I say a little louder. Nothing. His fingers drum the desk. He's playing tabla, accompanying the chipmunk voice and the synthetic drone of the music, dreaming of a world where he always gets the girl. "I'll take the damned cot!" I yell.

A door opens across the hall. A distinguished-looking older man in a beige safari suit eyes me. His thick white hair and white moustache show signs of obsessive grooming. "Why would one sleep on a cot?" he asks in an English that hints at a British education.

I look at him dumbly. The bus, the bumps and turns and sheer length of the ordeal have rendered me helpless.

"I know of a double room occupied by a young university boy," the old man says, raising his eyebrows. "Interested?"

Before I can answer he has rushed down the hall and knocked on a door. The innkeeper runs after him. The door opens and the two men disappear inside. "He will fix you up," says yet another man who appears in the doorway of the old man's room. "He knows these things, yes?" This man is younger, with a foppish Beatles

THE ROOM IS FILLED WITH THE SOUNDS OF GLUTTONY. THE OLD MAN STANDS AND RAISES HIS GLASS. "TO CANADA," HE SAYS. "IT APPEARS TO BE A NICE PLACE. AT LEAST IN THE PHOTOS I'VE SEEN."

haircut, and bushy moustache. He's tall and thin and swarthy. He looks like a man who can tell an easy lie. "You will have no problems." He picks at his teeth with a well-used toothpick.

"Actually, I'd just like a beer," I say. "I'd settle for a pop."

"We can do better," the swarthy man says cryptically.

The door at the end of the hall opens again and the innkeeper motions for me to come. The swarthy man picks up a shopping bag and walks down the hall. I pick up my backpack and follow, slowly, resigned to this weirdness, to another strange experience in a country full of them. A semi-crazed Brit in Delhi had told me, "India just doesn't stop," and I am starting to understand what he meant.

The room is large and well-furnished. The old man and the swarthy man sit on fine leather chairs. The innkeeper, his head bobbing with great joy, points to an empty king-sized bed. On another bed sits the student, dressed in grey pants and a white shirt. His hair is rumpled, his shirt creased. The look on his face indicates that he was either woken up abruptly or was caught masturbating. He manages a weak smile.

I sit on the empty bed and drop my backpack. "Drink?" the swarthy man asks.

"Yes!" the old man shouts. "Look at him! We all need drinks, but first we will require glasses!"

At this the innkeeper leaves the room. I look to the student, my roommate, and introduce myself. "I'm Ashok," he says wearily, shaking my hand.

"Our friend is ready to enter engineering school," the old man announces proudly. "I made his acquaintance this morning. Tomorrow we will take him to Mussoorie. It is beautiful and not so hot. The food is terrible and expensive. The scenery more than makes up for it, however. You should come as well."

"Mussoorie's not on my itinerary," I say. I haven't circled it in my Lonely Planet. The plan is to avoid the places tourists go, and Mussoorie is this country's approximation of Banff. "I want to go north. To Dharamsala and Simla. Kulu and Manali. Try and get to Keylong." Keylong, everyone has been telling me, is a stunner, on the other side of the Himalayas, on the Tibetan Plateau.

"Fine, fine, you will have time for that later," the old man says. "But tomorrow we are spending the day in Mussoorie and you will join us."

The swarthy man pulls two bottles of Johnnie Walker Red out of his shopping bag. He opens one and takes a swig and passes it to the old man who does the same. I'm not a Scotch drinker at all. I can't even remember if I've ever finished a glass of it.

The innkeeper returns with glasses and a funny smile on his face. He says something in Hindi. "Excellent!" the old man says.

The glasses are passed around and quickly filled. Triples easily. The old man raises his glass. "A toast. To our American friend."

I put the drink to my lips and take a sip. My stomach makes a half-turn. My toes curl. But the taste that lingers on my tongue is pleasing. My palate is a step ahead of my gut. The drink feels right, whatever that means, and so I take another sip and my stomach turns a little more. "I'm Canadian," I say.

The old man stands bolt up. "This is incredible!" he announces. "My son works at the Indian consulate in Toronto!"

The innkeeper claps. He obviously understands more English than he's let on.

"You must know him," the swarthy man says stupidly.

"I'm from Montreal," I say.

The old man sits again. "There's nothing wrong with that!" He takes a long sip of

AN ACTRESS LIP-SYNCHS TO A VOICE THAT IS JUST THIS SIDE OF CHIPMUNK. SHE DASHES FROM TREE TO TREE, COYLY HIDING FROM A FLACCID-LOOKING GUY WITH A CHEESY MOUSTACHE. I HAVE JUST DESCRIBED A SCENE FROM EVERY BOLLYWOOD PRODUCTION THAT HAS ENTHRALLED THIS CRAZY, COMPLICATED NATION. THE ACTRESS HAS FINISHED SINGING AND NOW THE ACTOR GETS OVERLY EMOTIVE AS HE LIP-SYNCHS HIS LINES. THE INNKEEPER TURNS TO ME AND SMILES.

his drink. "My son posts the Scotch via diplomatic pouch. No tax. Very convenient. Drink up. Another toast!"

The swarthy man downs his Scotch in a dangerous-looking gulp. He's a professional, I think. The old man does the same. I've just realized that the innkeeper isn't drinking, and for whatever reason I find this annoying. Ashok takes the tiniest of sips. "Go on," the old man says to him, laughing. "This drink is civilization itself." Ashok closes his eyes and gulps the Scotch down and holds his head for a second. He stays like that, still, and then his eyes are open and he is smiling triumphantly.

It is my turn. This situation must be the definition of peer pressure. I stare at my glass, close my eyes and before I realize I've done it, the glass is empty, my insides on fire. Just as quickly, the fire subsides and I see myself holding my glass out for more. I may be drunk already.

A man wearing a dirty T-shirt and a dhooti enters, bearing an enormous platter of tandoori chicken. "Fabulous!" the old man says. The platter is placed on the floor and the lowly-looking man leaves.

"Eat, eat," the innkeeper says and he picks up the platter and holds it in front of me. I take a piece, reluctantly. The taste is otherworldly. Perfection. Surely the scrawny chickens outside aren't the source of this.

The room is filled with the sounds of gluttony. The old man stands and raises his glass. "To Canada," he says. "It appears to be a nice place. At least in the photos I've seen."

He sits again, takes another gulp of his drink and leans toward me. He smiles, revealing teeth coloured a macabre shade of yellow. "You have come a long way to visit us. We are honoured. And what are you doing here, may I ask?"

This is the question. It is one that I can answer simply by saying, "Travelling," or "Visiting family," but it would not be remotely true. I don't tell him that I am here to find something. I don't tell him that I am here to escape a grievous disappointment back home. I don't tell him that I know only what I don't want to do with myself and that I think my future should be more than the end result of a process of elimination. I don't tell him any of this. I can't. I've just started to admit these things to myself. How can I possibly share them with strangers?

I down my Scotch and my stomach behaves. I have become acclimatized. I have come to India looking for answers to a question I am just starting to formulate—only to find that I enjoy Scotch. It's a start. I hold out my glass, and the swarthy man refills it. His hands leave grease marks all over the bottle. I take another piece of chicken. "I'm here to go to Mussoorie," I say.

Arjun Basu is the editor of enRoute *magazine. He lives in Montreal, a mere five blocks from the Whisky Café.*

THE TEA HOUSE ON THE MOUNTAIN
Rabindranath Maharaj

Maybe it's a good idea for us to keep a few dreams of a house that we shall live in later, always later, so much later . . .

—Gaston Bachelard, *The Poetics of Space*

Sometimes I would read of travel writers miraculously stumbling upon a remote gem, cached away from everything that had made them uncomfortable and itchy. I was usually skeptical of these miniature paradises and particularly of their descriptions: frozen in time, lush and verdant, wreathed in mist. I felt that these writers needed to isolate some redemptive nugget from their montage of irritation. But then I discovered just such a spot. In Trinidad, of all places.

During each of my summer visits back to Trinidad as an adult, I got the sense of an island hastily constructed and waiting to be pulled down, like a movie set with actors bustling along temporary streets and sometimes disappearing into temporary buildings. And as though it were a movie set, buildings constructed centuries ago were routinely destroyed, with the actors wandering aimlessly, waiting for another production to take over the island. The most recent was the bother about corruption and about American influence.

On my last visit, a recently retired teacher was complaining that the malls and shopping areas were being converted into American monstrosities. He placed his glass of Coke on the circular table set at the edge of his porch and glanced at his overdressed daughter. "This is the younger generation for you. Follow fashion. Monkey see, monkey do." He leaned back. "This damn nonsense start the minute the English pull out from here. Now them fellas did know how to run a place." After two weeks of listening to *mauvais langue*, a potent form of gossip, I decided to escape to Mayaro Beach on the eastern tip of the island.

On the road from the small agricultural town of Rio Claro, the approach to the beach is signalled when the teak plantations shift to coconut palms, and the small, modest houses with perfect lawns and croton hedges give way to newer concrete homes owned by employees of the various oil companies. The house where I was to spend the weekend was a two-storey structure, part of a semicircular compound at the edge of the beach. The first night, I slept on the porch, listening to the wind prowling through the leaves of the coconut palms, and the tumbling of the waves. Once, I heard a metallic knocking and footsteps, but when I looked over the balcony, I saw no one.

The next morning, I was awakened by a fierce argument. Two men, one accompanied by a woman and three boys, were quarrelling in the sandy yard in the middle of the compound. The single man saw me and shouted, "You get any water last night? Tell me one time."

"I just woke up," I told him.

He took this as some sort of confirmation. "You see? Is the same thing I was saying."

The man with the family looked at me. "You sure you didn't get any water?"

"I just woke up."

"You sure?" After a while, he added, "You better go and check again."

"Why you making the man waste he time so? It have no water in the whole compound."

"But I turn on the pump last night."

"Turn on, turn on, turn on. You don't know nothing about this damn job. I never had no problem when I was caretaking this place. Since you start caretaking is problem on all side." He glanced at me. "True or not true, mister?"

Just then, a stubby man emerged with a wrench from one of the houses. "I was a plumber. I will fix it." He tapped the iron water pipe with the wrench, held a steel crossbar with his other hand and torturously hoisted himself up to the tank. A woman came to the doorway and said tiredly, "Take care you don't fall down again."

After about twenty minutes of knocking and tapping, the ex-plumber announced that someone had turned off a valve. "It look like sabotage to me."

I headed for the beach, the argument still simmering. I walked along the shore, trying to memorize the pattern of the waves, the position of the driftwood on the sand, and the varieties of shell strewn about. Beyond the crashing breakers, a fishing boat skimmed the small rippling waves. Seagulls dipped into the boat's trail, foraging for fish trapped in the seine. Soon the net would be stretched along the shore, and carite and kingfish and moonshine heaped into aluminum pails.

When I returned to the compound, the ex-plumber, looking quite pleased, was sitting on a bench, nibbling at mango slices seasoned with lemon, pepper and shadow beni, a local herb. He raised the bowl toward me, "You want some chow?" I took this as a hint that he wanted to talk about his mediation. Later in the day, the bench grew crowded as friends and relatives dropped by. A group of government workers descended on another building in the compound and off-loaded a few cases of Carib, a local beer, from their vehicles. They discussed the political situation in a noisy, partisan manner. A foreigner could easily have imagined that they were quarrelling.

In Trinidad, these intricate arguments are often a prelude to astonishing revelations about shady deals, and for the next few days, I regularly encountered similar boisterous conversations, where opinions and "inside info" were flung at friend and stranger alike. A man in his sixties, a friend of my uncle, told me, "I hear you is a sorta writer. Make sure you don't say my name when you write about who greasing the Minister hand. Make sure you don't say that is Maniram who clue you in." He spelled his name slowly. "That is M-a-n-i-r-a-m." Before I left, he recanted and said I could mention his name.

After less than a week of this, I asked my sister, a doctor at St. Ann's Hospital, known locally as the Madhouse, if there were any quiet places nearby. She mentioned a tea house at Mount St. Benedict. I had been up the mountain a few times. The estate, about seven hundred acres of misty, forested mountains and sharp valleys and once-thriving coffee plantations, is studded with distinctive red-roofed and white-walled buildings. There are partially concealed chapels, natural trails favoured by bird watchers searching for euphonies and woodcreepers, a rehab centre, and the monastery, built a century ago by Benedictine monks from Brazil. I remembered it as a place to which troubled families turned as a last resort. This bushy Benedictine outpost, shaded by palmistes, was also a perfect place for young couples to visit, and there was a steady stream of cars trekking up the hill.

To get there, my sister and I had to pass through Tunapuna, a busy town about half an hour from Port of Spain, the nation's capital, and a few minutes from the University of the West Indies. As we crawled along the crowded road—here pedestrians veered in and out of the traffic and occasionally slowed to respond to an irate, swearing driver—I noticed that not much had changed since my last visit, two years earlier. The roads were lined with hardware stores and rum shops and vendors selling doubles and pudding and souse. Everyone seemed busy, but there was no discernible pattern to the constant motion; from a distance it might have seemed as if the pedestrians, many with cellphones clapped to their ears, were going round in circles.

Soon we were out of the tangled traffic and at the foot of the northern range. On both sides of the narrow, precipitous road were old wooden houses crowded together, but as we drove up, I was able to see the Aripo Savannah and the Caroni Swamp, and from this elevation, the landscape simplified into an uncluttered pattern of towns, villages, plains and mangrove swamp. We drove past the monastery and then up a winding road, almost missing the tea house, an incongruous building at the apex of a sharp curve. There were two cars parked close to an iron railing at the brink of the hill, but from the road, I noticed the tea house was empty. In Trinidad, buildings are usually renovated in an elaborate and gaudy manner, but the guest house and the adjoining tea house, built during the Second World War (and favoured by American soldiers, my sister mentioned), retained all the architectural characteristics of the period. The garden was noisy with bananaquits, tanagers and unrecognizable seed-eaters. I thought: This place is perfect. There was just the correct mix of desolation and sanctity.

We chose a table close to the garden, and a woman dressed in white brought over a menu that listed Dutch and Chinese and American and presidential teas and a variety of fruit-flavoured ice creams. A few minutes after we ordered, she returned with a tray smelling of cinnamon and honey and faintly of molasses. The home-baked bread and cakes were soft and warm, the tea perfectly blended. A young man, also dressed in white, emerged from the kitchen a few times, but for the rest of the afternoon, my sister and I were the only visitors.

THERE ARE PARTIALLY CONCEALED CHAPELS, NATURAL TRAILS FAVOURED BY BIRD WATCHERS SEARCHING FOR EUPHONIES AND WOODCREEPERS, A REHAB CENTRE, AND THE MONASTERY, BUILT A CENTURY AGO BY BENEDICTINE MONKS FROM BRAZIL.

From the tea room, partially encircled by the hill's arm, I saw starthroats and copper-rumped hummingbirds buzzing around a bird feeder wreathed in serpentine orchids and set against the edge of a slope. The waiter walked to the garden and, with his back to me, joined in my examination. After a few minutes, he returned to the kitchen. I tried to read his face as he passed.

On an island where there is an interminable stream of conversation, it was easy to be lulled into a pleasant languor by the singing of the birds, the remoteness of the tea house and the unexpected reserve of the workers. But all too soon, it was six o'clock and the tea shop was closed.

I returned alone to the mountain a few days later, just before my departure from the island. On the way, I paid a visit to the monastery, which was so quiet that my footsteps echoed intrusively along the aisle. An Indian woman was kneeling before a statue decorated with an impressive array of flowers: pink heliconias and blood-red ginger lilies. I remembered that non-Christians routinely sought solace here.

I walked up the hill to the tea house, taking some of the monastery's peaceful-ness with me. That afternoon, there was a family whose racial mixture could have placed them as Trinidadian but who gave no curious glances, and for the rest of the afternoon they were quiet. When the woman in white came to take my order, I tried to engage her in conversation, but she, too, was unusually reserved for a Trinidadian. She glanced at my notebook on the table but said nothing. When she returned to the kitchen, I walked out to the garden. This late in the afternoon and at this altitude, the place felt cool and breezy and somehow disconnected from the busy streets, the crowded houses and the impatient pedestrians I had left behind. A circlet of smoke, perhaps a bush fire, seemed far, far away. I remembered that the monastery was known locally as "Our Lady of Exile," and I wondered at the tenacity of the Benedictine monks setting up their buildings in this steep, forested area.

A few months later, back in Ajax, Ontario, when fall was shrugging off its appeal, I felt a twinge of nostalgia for the little island I'd left behind. This was surprising because Trinidad usually evoked memories of unwarranted conversations and a lewd, speculative friendliness. But on those chilly fall nights, I missed the sudden, brief thunderstorms, the rain tumbling on the aluminum roof like a hail of broken bottles, and pedestrians shaken out of their lethargy, hurrying like they might do for a train or bus in Canada. I missed the water softening the leaves of the jiggerwood and the pois doux and the tapana, and a few moments later, the sun's signature: brazen specks of garnet, a scatter of tinfoil. I missed the precise tranquility of the nights with the chirp of insects coming at such regular intervals that they sound like cartoonish chanting. I missed the cool fogginess of the mornings, and the drop of fruit on the wet grass.

When I was growing up in Trinidad, I had this romantic notion of travellers circling the globe and finally banishing themselves to some outlandish, far-flung corner. I imagined that I, too, would someday leave the island for a secluded cottage with a shaggy hedge overlooking a misty field, and a garden with small unfamiliar animals burrowing about. I had already written off Trinidad as incapable of hosting this romance. I'd forgotten this until my last afternoon at the tea house at Mount St. Benedict, which was strange because the dream may have played some part in my decision to leave the island. I had wanted to share this with the woman in white; instead I simply wrote in my notebook, "Sometimes home is right around the corner."

Rabindranath Maharaj is the author of The Lagahoo's Apprentice *("This may be the best Canadian novel yet written about the Caribbean"* The Toronto Star*),* Homer in Flight, *which was shortlisted for the Chapters/Books in Canada First Novel Award, and* The Interloper, *shortlisted for the Commonwealth Writers Prize.* The Book of Ifs and Buts *was published in 2002 by Vintage Canada. He was born in Trinidad and now lives in Ajax, Ontario.*

MY FIRST BROTHEL
Scott Gardiner

There was no doubt about the place. I don't remember the door; I don't remember stairs. What I remember is the sensation of entering, of leaving the sunlight and passing into the dark. The walls and even the ceiling were carpeted red. There was a smell of cigarettes, and vaguely moving skeins of crimsoned smoke. It was underground, this place; beneath the street. A red room without windows.

The absence of windows nearly made me lose my nerve. Windows, sometimes, could make the difference. I stood and knew that I was trembling, fighting back the urge to turn and shrink into the street; I had thought I was beyond this. Dark ovals of chewing gum speckled the carpet. A trail of chewing gum led me to where the women waited.

Two stretched across a pillowed divan in the corner, and another was draped against the bar. There were mirrors, reflecting rows of bottles, which in the dimness made the room seem larger. Mirrors, too, helped emphasize the women's nakedness. The one by the bar wore strings of beads as curtains round her hips and thighs. Tassels, like the fringes of my mother's lampshades, dangled somehow from her breasts. She played with one of these, languidly teasing the strands between her fingers. Red could be a tricky colour.

Gripping my satchel, squaring my shoulders, I put on my smile and walked to the bar. "*Guten Tag, Fräulein,*" I said in practised German. "*Sie haben einen grossen Fleck auf dem Teppichboden!*"

My road to this brothel had begun in Amsterdam, where I'd been staying with a friend. Quite some time earlier, I had run out of money and was beginning to feel my welcome had become a little overstretched. In two weeks, though, a girl I knew would be in Munich and I would have another place to stay. But that was still two weeks away.

One morning in the kitchen, I found a newspaper, pointedly opened to the Help Wanted section. It was a Dutch publication, but the advertisement circled in red ink was printed in English. A series of bright vermilion arrows converged on the circle in

DARK OVALS OF CHEWING GUM SPECKLED THE CARPET. A TRAIL OF CHEWING GUM LED ME TO WHERE THE WOMEN WAITED.

case I had missed it. The ad said that young, energetic and ambitious self-starters were wanted for a unique employment opportunity. Interviews, it said, were being held that day at a hotel on the Leidseplein. A suite number was similarly underscored in red.

My friend was at work, so I went to his closet and borrowed a suit. The pants were too long, but this I fixed with some folding and a few strips of tape. Streetcars in Amsterdam at that time worked on the honour system; if you got on at the back of the tram, you stood a fairly good chance of getting off again without being caught for a fare. At the hotel I had a very successful interview and was promptly hired and given a ticket for a train departing that afternoon for Frankfurt.

At this stage, I still had no idea what the job really was. What decided me was the ticket to Frankfurt. There was this girl in Munich—and Frankfurt was more than half that distance covered. I left my friend a note saying thank you and that I would return his jacket and tie sometime later.

At the platform in Frankfurt, I and two other young and energetic recruits were met by a man in a white van and driven to a suburban motel. There was to be a meeting that evening. Meetings, I soon discovered, would account for all time not spent working or sleeping. These meetings were sales meetings, and what I was now was a salesman.

Early next morning, after a six A.M. session during which bonus prizes were awarded to the most productive salesperson, and the least productive was fired, the two new hires and I were driven to a business district somewhere in Frankfurt. I was paired with the team leader, the driver of the white van. For the next two weeks, I would shadow him, absorbing technique. The team leader was in charge of four people and earned a percentage of their sales. But for the next two weeks, I would not be expected to earn a commission. I was observing while learning sufficient language skills to put this learning into practice.

None of the sales force was German. Mostly they were American—the team leaders and senior people, certainly, were American, and eventually I came to believe that head office was located somewhere in Utah—though there were also some Danes and English and Norwegians, and now a few Netherlanders. I was the only Canadian.

It was advantageous, I learned, not to be too conversant in the language we sold in. Before my training was over, I had also learned that the most important thing in sales is the salesman. The thing you are selling is yourself. If you fail to sell yourself, you are letting down the team. The two young and ambitious people I had started with back in Frankfurt had by this time been judged insufficiently ambitious. One morning meeting they were part of the team, like family. At the dinner session they were gone and their names never mentioned again.

By now we were working the northern city of Bremen. We never stayed longer than a day or two in any one place. The team leaders would take us out in the morning and assign us each a single city block. We never worked in residential neighbourhoods, only business districts. Our practice was to stop at each and every enterprise on the block we'd been allotted. It didn't matter what the business was—whatever the door, you entered it, the north side of the block in the morning, the south side in the afternoon.

That morning I had made my first unsupervised sale. It was to an accountancy firm, I think, or perhaps a legal practice. (Unless the place was a restaurant or a church, or an enterprise somehow defined by its premises, I often did not know what kind of business I was pitching.) I knew it would be a good one, though, when I walked in the door and saw a room full of women. Women were always better to sell to than men. This was accepted as a universal truth.

Now I was facing another collection of women. Very different from this morning's, though in other ways strangely the same. Five pairs of eyes and five pairs of nipples adjusted their gaze as I entered. Smiling my mendicant's smile, I gave a formal greeting and drew attention to the carpet. "*Sie haben einen grossen Fleck auf dem Teppichboden,*" I said, and dropped to my knees on the floor.

There was no better blemish than chewing gum for showing my product to its best advantage.

Pluri-Clean was a general-but-amazing-all-purpose-cleanser available only through certified sales agents. Pluri-Clean was marketed in one-litre bottles only—more expensive than store-bought cleansers, yes, but vastly superior. With one bottle of Pluri-Clean, a person would never again need any other type of cleanser. Pluri-Clean, I assured the ladies was "*fast ein Wunder!*"

The stain on the carpet was magically vanishing. I had been taught which kinds of spots were most easily dealt with (gum by far the most impressive) and which kind were not (mustard to be absolutely avoided in every circumstance). "Like a miracle!" I said again, knees on the plush red pile. As I worked the spot of spearmint, five nearly naked women arranged themselves around me in a circle.

One of them let loose with a stream of impenetrable German, but I knew from experience that she was telling the others the chewing-gum stain had been there forever. I spread my hands like a magician. "*Fast ein Wunder!*" Another woman, older, wiser, in beads more strategically cloaking than those of her colleagues, wondered if this process would bleach the carpet. I had heard this question often enough by now to recognize the theme, if not the words themselves.

NOW I WAS FACING ANOTHER COLLECTION OF WOMEN. FIVE PAIRS OF EYES AND FIVE PAIRS OF NIPPLES ADJUSTED THEIR GAZE AS I ENTERED. SMILING MY MENDICANT'S SMILE, I GAVE A FORMAL GREETING AND DREW ATTENTION TO THE CARPET. "*SIE HABEN EINEN GROSSEN FLECK AUF DEM TEPPICHBODEN*," I SAID, AND DROPPED TO MY KNEES ON THE FLOOR.

"*Nein, nein!*" I promised, a hand on my heart. The difference in colour, I assured her, would disappear once the carpet was thoroughly dried. This was chief among the reasons why our sales force never stayed in any town for longer than forty-eight hours.

Now they were laughing and chattering—a very good sign, though by no means the promise of certainty.

"Pluri-Clean," I said, still kneeling within the circle of skeptical hips, "*ist nicht giftig!*"

To illustrate the product's incredible non-toxicity, I sprayed some into my hand and licked it. We had been taught to squirt the liquid into the centre of the palm, but to touch the tongue only to unsprayed fingers. *"Haben Sie einen Kugelschreiber?"* I asked as they gazed in astonishment, and one of them hastened to find me a pen. I reached into my satchel and removed a spotless white towel. With the pen, I scribbled a deep blue stain on the towel's pristine surface, sprayed it with a little Pluri-Clean, and—*Wunderbar!*—the towel was virgin white again. (Our towels were carefully pre-treated each morning with ink-removing solvent.)

Now would have been the moment to spring to the window—Pluri-Clean was very effective in brightening glass—but as I had noted, this location was entirely without. I applied myself instead to burnishing a mirror cut in the shape of a woman's torso and soon produced a nicely polished squeak. This was cause of much merriment and a ribald spate of Q & A. The beauty of not speaking German was that I was unable to provide any answers beyond the ones I had been trained to provide. One of the ladies wandered over to the bar and poured me a drink. It was a slow afternoon, I gathered, with time and inclination to negotiate.

I departed, inventory satisfactorily diminished.

At intervals throughout the day the sales force was expected to rendezvous with the team leaders to replenish our satchels, exchange inked towels for fresh ones, and generally receive motivation against any flagging of effort. I was a few minutes early after leaving the brothel and so had time to find a phone and place an unsupervised call to Munich. That night, as I was being feted for the brilliant success of my first day's solo hustling, an emergency telephone call interrupted our evening meeting. My colleagues watched as my face turned white. There was silence at the table as I hung up the phone. "My brother," I choked, barely able to speak, ". . . a car accident. I have to get home!"

Early next morning, a train ticket in my pocket, I solemnly shook hands with the team leader, who expressed his deep sympathy for the death of my non-existent brother. Pluri-Clean had agreed to pay my fare to Amsterdam. I had an open ticket with Air Canada, I'd told them, and the connecting flight was out of Amsterdam. With a little luck I might be able to catch a flight home that night. When the white van disappeared around the corner, I walked back to the ticket counter and changed my destination to Munich. Then I placed another call.

"It worked," I said, and we laughed and I looked at my ticket and told her what time to pick me up. My two weeks of homelessness had passed. I was twenty years old. There was a girl waiting for me in Munich, and that day I'd finessed my first brothel.

The world was *fast ein Wunder*, and its stories all mine for the taking.

Scott Gardiner now lives in Toronto. His first novel, The Dominion of Wyley McFadden, *was published in 2000.*

THE GROWING SEASON
Nikki Barrett

September 14, 2001, Cape Town

We are restless, my Afrikaner friend and me. The fish aren't biting and the winds are gale force here at the southernmost tip of Africa, where two oceans meet. It's the off-season in the holiday town of Cape Agulhas. Sometimes we drive out past the lighthouse and down the ragged coast where he casts for kabeljou and I rake through the tumble of kelp and bones, on the hunt for sea treasures. I scan the rocks for starfish, and skim my eyes out across the sea, looking for the blow of whales. Some days we drive out through the wildflowers and the farmland, cruising through the growing season in his dun-red pickup. The wheat fields shimmer and wave, on their way from green to gold. I marvel at dappled blue gums with their waggly branches, or majestic blue cranes dipping slender beaks into rusty soil. I giggle at fields of ostriches all googlie eyes, shaggy feathers and wobbly necks. How do they manage that expression of shock mingled with superior resignation? Oh, to be an ostrich, to pull your head out of the sand with that kind of defiance.

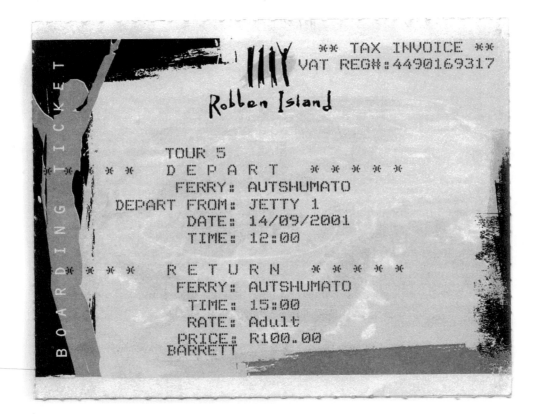

These are our outings, our adventures, R's and mine. He content to drive, off-duty from the South African Police Service; me content to look out car windows, my thoughts splayed by the electric yellow of canola fields and the whirring blades of windmills. But today our boredom is as big as the sea we live against. We need a real excursion, something more probable than a bay full of fifty-ton whales who survive on microscopic plankton. We need something more real than the lurid stream of CNN reports of massive-scale terrorism in the United States.

One hundred rand for the tour, *finished and klaar.*

On our last trip to Cape Town, we watched the rugby and went to a *Boerdans*, a wild farmer's dance where I held my whisky while R held me, whirling me about in a mean two-step. "Are you sure you want to come to Cape Town with me today?" I ask, knowing this time will be different. "I can go alone. I don't mind. And I'm not sure you'll like the show I want to see." But no, he wants to come with. "Really *bokkie*." And it's not so safe for a woman to go alone. Carjackings on the N2. Rape. Murder. And yes, he'll try anything once. I phone and book our tickets.

In the car I explain. It's the new Athol Fugard play, *Sorrows and Rejoicings*. It's all about the lingering effects, the fallout of apartheid. He doesn't sigh, doesn't roll his eyes even. He's humouring me today. It's my turn, my day. I simply read the cartoon bubble above his head that says, "Please, Nikki, no politics."

"Athol who?" he asks.

Before the play, we are going across to Robben Island. That he is excited about. His parents used to take the ferry over to the island for all-night *jolls* at the prison mess hall. The fishing was good there. As we drive past Fairfield farm, I can see him anticipating an island picnic. He is, isn't he? I keep my mouth shut, my eyes fixed on the puff adder flickering across the road. I keep the cartoon bubble over my head as empty as possible.

In the New South Africa, a trip across the bay to Robben Island costs you one hundred rand. That's about twelve American dollars, which is good if you're paying in dollars, not so good if you're paying in the ever-weakening rand. The island, once the maximum-security prison where Nelson Mandela and other political agitators were treated so savagely during the struggle to free South Africa from apartheid, is now a World Heritage Site, one of the top tourist destinations in South Africa. Ads running in the *Cape Times* encourage investors to associate themselves with the lucrative brands of "Nelson Mandela" and "Robben Island" by funding development around the new Robben Island gateway. At the ticket office, there is no information describing the tour. It's straightforward. One hundred rand for the Robben Island tour. *Finished and klaar*, as the Afrikaners would say.

Table Mountain is stark against a cutting blue sky as the ferry shivers and hums out of the harbour, leaving Cape Town behind us. God, R loves to be on the water.

Look at him. "Look at that sea," he says, "So flat, so calm. Perfect day to get me some perlemoen." I love the way he reads the sea and the wind, sizing up days in terms of their fishing and diving potential. He is not a policeman who fishes but a fisherman who polices.

And me? My identity markers are thin on the ground these days. I no longer say who or what I am. I simply say where I was born, followed by the places where I have lived, as if geography might suffice. Born in Zimbabwe to South African mother, Rhodesian father. Live in Canada mostly. Have lived in England, Scotland . . .

As we walk up the gangplank, a photographer offers to snap romantic shots of the couples boarding the ferry, in some bizarre parody of a pleasure cruise. *Please.* Once on the ferry, we are sardined with mostly tourists: Germans, Brits, Austrians, and some Namibians drinking cane, a clear, potent alcohol, mixed with orange juice. There are South Africans too, black and white, including four Afrikaner women with matching blue bags covered with images of leaping dolphins. Cameras click. The video recorders pan round and round. Penguins bob up and down. Cellphones sing and trill. The dolphin bags open and close.

The atmosphere is cheerful but strained. R bristles every time the Namibians swagger past to the cabin for more booze. There is some confusion, everyone undecided about the appropriate demeanour for this cozy journey. The tourists, armed with recording devices, are anticipating a sombre foray into South Africa's very recent past, while the Afrikaner women are out for a jaunt on this day that flirts so boldly with summer. And R and I?

When we reach the island we are herded onto a bus. We are told a one-hour island tour will be followed by the prison tour. R says nothing, but I know he would rather grab a beer at the *shebeen* where his parents used to go, check out the colony of jackass penguins maybe. He's not interested in history that is barely history.

After the dull coach tour, we all clamber out into sunshine and are introduced to a slight Coloured man, Derek Basson, a former political prisoner who tells us he spent five years in the prison he stands in front of. With the prison, dull and shabby, behind him, Derek explains how he was convicted of sabotage though, in his opinion, it should have been arson. He threw a petrol bomb at a post office as part of his contributions to the struggle to free South Africa from apartheid. Before he leaves us in Derek's hands, the bus guide repeats his one tired joke: "So, who's ready to go to prison now?"

Derek, prisoner turned prison guide, asks us to follow him. Fifty tourists file into a communal cell, bunks at one end of the grey concrete room, benches arranged in a semi-circle for us to sit on. He closes the cell door. This is the extent of the tour: Derek in a communal cell, telling us about the brutal, inhumane conditions in the prison and about the camaraderie, the heroic resistance that surfaced in spite of them.

We sit side by side, R and I, on the grey bench in the front row of the cell. Derek paces. Up and down, walking over and over the thin mat that once served him as a bed. He looks right at us when he talks. There is no script. With disarming intimacy he randomly shares pieces of his prison life. He speaks in eloquent English but with a thick Afrikaans accent. Afrikaans is Derek's first language. While an inmate, he used to teach Afrikaans to his comrades. He explains about the hierarchy of privilege based on colour. Blacks received the most meagre food and clothes rations. "Sandals. All we got was sandals made from tires. They rubbed your feet so much,

BEFORE HE LEAVES US IN DEREK'S HANDS, THE BUS GUIDE REPEATS HIS TIRED JOKE: "SO, WHO'S READY TO GO TO PRISON NOW?"

hurt them so much, you ended up not wearing them at all." It is these details that seem to rile him the most, the injustice of being denied equality in the most basic of arenas—food, clothing, bedding.

R's big hands grip the edge of the grey bench. His discomfort is palpable. When I glance at him, I can see his teeth are clenched harder than his hands, and I understand the word "seething." He is still as stone as Derek's words tumble forth like gravel, slow and measured: "I detect the mood in this room is sombre. But I want you to know I am not angry anymore. There is no point in anger. You know, there are some former prison guards who came back here to work, and now, now we party together. And let me tell you, when you've had a few drinks, inhibitions go away. You say what's on your mind. We drink together. It's something to see our children play-ing together. That is something."

After about forty minutes, people start to shift, shuffle feet, move a dolphin bag from one shoulder to the other. The divisions in the hushed room are clear. Some people are moved to the point of tears by this extraordinary moment in history, the triumph of human will that took place on an island reserved for outcasts and exiles, madmen and lepers. Some are wondering when they will get to see Nelson Mandela's two-by-two-metre solitary confinement cell or when they can pick up their romantic ferry photo. R, along with three of the Afrikaner women, is squirming, vis-ibly agitated. *Yes, okay, this is the New South Africa, the Rainbow Nation. Enough of the ANC rhetoric.* The "New South Africa" and "Rainbow Nation," the *Dictionary of South African English* had warned me, are two epithets that are already used deri-sively, sarcastically in a nation grappling with extreme violence, poverty and an astounding AIDS crisis. The dolphin women are skeptical of Derek's assertions— designed to attract foreign investment—that South Africa is an economically and politically stable country with an exciting future. One woman raises her eyebrows suspiciously as if to say, "Propaganda." The fourth dolphin woman, however, is listening intently. She raises her hand, not her eyebrows, and asks Derek timidly, genuinely, "Did you kill anyone?"

"No. The post office was closed. It was late at night. It was never the intention of the freedom fighters to kill innocent people. The struggle was only 20 per cent vio-lence." Derek looks directly at R, and I know that R reads this intimacy as audacity, as confrontation instead of two people seeing eye to eye. I have never been this close to R's anger. Here in the communal cell, at the edges of Derek's gesture for recon-ciliation, violence simmers just beneath my friend's skin. Oblivious tourists glance at their watches.

"You are South African, Afrikaans, aren't you?" Derek's question is for the little woman, but he sweeps his gaze around the room, settling it first on R and me and then across the rest. The little dolphin woman is obviously uncomfortable. She is being singled out. She struggles for words. It would be easier for her and Derek to break into Afrikaans, their first language. She says, rolling her *r*s fiercely with the typical *brei*, "Both sides done mistakes. We must try to get it right now. That is the important thing."

My eyes brim with tears as I watch this small Afrikaner woman trying to understand, making this small effort to break from her school of dolphin sisters. Derek says to her, gently, "It's true that apartheid was led mostly by the white Afrikaans, but I am not angry anymore. I have let that anger go. If there are any racists in this room, I want you to think about what your religion, your politics might teach you. Who does it teach you to hate? I encourage you to leave your comfort zone. Learn an African language. Try and encounter someone who is different than you and learn from them. We are all the same when we are born. We are equals. We are equals."

R is fierce with indignation, his anger huge. I feel it there beside me. *Equals?* I am afraid the flimsy façade of the prison tour is about to crack open into a skirmish of sorts. *Equals? You terrorists committed atrocities in the name of freedom, then drive our country into a ruinous state of violence, disease, poverty, economic decline. Equals?* I can read the cartoon bubble above his head. I nudge R's thigh with my knee in order to say . . . to say . . . what? That I, too, find this eerie, the way this struggle, so recent, so raw, has been packaged, branded—history, revolution so quickly turned into an economic opportunity? *Please.*

I want to explain, too, that I know R has grown up on the other side, has been shaped by a misguided belief system that was confirmed for him by the worst violence and human degradation which he had seen on duty. I want to say that I will try to understand but I cannot accept. I am not bothered one smidge that unsuspecting South Africans like him might be manipulated into confronting their recent pasts, that they are trapped for a fleeting hour in a cell, listening to what they think of as a simplistic one-sided take on history. Can I go on loving him in spite of the hate and resentment he harbours? For the first time, I feel the magnitude of the gulf between us, large as the Atlantic that cleaved our childhoods.

That night R and I sit in the dark of the Baxter Theatre watching *Sorrows and Rejoicings*. The performances are stark and intense, but the play, about an exiled writer who cannot come to terms with the lives he has ruined, is like a ferocious punch that misses its mark, goes flailing into space. Apartheid was good for art, the

Sunday Times says. Oh, how art thrives on resistance. Oh, how we become lost, collapse in on ourselves, without clear enemies. That strange lure of opposition, of defining oneself against something. There in the dark, I think of my home so far away, think of me living now in such a lonely place under the steady blink of the Agulhas lighthouse, think of the sickening luxury of self-imposed exile, the strange prisons we construct for ourselves. Where is the rejoicing?

The whale-sized dolphin woman rolls her eyes, huffs a little and asks Derek in a voice thick with superiority, "Can we go and see the rest of the prison now?"

Derek opens the cell door, and all of us file out—perpetrators, victims, consumers—uncertain of our complicity then, our roles now. We are as responsible for creating joy as we are for eradicating the errors, the sorrows of the past, are we not? It's not about blame. It cannot be about resignation. It's about where we go from here. R is here beside me, and I know instinctively that the hour in the cell could split us forever. What dawns on me as we file past the place where Mandela spent eighteen years, is that had my family and I not left Rhodesia when we did, the gap between R and me might not be this wide. My African childhood, uprooted, transplanted in Canadian soil, enables me to draw a distinction between terrorist and freedom fighter. I am able to register suffering on both sides, to see the dangers of clinging to hate. I am no longer an African who moved to Canada; I am a Canadian transient in Africa. I feel the difference, a change in the trajectory of my identity, the core of me reoriented for good.

The whale-sized dolphin woman chirps on her cellphone, planning the evening *braai*. She says to her friend, "Summer is on its way. Finally we can do some real drinking." Drinking. Amnesia. They are lifestyles here. R and I step out of the prison. We have a play to go to, but part of me wants the simplicity of the sea and the wildflowers, ostriches and whales. I am overcome with sorrow and joy for the two of us snagged on this juncture in history, caught at the end of Africa, between two oceans, between an off-season and a growing season. I reach for R's hand, wink and say, "Let's go see the jackass penguins."

Nikki Barrett was born in Zimbabwe (then Rhodesia), and has lived most of her life in Canada. Her writing has been published in Chatelaine, Write *magazine,* Blood & Aphorisms, Pagitica *and* enRoute *magazine.*

THE BALLET OF PATRICK BLUE-ASS
Patrick Woodcock

When I flew into Keflavik airport in February, it was for two reasons only: I needed both darkness and isolation to focus on a book of poetry I had begun fourteen months earlier in Moscow. It was NOT to become a ballet dancer.

Whenever I've met other people who have travelled to Iceland, they all retell the same story. They flew to Iceland in the summer months, when the weather is favourable for camping, hiking or biking. They wanted to visit the country of poets, the land of 100 per cent literacy, to see theatre in and out of doors. They love to talk about how unique the country is. I usually agree and politely try to change the topic of conversation. Their Iceland isn't mine; they ventured there for reasons that, for the most part, mean little to me.

Iceland is stunning in the summer. There is a certain grace to its countryside that can only be seen then, especially since summer is the only time the Number 1, Iceland's only national highway, is accessible. But for me, the problem with summer is more personal. I have inherited from my Irish father a skin that, on the white scale, is more clear than pale. I have never been able to tan; the only sunscreen that has ever worked for my wan cheeks is the roof of a house. Therefore, ever since childhood,

I've had an aversion to sunlight. I think Woody Allen had a line that says it best: "I don't tan, I stroke."

By the time I left Iceland in May, there was never any darkness, and nighttime brought a hazy dreamlike dusk that played havoc with my mood. I always felt like I was walking in that alcoholic fog Eugene O'Neill wrote so well about. I tried covering my windows with a layer of tinfoil and tape, followed by two winter blankets. It worked—I couldn't see my hand an inch away from my face. But I still knew there was light outside; patient and unmoving.

The Iceland I wanted was the tourist-free, dark, cold, unforgiving home of volcanoes and glaciers. I flew from Boston on a practically empty plane and arrived in an agonizingly loud hailstorm that sounded like Norse gods were tearing apart the fuselage. I was both amused and uneasy during the forty-kilometre bus ride from the airport in Keflavik to Reykjavik. I sat behind the bus driver and could see no more than three feet out the front window—snow, rain and hail were all battering us incessantly. I was obviously the only tourist on the bus, being the only one not sleeping. I just sat there drinking from a small bottle of vodka and shaking.

During those winter months, it would be Iceland's wind, my nemesis, that would provide me with the most misery and frustration and consequently the most entertainment. The wind in Iceland hugs you like a drunken uncle. There is no sign heralding its arrival; it catches you off guard, holds you, ignores your struggles, and only lets go after you are exhausted, frustrated and completely embarrassed. It is the demented choreographer of the ballet of the absurd in which you are the acrobat. After contorting you into pirouette after pirouette, it forces you to attempt a few "I'm losing my balance" arabesques only to conclude with—much to the approval of the university students I passed daily—an "I give up" grand jeté, which usually leaves you looking for your camera, Walkman or wallet beneath a parked car.

And there is nowhere to hide. Alleys, storefronts, even culverts, are all amphitheatres and dance halls for this shrieking demon. It attacks from all angles to remind you of one thing: you are in Iceland, and in Iceland, the wind is omnipotent, owns you and can devour you.

And how does the Icelandic government try to aid you in your fight against this tempest? Well, it sprinkles volcanic ash over the sidewalks to help you with your traction. Unfortunately, this only serves one purpose: to cover your clothing in volcanic ash. I am certain the Icelandic government has a clandestine agreement with every laundry detergent company selling its product in corner stores.

I did not have a washing machine, so I washed my clothes in my bathtub with a broomstick. I fell daily, I purchased more detergent than bread or vegetables and was given the Sagaesque name "Patrick Blue-Ass" by a bartender at The Dubliner, Iceland's first Irish pub. "You fall down more than our regulars," he observed one day, and later added, "but more gracefully."

A few weeks after my arrival, my roommate, a filleter named John from Newcastle, awoke me to watch the Icelandic news—Hekla, a volcano roughly 110 kilometres southeast of Reykjavik, had erupted, and thousands of Icelanders travelling to see it were trapped in a blizzard. The anchorman announced that even with the help of the army and volunteers, it would still take days to rescue all those stranded. I returned to my bedroom in a rare state of contentment, eager to write, feeling I had finally found the foreign country I'd been searching for. One that was invigorating while being ruthless and demanding.

Iceland was and still is, as Lowry wrote years before about Mexico, a country of "desolate splendour." It is a place where a wind suffused with a devilish playfulness creates radiant undulating snowdrifts, re-shapes vast majestic panoramas and, if you are not prepared, demands the occasional dance or two before allowing you to return to the safety of your apartment. It is there that you are left alone to rest, write and practise the inevitable "I just lost my hat" ballotté for the next day's recital.

Patrick Woodcock is the poetry editor for the Literary Review of Canada. *His fourth book,* The Challenged One, *has just been published. He has fallen down in seventeen countries, most recently, in Bosnia.*

AFTERSHOCK
Jill Lawless

I grabbed the driver's shoulder—"Stop, stop!" Wrenched at the door handle, rested forehead on forearm, and forearm on window frame, and vomited a thin, clear cascade into the Indian dust.

Sat up, gulped from a water bottle. A couple of deep breaths, tangy with earth. Calmed the stomach, contorted with hunger and nerves. The brown eyes of the driver—I'd already forgotten his name, damn—flashed alarm in the rearview mirror. The stream of people trudging along the roadside, hauling sacks and bundles and small children, diverged around the puddle and flowed past us toward the city and solidity.

Dozens of villages had decanted their populations onto the road that led to the city. The villages had crumbled like sandcastles. From the road, you could see what was left of them: small, jagged mountains of debris rising from the desert.

We were driving toward the epicentre of an earthquake. There was a town at the epicentre. Had been a town. My stomach churned.

I leaned forward, stretched out a trembling arm. "Okay. Keep going."

I didn't want to keep going. This was not my beat, and I'd used up my last shot of adrenalin somewhere between the cracked and tilting city a hundred miles back down the road and this teeming crossroads.

The first bit had been easy: Just keep moving; get as close as you can. Flight, airport, another flight, taxi. Inquire, haggle a bit, find a car and agree to leave at dawn. Go to bed and lie awake, thinking of aftershocks.

The city hadn't looked too bad. Squat buildings had sprouted cracks and gashes, and high-rises tilted at dangerous angles; but the luxury hotel was still standing, and the shops were open.

Heading back toward the city, it was like rush hour: buses grumbling under roof-rack suitcase mountains; jammed cars of all descriptions; open-backed trucks, their flatbeds packed with passengers like vertical sardines; families on tractors. West, toward the destruction, went the first of the relief trucks, laden with hastily assembled cargoes of clothing, water and biscuits; white government jeeps; and cars full of passengers with shiny white faces: journalists.

Our progress slowed as we drove west. The road developed bumps and fissures, and the buildings that dotted the roadside had been reduced to jumbles of bricks and concrete and timbers and tiles. Amid one pile, a filing cabinet stood inexplicably upright, gleaming and unscathed. It was the tallest object in the landscape.

We came to another crossroads and slowed to a crawl. Hundreds of people stood or sat beside the road; some leapt into the traffic, trying to flag down already crammed eastward-bound vehicles. Five women in rich maroon saris, tin water pots glistening on their heads, walked in elegant single file along the road, then turned—defiantly, it seemed—and headed across the desert for a rubble drumlin half a mile away.

We crawled on through thickening devastation and reached a town turned inside out. The buildings had been eviscerated, their innards strewn on the dusty ground: pipes, refrigerators, clothes and blankets, wall calendars, images of gods, and pictures of children.

Here I was. I had a mobile phone (no signal), a laptop (no electricity), a satellite phone (ditto) and a notebook (blank).

I got out of the car, took a few steps. I had no idea what I was looking for. I soon found it.

"Christ!" blurted the perspiring, notebook-clutching figure who appeared out of the dust. "Terrible, isn't it? Where've you been and what have you seen? I've just been to the military hospital, what's left of it. They're operating in the open air. Amputations galore. Bloody awful."

"I've just arrived," I said. The stranger boasted an English accent and a vest bulging with external pockets—a combination that never fails to intimidate. His broad face was a luminous, glistening pink. "I'm just getting my bearings."

"Do you have a car? Brilliant! I've mislaid mine. Let's go to the old city; I've heard the damage is worst there."

It was a plan. I felt better, having a plan. We drove on into the shattered town, stopped beside a gate to the old city. You couldn't drive in or even walk—you had to climb.

We picked our way into the heart of the town: hopping, teetering, scrambling. Here and there, concrete slabs formed precarious bridges. I stepped on one tentatively; it shifted squelchingly underfoot, with a smell that burned my nose and caught the back of my throat. Looking down, I glimpsed the bloated beige flank of a cow. The smell got stronger the deeper you went. A little farther on, an outstretched arm and a woman's bare midriff, the flesh soft and greying.

People squatted atop the heaps, handkerchiefs tied round their faces, peering through gaps in the rubble. For survivors or salvage; I didn't know which. One man crouched, painstakingly enlarging a hole. Now and then, he pressed his face to the gap, then reached in an arm and pulled out a battered pan or an item of clothing, which he folded neatly and placed in a battered suitcase at his side.

My English friend scribbled feverishly in his notebook. I uncapped a pen, flipped open my own notebook. Paused. Wrote "suitcase" and "children's clothes."

"I can't give a shape to this," I thought—my clearest thought of the day. "I can't put this into six hundred words. Or six thousand."

The Englishman was speaking to people, quietly and deliberately. Simple questions: What happened? Where is your house? Your family? The answers were obvious, but people answered without anger or tears, in what English they had. "It's shock," I thought. "It was only thirty-six hours ago; it hasn't sunk in yet."

"This is great stuff," he said. "I've got to file. Shall we go back to HQ?"

He directed the driver to a large hotel. On the wide lawn behind the listing building, the world's press was imposing its own order upon disaster. Tent clusters and sleeping bags dotted the grass. Trestle tables had been set up, generators hummed, satellite phones whined and fingers tap-danced on keyboards.

I hauled my knapsack and my laptop and the flat, dense brick of my satellite phone from the trunk of the car and staggered to the nearest cluster.

No one paid me any attention. Surreptitiously, I explored the dense tangle of wires and sockets and found a spot to plug in the phone. It hummed gently. I placed it on a clear patch of grass, angled its lid toward the sky, watched the little signal bars sprout on the tiny screen. Then I punched in a phone number. It rang. Magic.

"Hello. Hello, newsdesk? It's me. I'm in India. Yes, fine. No, terrible. Look, can you take dictation?"

I took a breath. Thought of what I'd seen, thought of six hundred words of crisp wire copy. "The residents of this earthquake-shattered town . . ." I began, faking it, and ten minutes later I was finished: " . . . a child's teddy bear."

The news editor came on the line, booming across a great chasm. "Good stuff," he said. "Look, try to find some Americans or even Canadians. A lot of people have relatives over there. We need local angles. Tragic families are good. Miracle survivors are even better. Got it?"

I got it.

Then, fortified with sardines on toast—courtesy of the Englishman—I unrolled my sleeping bag and went to sleep. I slept so soundly that I didn't feel the aftershock at dawn that jolted the residents of the town from their outdoor beds, driving them instantly upright, hearts pounding, ready to flee.

The atmosphere in the camp was chaotic and congenial. Journalists are territorial, but here the caginess and rivalry were muted. Television spoke to print, and photographer to reporter, sharing scoops, gently prodding for information. Comrades who'd met in previous wars or disasters renewed their acquaintance with offhand bonhomie. Around the campfire, the old veterans would reminisce about jeeps and guerrillas, artillery fire and malaria. Sometimes they spoke of dead colleagues, killed in the line of news-gathering duty.

These stories fascinated and terrified me. I was not like these people, brave and self-important. I did not want to go to a war. I liked my job, but I was rather homesick and increasingly, shamefully, certain I wanted a quiet life.

On the job, their blank and professional faces were as hard to read as those of the survivors, who met my gaze steadily, calmly. "What do they feel," I thought, "the journalists and the survivors? What do they think of me?" I wanted them not to hate me, but it was so hard to tell.

I spent my days loitering on the fringes of misery, scuttling from rubble heap to field hospital and back. Finally, I got lucky. I stopped to talk to some British rescue workers sunning themselves on a patch of grass between shifts. They were exhausted but elated; they'd pulled someone out alive. An American.

At least he sounded American. A young lad, about twenty, in remarkably good shape for someone who'd been buried alive for two days. Bit of a miracle, really. It had been a high-rise building by this town's standards: eight storeys. The top five were more or less intact, but they'd collapsed onto the bottom three, just pancaked them. The Turkish rescuers had swept the building with dogs a couple of days before but had found no signs of life. Then yesterday, a neighbour had come to the Brits' camp and said he'd heard someone calling. They'd been skeptical but went along, banging on the rubble and calling out; to their surprise, a weak voice had responded.

It had taken them two hours to reach him, shifting rubble and inserting props and inching their way forward. They pulled him out and put him in an ambulance. The boy said he'd been in bed asleep when the early-morning earthquake struck. There was shaking and a huge noise, and he'd woken up with the ceiling six inches from his face.

He'd sat in the ambulance and drank some water, and they tried to take him to hospital but he refused. His family was still inside: his mother and brother and an uncle and aunt and a cousin. When he'd called out after the earthquake, a female voice had responded from nearby; but after a while it had stopped. He even drew them a plan of the house.

They told him he needed to see a doctor, but he wouldn't listen. And in truth, there wasn't a scratch on him. Some of his other relatives had arrived, and they took him aside and huddled with him near the building, and there the rescuers had left him.

A miracle survivor. I knew what I had to do. The high-rise building stood on its own on the edge of town, set back from the road; a tall, middle-class oasis, pale pink and white. The central elevator shaft had split away from the building and leaned toward the ground. The residential wings on either side also leaned outward, surrounded by three-storey skirts of rubble. It looked like a tree split down the middle by lightning.

Since the rescuers had left the site—one miracle deemed all the tower would yield; lightning unlikely to strike the same place twice—an earthmover had arrived to begin clearing the debris. A large crowd watched with silent, sombre faces.

I edged into the crowd, making tentative—and, I hoped, tactful—inquiries. "The young man who was rescued yesterday," I began. "Do you know him?" The bystanders either did not understand or had no answer, and they turned their backs.

I retreated in defeat to the margins. A jolly television reporter hailed me. "Looking for the guy they rescued? He's standing over there." And he pointed to a lithe young man in brown trousers and a short-sleeved shirt. "He's been here ever since they pulled him out. He hopes they'll find his family. But you'll never get near him. His relatives are keeping everyone away."

I looked at the youth, who appeared clean and dapper. He stood looking toward the building, one hand holding a paper mask to his face, the other on his head: a posture of frozen surprise. I couldn't see his eyes.

I knew I had no choice. I began walking toward the youth, in what I hoped was an open and friendly manner. Before I'd gotten very far, several of his relatives broke off from the crowd and advanced upon me, shaking their heads and waving their arms.

"Told you," said the television reporter. "It's a bugger."

I left the compound and walked around the perimeter fence, until I was opposite the young man, separated by chain-link but only twenty yards away.

"Hey—excuse me," I called out. "Where are you from?"

The youth turned and looked. He had deep black eyes.

"Is there a message I can give to anyone?"

The relatives were shaking their heads, and the young man seemed to register my notebook and pen. "Go away," he said, turning back to face the tower.

"No, look," I said, desperate now. "I want to help. I can take a message, tell people you're all right. Your friends or your fam—"

"My family!" The young man spun around, strode forward and shook the chain-link fence with both hands. "My family is here! We were all visiting my aunt and uncle: my mother, my father, my brother and me. It was the Christmas holiday. We were almost ready to leave. Now I am here and they . . . they are in there.

"I must stay here and find my family. If you want to help, get digging. Otherwise, you are just a vulture and you can fuck right off."

He turned away again, and the relatives rushed the fence. I leapt back and scurried off.

"Any luck?" asked the television reporter.

I considered. "I can get a story out of it," I said.

The next day I returned with the Englishman to the ruined old city. We clambered across the new alpine landscape to a hill where a knot of young men stood watching. Two middle-aged men, one large and bald, the other compact with a mop of black hair and a moustache, were tunnelling by hand into the debris.

"That is their mother's house," a young man whispered to us. "They have been digging for three days."

But the men had stopped digging. They nodded to one another, reached in and pulled in unison, gently. They eased a woman's body from the hole like a cork from a bottle. She was about sixty, stout and grey-haired. Her skin was grey and deathly, but her dirt-encrusted sari was as neatly wrapped as when she had put it on, on the last morning of her life.

Her two sons stood and wiped their foreheads with the back of their forearms. They wrapped their mother's body in a blanket, then stood beside it, looking down, their hands clasped in front of them.

The Englishman nudged me, and we edged our way down the slope. We shook the hand of one man, then of the other. "I'm very sorry," I said. The bald brother looked up. "Thank you," he said. His dusty hand gripped my sweaty one.

We returned to the car and sat in silence. At last I spoke.

"Do you think I can catch something from shaking hands with those guys?"

"I was just wondering that myself," the Englishman said. Then he leaned over the front seat. "Come on, driver! I've got a story to file."

A former Toronto theatre critic and editor of Mongolia's first independent English-language newspaper, Jill Lawless is the author of Wild East: Travels in the New Mongolia. *She is a journalist based in London.*

La Manche
20 July '01

TWO DRAWINGS
Michael Winter

Abandoned
La Manche, July 20

I was swimming here with a woman who'd come to live in Newfoundland for the summer. I was going on day trips in my car. This one's about forty minutes south of St. John's. We packed a suitcase full of picnic things, English plates and Duralex water glasses. We swam naked in the water, which is backed with a cold waterfall. We ducked under the falls. There is a trail with a walkway over the water, and you can hike between communities. This one is abandoned. A puffin dove. A few humpbacks out by the point. The woman sang a Gillian Welch song on her guitar. I wondered if I could fall for her and then I realized I was wondering. She said, "I could bring you joy."

Indiscriminate
Terra Nova, September 20

I was caribou hunting the morning after a tropical storm smacked into Newfoundland. The water rose two feet, washing away my campfire. My tent is in the woods to the right. I decided to camp across the river from a family of beavers. As I drew this, a caribou appeared by the big rock, downwind. He did a move I associate with wild horses: he swivelled the weight in his chest, which caused his front legs to

twist and turn in the water. At night the beavers paddled across the river, climbed the bank and gnawed on the birch around my tent. Their work was tremendous and indiscriminate. The expression is not as efficient as a beaver. I worried for my forehead. The tent just big enough to house me. How good is a beaver's eyesight if he waddles past and considers my head?

Michael Winter wrote a book called This All Happened. *A lot of people think it's autobiographical, and he's glad he convinced them of this. He lives in St. John's and Toronto.*

HEADLANDS
Jonathan Bennett

For James

It's still early and the morning sky is empty, neither black nor blue. A small mob of grey kangaroos has come down off the headland. They graze in the light scrub, moving only a hop or two at a time. In this scrappy light, they are easily mistaken for rocks or stumps or shadows. My mug of tea rests on my leg, the concentrated warmth of it calling attention to the outside chill. My bare legs, hanging off the front verandah, move a little involuntarily, twitching to keep warm.

In the garage I turn the key in the old, orange Land Rover. My brother instructed me to douse the engine in WD-40. "Be nice to her," he joked, "and she'll start."

Thankfully the old girl does turn over, the clutch having given about half a metre before jamming against the metal floor. As I grope to fulfill the demands and desires of a 1967 British gearbox, I can almost feel my father sitting beside me, tossing in words of encouragement. The engine roars and the kangaroos bound into the reaches and folds of the headland.

I stop at the wharf beside the tea-coloured river and pick out two very large, discarded fish heads from the fishermen's bins. In the half-light of this still morning,

The raw atmosphere for imaginings.

221

I thread a piece of rope through their mouths, aghast, and tie them to the bull bar on the front of the Land Rover. You need these fish heads to stink in order to catch bloodworms, an unsurpassed fish bait. In a few days' time, after having hung in the scorching Australian sun, they will be perfect. It's a simple cycle: rotting fish to catch worms, worms to catch fresh fish. Today, however, the heads are new. Still, I will try.

You can imagine Hat Head just from its name. It's a long day's drive north of Sydney, up the murderous Pacific Highway. Drive through Taree, Forster and Tuncurry, Port Macquarie and, at Kempsey, you make a right turn and head back for the sea to find the windswept headland, upon which a large hill shaped like a hat—a misshapen fedora, a punched-out Stetson—juts into the Pacific Ocean. A few hundred people live here year-round, the population swelling in the summer with holidaymakers and surfers, fishermen and bush walkers.

I drive fast but stay close to the shore where the sand is firm. In all the times I've returned home to Australia, revisiting this stretch of coastline, I've never travelled the beach from end to end. No matter how far I go, the beach just seems to continue, to disappear into the haze and wind ahead. Should the orange Land Rover break down or the tide turn and come in high and sooner than expected, I am a stranded Crusoe, four-wheel drive or not.

The sky is lightening now, and a few solitary fishermen cast their lines into the surf, reeling in the first dart fish and whiting of the dawn. Seagulls hover out beyond the breakers, concentrating on schools of fish that rise and fall in swarm-like formations from the bottom of the ocean as they are chased by larger fish. To my left, sand dunes veined with thin runners of grass and the odd burnt stump of a tree go on forever, disappearing into oblivion, into the haze of scant light and sea spray ahead of me. With my bare feet on the hot metal pedals, I push the Land Rover to go faster. Behind me, my tire tracks recede only to be erased by waves sliding up the beach.

The tide is low and I scan the sea, the breakers. I find a deep gully of water between two shallow sand flats where the fish feed. Reversing the Land Rover up the beach into the soft sand, I point its nose down at the sea. If it will not start later, at least I'll have a modest hill to try to jump-start her. I learned these secrets as a boy, by watching my father and my uncle John. I saw first-hand what happened to ignorant tourists in lightweight jeeps bogged in fine white sand. We'd have to stop and help dig them out, or winch them free in the worst cases.

My fish heads are too new. Standing in the surf up to my knees, I wait as each new wave washes in: when it pauses, caught between advance and retreat, I drag the fish heads across the sand. I watch for the tiniest indications of bloodworms poking their heads up through the sand, smelling what they think is a meal. I swivel my hips, digging down into the sand, hoping to feel small, hard shapes on the heels and balls of my feet. Pipies are clam-like bivalves, and I bend to collect them one by one, putting them in a bucket tied to my waist.

I smash two pipies together and their shells burst open, exposing blond flesh and opaque tentacles. The insides of their shells are smooth and opalescent in the new morning light. I drag the fish heads across the sand once more as a wave goes out, and as it does, I see a small break in the diminishing water's film, something interrupting its evenness, like an arrowhead pointing at me. Kneeling beside it, I wait for another wave to come in, which washes against me hard, soaking my shorts and most of my T-shirt. The water is cold. I want this bloodworm now.

The wave withdraws and I wag the pipi over the area where the bloodworm's head split the rushing water only moments ago. The head emerges again; this time I am close to it and I tempt it with the pipi's flesh. I manoeuvre my fingers in behind its head, ready to pinch and pull in one swift motion. But I must not rush.

As children of eight or ten, we would try to catch bloodworms. My uncle John would offer outrageous sums of money—sometimes even five dollars—if we could pull one worm up whole. The chance at these winnings was enough incentive to

Be nice to her and she'll start.

keep us occupied for hours while he and the other adults fished and wormed. His money could not have been safer.

Bloodworms live in the sand and sea and are as thick as a ten-year-old's baby finger. They can be just as long as a boy is tall, a sort of seafaring millipede, and are difficult to catch because of the innumerable tiny legs that run down either side of their bodies. If all the legs are not going in the same direction, then the head will simply rip off. To make matters worse, bloodworms are extremely fast in retreat. Twice I wait for it to come to the surface, nibble and recoil, my thumb and forefinger lingering gently around the neck, before I strike.

I get the worm first try. I feel it arching, its momentum heading upward, and I pull it from beneath the sand with all the precision of a surgeon in mid-suture. I fish with it as bait for about an hour, using segments of it at a time. I catch two bream and put them in a bucket of sea water where they swim in circles. Not big fish, but with the sand under my feet, the salt in the air, and the horizon before me, I feel elemental. This is why I have travelled up here. Lolling about in the last licks of wave are my two fish heads, bound, dead. After a time, I decide to drive farther up the beach, but before I do, I upend the bucket in knee-high surf, both fish swimming free.

Driving again, I am looking for signs of a sudden tidal shift. Yesterday's paper said it wouldn't happen until late this afternoon, but I drive distracted nonetheless. The beach continues to unfurl ahead of me in slight variations of dune, scrub and surf. A piece of driftwood. A washed-up plastic bag half-filled with sand catches the wind. This is how I remember the drive from my childhood, but now the possibility and concern of being trapped by the tide is no longer my father's or uncle's worry. I drive on.

In the distance a sharp wall of dark rock breaks the horizon as if thrown down by a spiteful God. It punctuates the beach, a piece of geographical exclamation, halting my progress northward, ripping me clear of my thoughts. A sign announces South West Rocks and a turnoff to Trial Bay Gaol.

The gaol, constructed of locally quarried pink and grey granite, closed for good in 1903 but was briefly reopened in 1915 to hold First World War internees from Germany. They were allowed out onto the beach during the day, so the story goes, but were locked up at night. I climb up on one of the low walls. Looking out to sea, I can't help but scour the distance for a glimpse of Hat Head. All I see is beach and haze.

In the lee of the cliffs, I sit on the sand where the internees must have spent their days. I imagine two lovers, freed from nightly lock-up, finding each other in broad daylight, their white bodies wading at the shore. In real life, he has made promises to another woman, but shut away up here, he finds himself drawn to this new woman, the curve of her mouth in the morning, the way her hair falls in the bright light.

She is younger than he is, I think. She makes her choice and they swim, touching only below the water, swimming deeper into the ocean until neither can stand. Their love is made suspended amongst porpoises, concealed from the island gaolers patrolling the beach.

They must have feared the future. Would they know freedom again and, if so, would it kill their love? The sun rises wholly, and I am miles from Hat Head. I have travelled to the end of a beach that I had always imagined to be unrelenting.

The next few mornings the kangaroos return and I watch them until the light firms and they melt into the landscape of the head. They dissolve one by one, between mouthfuls of tea, as I look down at a bull ant that is getting too close to my bare leg, or crane my neck to catch a glimpse of a pelican employing an updraft. I fish each dawn, first repeating my worm hunt, then throwing back the catch. I get more adept with each day. The fish heads decompose and ripen, until maggots writhe in their eye sockets. Fish eating worms, worms eating fish. Daily too, I press ahead to Trial Bay Gaol. The beach no longer a fearful passage limited by memory but the raw atmosphere for my imaginings, the source and cause of those stories still yet to come.

Jonathan Bennett's first novel, After Battersea Park, *was published in 2001 to critical acclaim. His next book,* Verandah People, *is a collection of short stories and will be released in 2003. Originally from Sydney, Australia, Jonathan now lives in Port Hope, Ontario.*

THE MOTHERHOOD ROADSHOW
Alison Wearing

When I was pregnant, people were always warning me that "children change your life."

The comment bored me. Since the day I'd left home at seventeen, I had changed jobs, addresses, countries and living languages more times than I care to count. "My life's never been the same two years running," I would think. "What's so monumental about this change that everyone feels the need to warn me?"

I should have noticed that what they were actually saying was "children chaaaAAAWOWOWOWOWAAAnge your life."

If people had only enunciated properly, I might have paid more attention.

I'll freely admit that I went into motherhood a bit naively. I thought having a baby would be like having a cat. Feeding, litter/toilet-training, dangling toys from a string. I knew there was more to it, of course, but I assumed that to be the general idea. It never occurred to me that I might not continue to live after the birth the way I had before. Being in a relationship, I'd already caught on to the notion of monogamy and remembering to call when I wasn't going to be back for dinner. Besides diapers and barf blankets, what else was there?

I had a beautiful pregnancy. Manageable nausea and no strange cravings apart from that awful powdery white cheddar cheese popcorn. I took long walks, read long books, travelled to Israel and Cyprus, house-sat a huge mansion filled with wildly expensive art, went hiking in south Texas, even finished writing my own book while the fetus was still the size of a fig. Change? Ha.

Prior to giving birth, I enjoyed spending hours of every day in complete solitude and adored places of isolation. While I cherished the company of good friends, I had always had a strong allergy to groups of any kind.

Almost from the moment I slipped my hands under my baby's arms and pulled him from my body, however, it became clear that the job of caring for children is a task for a community, not one person on her own. The image of a solitary parent sitting in a house by herself, trying to meet the nearly constant needs of an infant is, in fact, the picture of a form of insanity. Nature never intended children to be raised in anything short of a communal setting.

The price of my life of independence, privacy and mobility, I realized, was that I had virtually no sense of community. My closest friends were flung over three continents; my family spread from Vancouver to Halifax. I don't know why I didn't notice until after I gave birth that none of my friends in the area had babies, but I didn't.

I had done enough solo travelling to know how to cope when everything that I believed and took for granted was upended. But this—*this*—was utterly different. This time, everything around me was familiar and I was the part that had changed.

"Try playgroups!" people said when I explained my feelings of isolation.

Now I don't know how this statement resonates with other people, but these words, when spoken in that cheerful voice people use when they're trying to be helpful, felt like the death penalty to me.

Eventually, though, I swallowed my apprehensions and decided to give it a try. On a blustery day in January, I zipped my little guy into his bunting bag and trekked to our local family centre. It was filled with brightly coloured plastic gadgets, rangy kids already buzzing on too much sugar at ten in the morning, and fluorescent lighting. I was welcomed very sweetly and invited to join a circle of mothers. We were told to introduce ourselves with our name and our favourite snack.

Once we were familiar with each other's eating habits, we gathered our children onto our laps to learn the words to a piece of music entitled, "Inky Linky Pinky Stinky," which we sang together more times than I thought humanly possible.

When it was all over, I went and stood in the glorious blizzard outside. "Let there be no doubt, Alison," I said to myself. "Life has chaaaAAAWOWOWOWOWAAAnged."

I considered advertising for friends. "Creative mother of small child seeking like-minded people in similar situation to share our children and conversations that extend beyond the merits of teething gel." But I could never get the wording quite right. I talked to any interesting-looking mothers with infants whom I chanced to meet. They would smile politely when I suggested we do something together, go snowshoeing, whatever, but we never, ever, did.

My solitude melted into a loneliness I had never before experienced. Being alone (with my baby) was exhausting and draining. I had found almost no one with whom I felt a meaningful connection, and I couldn't bear the small talk and niceties that the get-togethers with other moms required. Not to mention all the sitting around.

This, together with severe sleep deprivation and the realization that I could no longer even go out for a walk to the bloody driveway and back by myself, led me into what is clinically known as post-partum depression but which should be renamed, to my mind, Women Very Sanely and Rationally Understanding What is Happening to Their Erstwhile Free and Independent Lives.

The day I received an invitation to a toy party, I felt my life was as good as over. I did the only reasonable thing. Called a travel agent and began pricing tickets to Mexico.

When I announced my plans to spend a month in Mexico to my partner, he was very supportive. He knew I was a traveller by nature, meaning that my soul is fed by journeys; and that if my spirit was flagging, this was exactly what I needed. At seven months of age, my son was still nursing exclusively, so I wouldn't have to worry about him catching any intestinal nasties. It seemed an opportune time to travel.

———

I'll never forget the feeling as I waved goodbye and walked through the airport to the departure gate: every inch of my skin was tingling.

Flying was a breeze. We slept, nursed, played with ice cubes, did a lot of bouncing up and down on the empty seat beside us, drummed on the tray table. Arriving in Mexico City filled me with excitement. As our taxi buzzed out of the city, I peered out at the vibrant, colourful street life: open-air shops and fruit stands, restaurants painted in gorgeously audacious colours and bursting with people, music and cacophonous voices. The lyrical lilt of Mexican Spanish made me smirk with delight.

The taxi brought us to Tepoztlan, a village in the mountains south of Mexico City, to a rental house I had found through an ad in a Canadian literary journal. We arrived after dark. The proprietor, a British woman, met me at the gate with a flashlight, furrowed her brow when her beam of yellow light caught on the baby slung on my hip— "You didn't tell me there was a baby"—and led me to a small house in her garden. "The front door sticks a bit," she said as she kicked it open. "The lights are here." A bulb dangling from the ceiling lit up a tiny kitchen. "Toilet is there, bed's upstairs. There's no hot water until morning. I'd watch where you put your baby, there are scorpions everywhere. I put a loaf of bread and some eggs in the fridge for you. Shouldn't need anything else until morning."

She offered me a perfunctory "good night" and closed the door behind her. I stood there, pack on my back, bags at my feet, baby on my hip, for ages.

The trip, door to door, had taken about fourteen hours. I was bathed in sweat. When I peeked into the bathroom at the little tiled shower, a scorpion skittered along the wall away from the light. There was no place to put a baby down. I ate a few handfuls of bread and tried to cook up some eggs, but I couldn't figure out how to hold the match and turn on the gas with only one hand (the other hand was holding the baby), so I gave up and had more bread. I tried to get our things upstairs, but the tiny winding stairway was so narrow, I couldn't squeeze through carrying both a backpack and a baby. I dropped the pack and let it tumble down the stairs. After lifting back the sheets to check for scorpions, tucking the mosquito net in all the way around the bed, nursing my son to sleep, and crying a little, I fell sound asleep fully clothed.

I awoke to the crowing of roosters. Opened my eyes and watched an enormous black spider rappelling down the length of the mosquito net. I ducked underneath, scooped the spider into my shoe and dumped it out the window. When my son woke up, all jolly and gurgly, I sat with him on the front steps of our little house and adjusted to the heat, the texture of the air, the scent of my surroundings.

It wasn't long before Ann, the proprietor, appeared.

"I'll take you up to the market this morning so you can do some shopping. I can't imagine how you'll manage on your own. I mean, with a baby . . ."

We drove up to the market and left the car at what Ann called "the car park with the best view in the world." I agreed. Lush mountains on all sides, vermilion flowers dripping from stone walls and terraces, and a bird's-eye view of the marketplace. The sun carved light from every bit of stone.

I tied a hat under my son's chin, perched him on my hip and toddled to catch up with Ann.

"Oh, I used to be a journalist," she replied to my questions of how she had ended up here. "I met my husband in Chile, and we moved here almost forty years ago. He was Mexican. Died ten years ago, just about . . ."

We reached the market with its sacks of fresh spices, tables heaped with every imaginable fruit, mountains of fresh vegetables, fabrics, hot plates frying up tortillas, quesadillas, itacates. The vendors, mostly indigenous women with dark skin and broad smiles, called out to us as we passed. "*Hola gordito!*" they laughed, reaching out to touch my son's pudgy white arms.

"They're calling your baby 'little fatso,'" Ann laughed. "He is so much bigger than Tepoztecan babies. They can hardly believe their eyes. Then again, I'd say he's big by any standard. How do you manage?"

I wound around the maze of stalls, gathering food and supplies in one hand and balancing my baby on my hip with the other.

"Look at you, you can hardly move," Ann said, taking one of my bags. We lumbered back to the car and heaved the bags into the trunk, then turned to enjoy the view one more time. "I don't think I adjusted well to family life," Ann began, squinting into the distance. "I just put so much of myself into it that part of me shut down. It's an enormous sacrifice, but I think if you're a good mother it has to be."

We drove back to the house in silence. I thanked Ann and schlepped my bags inside. I was exhausted but couldn't sleep. Stared out the window instead, wondering what on earth I was doing there.

First thing the next morning, I decided to master the art of carrying a baby in a sling (a long piece of fabric that secures a baby on the hip and ties together at the shoulder). Someone had given one to me months before, but because it's practically impossible to wear with bulky winter clothing, I'd never used it. I unrolled it from my bag and tried to wear it as I had seen some of the women in the market doing the day before. It took a bit of shifting and fiddling, but within a few hours, I'd decided it was the most brilliant contraption ever designed.

With my son slung comfortably and contentedly at my breast, I could light the stove, chop vegetables, carry groceries over long distances, even hike in the mountains. I explored the enchanted village with its narrow cobblestone streets, bougainvillea dripping over balconies and walls, houses rich in ochres, crimsons and terracottas. Most days we walked into town, where my son was taken into the welcoming arms of one of the market women, who laughed and shooed me off to do my shopping and snacking with both arms free. I took showers at night, wrote in the early morning, filled an entire journal in a few weeks.

I am breathing for the first time in months. Breaths of colour and light. I feel exhausted but strong; so strong. With every detail of this exquisite place, I am inspired. Inspirited. Nourished.

I sit amidst a chorus of birds. Calls for beauty. I float on song. Dry waves. The flowers within view are of a colour that feeds, seduces, my eyes. I open myself wider and focus, feel myself absorb that colour until it is part of my body. My flesh is a radiant violet.

My life has changed, but my core is the same. Intact. Alive. With every day here I feel myself coming back to life.

I washed my son in a bucket outside in the garden. Washed our clothes in the same bucket while he sat beside me, marvelling at the texture of avocado as it is squished between the fingers, smeared onto the belly and into the hair. I basked in the simple peace of our existence. And enjoyed being a mother.

Ann and I became friends. I grew to love her wry humour, her honesty, her opinions. She grew to love having a baby around, applauded his squeals, laughed at his efforts to crawl: "Look at you! You're a beautiful blond seal!"

On one of our last mornings, as we sat in the garden, Ann spoke of maybe selling the place and moving back to Britain. Even after all this time, she said, Mexico didn't really feel like home. "Though I'm not sure Wales will either," she added.

"I know what you mean," I said. "Sometimes I feel like such a foreigner at home, and so at home, briefly, in other places." And then I looked at my son, merrily removing teabags from the box, examining each one as though it were a precious stone, and laying it on the grass. He has no idea he is in Mexico, I thought. He makes magic with whatever is in front of him, wherever he is.

When my son was eighteen months, I took him to Vietnam, but I can honestly say that after spending almost a month in Hanoi, I have no idea what the city is like. I spent so much time with my head down to toddler level, watching for approaching hands or runaway traffic that I scarcely looked up. Large cities and small legs, I've learned, are not the happiest travel combination.

Fairly regularly these days, I am asked, "Where to next?" To which I can only respond that, for the moment, I am quite content where we are: tobogganing down the hill behind the house, skating on the pond, snowshoeing over to our beautiful little studio at the edge of the forest, letting the car sit abandoned for weeks. My partner and I talk of spending a year in Finland, visiting friends in the Czech Republic, building a cabin on Manitoulin Island, maybe travelling to Bhutan. But today, it feels wonderful to enjoy this extraordinary, fascinating, awe-inspiring moment right-right-right here.

Alison Wearing is the author of Honeymoon in Purdah: An Iranian Journey. *She lives with her partner and son.*

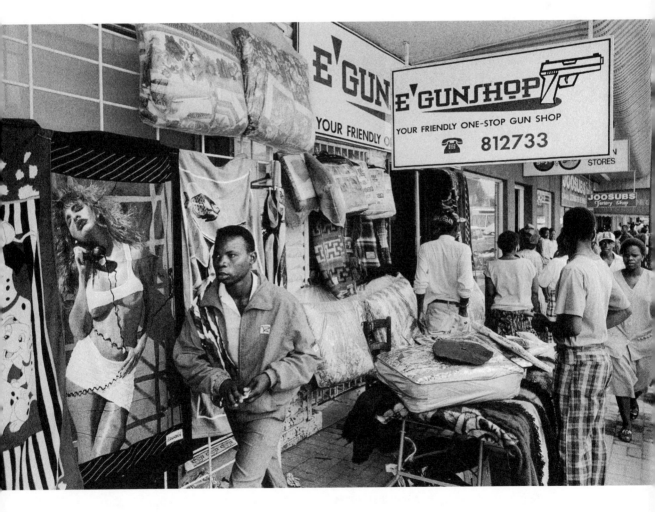

STATION ROAD
Sandra Shields

It was three in the afternoon and Station Road was thronged. The street got its name from the train station built here during the 1890s when this South African town, Mafikeng, was a sleepy outpost of the British Empire. Makeshift stalls lined the sidewalks, overturned cardboard boxes with wares spread out on top: bananas, umbrellas, Nelson Mandela posters, bags of peanuts, cigarettes, cheap perfume, a box full of day-old chicks all soft and yellow and peeping. Horns honked as minibus taxis headed out of town. A vegetable seller called me over to ask if I was really leaving and could he go back to Canada with me.

The only white street vendor on Station Road sat in front of the butcher shop with a picnic cooler full of milk at her feet, and the automatic shotgun of the shop's security guard watching over her. She was an Afrikaner woman with a quiet voice and thick glasses. I had money in my pocket from a friend who wanted me to buy myself a farewell beer, but after a year in South Africa, I had drunk more than enough beer, so I bought a two-litre Coke bottle full of fresh farm milk instead. I tried catching her eyes but they were small and floating at the bottom of her glasses. She didn't say much, just handed me the milk and went back to her knitting.

Six years before, I had spent several months in this dusty little city, falling in love

Mafikeng, 1996.

DAVID CAMPION

DAVID CAMPION (pages 236/237)

with a man who then followed me to Canada where, together, we watched apartheid come to an end on the evening news. At the beginning of 1996, we left winter behind in Canada and made our first return visit to South Africa on a one-year open ticket. We had arrived full of hope and intensely curious to see how the place had changed.

It was a Saturday morning in the middle of summer when we drove back into Mafikeng. The city is in the north of the country, up against the border with Botswana, and its claim to fame is that the Boy Scouts were started here during the 217-day siege that began the Boer War back in 1899. At first, everything looked familiar, the same red plain spread out around us, running off in the direction of the

Kalahari Desert, palm trees still graced the main streets leading into town. The wealthy homes lining the road were unchanged except that the fences were taller. The high school David had dropped out of was still there.

We soon reached the central shopping district where the sidewalks were relics of the colonial era, built like verandas with overhanging roofs. The stage-set was the same but the cast had changed colour and swelled in number. People spilled into the street and crossed wherever they wanted. Pieces of cardboard and old plastic bags lay in the gutters. Every few feet, vendors leaned back against the storefronts with goods spread out around them, their faces impassive.

We parked and got out of the truck to walk down the block to the shop where David used to work. Hundreds of blank and staring eyes hit our white skin. We walked faster. It turned out that most whites didn't walk much at all anymore. From their cars they waved grimly at one another. Behind the razor wire that protected their homes, they told true crime stories. "Get one of the fifty-thousand-volt shocker devices," an old friend advised over rum and cokes in his plush living room. Exotic fish were swimming in the tank built into the wall above his head. His wife nodded, "The tear-gas guns are good too," she said.

It took me months to learn to walk these streets comfortably again. Like everyone else of my colour, I watched from the car window until, by degrees, I eased out of that protective shell. The wide stares remained, but I learned to stare back—not so much staring as meeting people's eyes and acknowledging a shared humanity. Like the woman selling milk, whites in South Africa kept their eyes to themselves. People in Canada do the same, so I was good at it. In taking to the street, I tried to escape the dimensions of my own skin and followed the lead of everyone else out there by saying hello.

It was embarrassingly simple. All that was required was to meet the eyes of others and, as you did so, give a polite nod and say, "Good morning." The Tswana have a better word for it. "*Dumela*," they say. It's a smooth word that slips out easily and means "I greet you for the first time today."

For a while I was an actor with stage fright, worried I would flub my lines, too focused on how many people were in the audience. I felt exposed. In South Africa, most of the people who aren't white are accustomed to living their lives in full view of others. Few own cars, so getting around means walking. Women carry their shopping home on their heads. Tired workers lie down in the park to take a nap. The public space is common ground, and ignoring one another would make it a lonely place. Instead, Mafikeng has the feel of an ad hoc carnival. The cheapest eats are on the sidewalk. Women set up portable kerosene stoves, and in the mornings they make *vetkoeks*, lumps of bread dough dropped into boiling oil. "'Fat-cakes' is what they are called," a woman told me, patting her round thighs, "because they put fat here."

I stopped being scared of walking down the street, and I got high on human

DAVID CAMPION

interaction instead. Overwhelmingly, people returned my greetings with readiness, and I rarely experienced the hollow feeling that hits your stomach when you say hi to someone and they pretend not to hear. My greetings were returned with a grace I tried to emulate and an enthusiasm that could turn "Hi" into an hour of conversation. The end of apartheid did not mean the end of poverty, of course; the economy was struggling and the rand kept dropping. But though people were poor, a wealth of friendship and support was available on the street.

By the time our year was drawing to a close, I had also learned to squat. A side trip to the opposite edge of the Kalahari Desert had given me two months of life without chairs, an exercise that stretched my mind as well as my ass and gave me the ability to sink onto my haunches for long stretches at a time. Squatting is a polite gesture. It says, I'm interested in listening to what you have to say, I'm not going to rush away. It extends respect. The street looks different when you stop and sink down on your heels.

One morning I met the owner of a sidewalk beauty salon, a man named Micah in freshly pressed slacks and shirt who had arrived before seven that morning to claim his spot just around the corner from Station Road. He said that a man must look smart even when he has troubles, even when he has no money. He didn't elaborate but offered an overturned paint tin on which I sat as we talked about how much Mafikeng had changed. Micah told me about a nearby town where whites still thought they were in control. He said, "There are bars there where I cannot go; I will get yelled at like a dog if I go there."

My eyes scanned the street as we spoke. Posters in the windows of clothing stores offered credit cards to anyone who could sign their name. The crime rate was reflected in the uniformed guards standing with their big guns at shop doors. The BMW dreams of kids raised on American television rubbed shoulders with the homeless boys in bare feet who sniffed glue. The edgy aggression in the crowd bespoke a growing desperation about the economy. The pulse of the country was there in the street, the troubled past and the turmoil of the present mingling on a Saturday morning.

We had been talking for almost an hour when an ample nanny came along with two young girls in tow, one with blond curls, the other black braids. The day was getting hot. The woman stopped and bought the children bottles of strawberry milk from a nearby vendor. The little white girl and the little black girl squatted on the sidewalk to drink, looking around with calm regard at the dozen people in the immediate vicinity. A taxi roared past, horns hooted, the girls drank their milk, and we all watched. Grins broke out, glances were exchanged and, for a moment, everyone smiled at the future and dared to hope.

Sandra Shields has collaborated with her husband, photographer David Campion, for the past ten years. Their book, Where Fire Speaks: A Visit with the Himba, *was published recently. They live in Vancouver.*

WHERE THE BIRDS ARE
Katherine Govier

A pair of bald eagles are fishing over the harbour at Natashquan, Quebec. Red rock cliffs are laced with lime-green mosses under a milky sky. On deck, four French birders, so laden with gear I had taken them to be a film crew, stand shoulder-to-shoulder, elbows up at right angles, binoculars to eyes, silent, intense. One grunts. All drop elbows. Then the bearded one shouts in discovery. Elbows shoot up. Heads train to the right. Mass exhalation.

I sidle up. Raise my new Travelite Nikon V 8x 5.6 binoculars and look through—which end? The one with the label. Or the one bearing rubber protective eyepieces. Aha. A spectral forest appears in the lens: my eyelashes. I blink them out of the way. Porous grey wall turns out to be one of the steel pillars of the ship. I swear, dizzy with all this refocusing, try once more. Hey! For a fleeting few seconds, I capture the speck retreating to a clifftop.

The Four French Birders, or FFB as I call them, drop elbows, maintaining synchronicity. And at that moment, as if their communal sigh has propelled it, the bird

Mother and daughter.

takes spectacularly to wing again. Soars into my circle of eight times magnification, a visitation. The huge bird is suddenly mine, his curved beak, his white head feathers, his powerful broad wings, his predator's intensity as great as that of the birders on deck. "Wow," I say. The FFB do not acknowledge me.

I am a newcomer to birdwatching. Last night at 11:30 P.M., my daughter, my friend and I boarded the *M. V. Nordik Express*, at Havre St. Pierre, on the north shore of the Gulf of St. Lawrence. We are travelling east along the coast of Quebec, crossing into Labrador at Blanc-Sablon; then we'll ferry over the Straits of Belle Isle to the northern tip of Newfoundland and travel down through "the Rock." Our mission is to see the waterfowl that come here to nest in a landscape that has barely been touched since the Basque whalers departed.

The *Nordik* is a supply ship for the nine hundred kilometres of coastline guarded by rocky islands and deadly shoals. The shore is little more accessible today than it was five hundred years ago, when it was plied by sealing vessels and pirate ships. An ungraceful ship resembling a construction site, the *Nordik* inspired our trust as we watched it being loaded with goods for coastal communities not reachable by road—groceries, beds, lumber, and the dune buggies that the locals, or "coasters," use for transport. Cars belonging to tourists bound for Labrador are individually crated and lifted on by crane.

Last night the mid-decks were crowded with the beautiful faces of the Montagnais Indians. The *Nordik* is their *rue flottante*; tireless children in BUM T-shirts camped out in the cafeteria and squealed as they played tag between decks. A contingent of Eddie Bauer–clad, ecologically sensitive–looking tourists appeared to be queasy as the grey waters slammed against the hull. Our cabin is tight for three. Only one person can stand at a time; the others go to the hall. My daughter was aghast at the tight accommodations. She registered her protest by retiring to the cafeteria to read the Newfoundland Labrador guidebook, where she searches for four-star hotels. "Don't they have a Four Seasons?" she asks.

I wonder if I should have taken her birding. Most of her friends are off looking for boys. But she is above that sort of thing. I wanted an adventure. She was keen for that too. I wanted wilderness. She was a little guarded about the wilderness part. I wanted to see birds, and I thought she might want that too. As a sport, it sounded like a good thing to her, not too energetic. Now I wonder aloud if she's interested at all in birds. "What do you mean, Mum?" she says to reassure me, while resolutely pulling shut the thick curtain on her lower bunk. "Yesterday I got quite close to those whatchamacallits."

The "watchamacallits" may have been least sandpipers or they may have been golden plovers. We saw them yesterday on Île de la Fantôme in Mingan Archipelago National Park, at the edge of the water, a cluster of small, busy, long-legged birds, starting and stopping, pecking in the gleaming conjunction of sand with its veneer of water. They were brown, flecked with red, gold and black. They were indifferent to us and like pure electricity in their movements, tricks of light.

At dawn today we pulled into this exquisite harbour town, population one thousand, with its stunted trees and pink beach rocks with seaweed of a violent green growing in the cracks between. Natashquan is the birthplace of Gilles Vigneault (who wrote "*Mon pays ce n'est pas un pays, c'est l'hiver*"), but our visit coincides with the short window of summer, mid-August on a rare good day. Already, many of the migrating birds have gone south, leaving behind the hardy gulls, the Arctic terns, the guillemots. And the eagles. A hundred feet above us, they soar and circle, head down, scouring the water for prey, patient.

As we move beyond the harbour, we feel the buck and leap of the ship. The huge circle of the horizon and the flat sea water is like a sundial, our ship the compass blade setting direction. My daughter is miserable. She was unable to sleep in our wee cabin. She ate two sausages for breakfast and is now suffering *mal de mer*. The only Scrabble game is in French. We play but there are too many *e*'s and not enough *y*'s and I lose, which is a rare thing and gives no end of pleasure to my friend and Emily too. We go out on deck to get some air. Emily slumps down and talks about how she'd like a Jacuzzi bath. "How many more days are we going to be on this boat?" she says.

"Two."

Forever.

My birdwatching progresses. By midday I can pretty much tell a tern from a gull. We stop at Kegaska, where, says my book, Acadians settled until they were (improbably) driven out by a plague of dolphins that ate up all the seals. The line of gulls on top of the fish-plant roof mirrors the line of birders on the deck of the boat, all evenly spaced, all with heads angled the same way.

We're en route again. A coaster points out cormorants ("shags") and guillemots. He shows me an island where, in the 1800s, there was a big Hudson's Bay trading post, as if he'd seen it with his own eyes. Then you could see five hundred boats here in season; now we do not pass a single other craft. But as we enter the Strait of Belle Isle, the whales blow and breach all around. We rush from one side of the boat to the other with enough urgency to tip a less sturdy craft. The birds and the whales relentlessly squandered in the past are now so rare that people compete intensely for a glimpse.

The female of the FFBs speaks to me. "Are you seeing the same birds I am?" Probably not. They are seeing a storm petrel, which my friend has correctly identified. They are searching for its near-relation, the Wilson's petrel. The difference is all in the black tail stripe, which on the one is straight and on the other slightly notched. I am merely seeing a small white and black thing tossing in the wind around our bow. But in a half-hour the bearded one of the FFB jubilantly announces that he (and he alone) has identified a Wilson's petrel. There is much shouting and jumping around; and the three of their number who did not see the Wilson's petrel depart looking seriously vexed.

We are off the boat and none too soon. Emily goes off to the local hotel for dinner by herself. Unfortunately we show up there too, because there is nowhere else. She pretends she doesn't know us. We pass her later, walking jauntily home in the dark along the highway that cuts across the huge rock. It appears she just wants to meet Labrador on her own terms. She is further cheered when the next day, Norm and Gloria Letto, the hosts of our bed and breakfast, lend us their big red pickup truck. Emily sings in the open back as we tool along in a northeasterly direction. We stop at the L'Anse Amour lighthouse, name changed from the ghoulish original L'Anse aux Morts, which referred to the hundreds of shipwrecks that occurred in these treacherous straits. With fog 90 per cent of the time and storm the rest, and a current so strong it would pull you off course at a speed less than twelve knots, it was Russian roulette for sailors. But today is a perfect day. From the top of the lighthouse, we look down on the cove to see whales at play.

We go all the way up to Red Bay, Labrador. This is the end of the road. From here, you mush it. In a desolate yard, husky pups are tied up to individual stakes, howling, by a sign that reads Dogs for Sale. Yet in that weird Canadian way, in this forlorn spot there's an elegant Parks Canada museum. We walk through the mist on a little island to an archaeological dig of a sixteenth-century whaling camp. The tiny flowers we see growing low on the ground are only found here and in Arctic tundra.

The next morning Norm announces that we have "a flat wind" blowing offshore. He will take us out to Perroquet Island in his twenty-two-foot fibreglass boat, to see the puffins. Gloria will stay home to preserve bakeapples, which are in season. The little berries are now so popular that a bylaw has been passed requiring pickers to get a licence. Gloria says this is because Newfoundlanders come and pick them before the berries are ripe, using scissors and "ruining it for everyone." Scarce resources make for tense neighbours.

We hop into Norm's outboard and head out into the frigid water. A fourth-generation fisherman forced into retirement by the cod moratorium, even Norm is excited to see how many thousands of puffins swoop and sputter over our heads. They are chubby birds carrying their colourful bills importantly before them. Flying seems to cost them much effort; they compose themselves in evenly spaced groups of four, or forty, like squadrons, and cross over our heads just feet above us.

"They comes from the north," Norm says of the puffins. "They's still young in the burrows because they've got a loaded bill. You don't see the young fly until September."

We land, and scramble up the rocks, which tumble over each other like giant tiles. The puffins abandon their burrows, but the black-backed gulls scream in out-rage as we climb. We can see the openings to the puffin burrows in the grass, but we cannot see deep enough to spy the young; they hide from predators as far as four feet along the tunnel. When the prescient John James Audubon visited this island in 1833, he wrote that he could hear the cries of the young coming from underground, "like voices from the grave."

Norm knows the birds of the region by their traditional names. On the way home he shows us "tinkers," "turres," "beachy birds" and "sanders." "Tinkers" are razor-bills and resemble the extinct great auk, a funny-looking black and white bird with a thick bill. "Turres" are the thick-billed and common murres, and the "beachy bird" is a least sandpiper. I note the difference between Norm's sense of the birds, and that of the French birders. To the locals, the birds are practical, of use, part of land and season. To the birders, they are exotica, representatives of a fallen Eden. To we city dwellers, they are the foreign inhabitants of this big empty place, and we look to them with curiosity and a little longing.

WE LAND, AND SCRAMBLE UP THE ROCKS, WHICH TUMBLE OVER EACH OTHER LIKE GIANT TILES. THE PUFFINS ABANDON THEIR BURROWS, BUT THE BLACK-BACKED GULLS SCREAM IN OUTRAGE AS WE CLIMB.

When we board the ferry to cross over to Newfoundland, we see a man getting off with a knapsack and a determined look; he sets off up the hill to pick bakeapples. "I wonder if he's aware of the legislation," mutters Emily. I suggest she confiscate his scissors.

By the time we get through Gros Morne National Park, Emily has eaten cod tongues, danced to Celtic music and stopped asking for a Jacuzzi in her room. But she still thinks this is a weird holiday. While staying in the best hotel in St. John's (Emily won), we meet John Pratt, the St. John's lawyer and ornithologist. I ask him why we like to watch birds. His answer is that it is partly because we can. "They're the most observable of animals," he says. "Mammals had the luxury of being able to be afraid of humans. Birds don't have that luxury, their lives are so hard." They will stay to feed even if humans approach. But they are, though tantalizingly close, still unknowable. He talks about their reptilian coldness, their me-first-ness and their "driven intent to survive." "What birds can do defies our ability to define it even now," he says. "They are enigmatic."

We end our trip with a visit to the famous gannet nursery at Cape St. Mary, Newfoundland. We set out on a high cliffside trail where sheep have curled themselves inside little grassy hummocks. We're heading for the flat-topped "sea stack," an independent rock out of reach of land predators. The gannet is a graceful flyer with a six-foot wingspan. It can plunge-dive for fish, reaching speeds of one hundred kilometres an hour.

We hear it first, a rhythmic squawking over the sea. We smell it next. Then we see the breeding rock, alive with gannets, the great white adults flying on and off as their grey offspring merely stand and flap, training for flight. Experts claim 5,300 nesting pairs are here. Awestruck, I leave Emily sitting on a rock twenty feet from the stack and run back for film. When I return, she has braved the smell and the flies on this uncharacteristically still, hot day. Her binoculars lie on the rock beside her as she babbles excitedly about how she saw the gannets spread their tail feathers in order to slow their flight as they came in to land.

I tell her what I've read about how gannets mate for life (Imagine! In this day and age!). While nurturing young, they still engage in "sexual behaviour," that is, nape-biting and preening. We watch them hook bills and try to push each other off the rock. We sit for ages looking for the behaviour called "sky pointing," where one bird points her bill and her long neck skyward to signal to her airborne mate that she wishes to leave the nest to get food.

And we see it. "Look, look," says Emily. The female points, and her mate returns to spell her off on the nest. We hug each other so as not to fall off our perch in the sun, with the sea calm beneath us and the frenzied nursery right before our eyes, and we think we see ourselves in the birds, or the birds in ourselves, and we are happy.

Katherine Govier's new novel Creation *is set in Labrador. She is the author of six previous novels, as well as three collections of short stories, and will follow the anthology* Without a Guide: Contemporary Women's Travel Adventures, *with a new anthology of writers' pilgrimages. She has won the Marian Engel Award and the City of Toronto Book Award, and is a contributor to the bestselling anthology* Dropped Threads.

PHOTOGRAPHS
Rui Umezawa

I looked up, squinting in the bright sun, at the immense statue of Chairman Mao. I took a deep drag from my *Fenghuang* and coughed into my hand. Wretched stuff until you get used to it.

The crowd of students at Beijing University shimmered in the courtyard over which the Great Helmsman stood guard. Skinny arms hit a volleyball back and forth. A man and a woman in matching blue track suits rubbed against each other. The autumn sun was still warm, and the graffiti on the bench where I was sitting was as sick as anything I'd seen back home.

The foreign students dormitory was just a minute's walk farther down campus— a sort of United Nations of geeks. Bookish men and women from all over the globe getting along remarkably well, all things considered—Turks, Greek Cypriots, Czechs and Slovaks when their country was still united. Even the North Koreans ate with us, albeit in their own, self-designated corner of the cafeteria. There were usually Palestinians, too, but this was 1982. They were away at war, because Israel had invaded Lebanon a few months earlier.

She'd been studying me, apparently, for some time through those cat's-eye glasses. She said hi, smiling guilelessly in her plaid jacket, wide black slacks and nameless sneakers. "I'm in your History of Modern Literature class," she said. "You haven't been around in two weeks. I was worried."

A broad smile revealed a row of crooked, spotted teeth. In the periphery of this vision was a girl with pigtails and perfect skin, sitting on the grass at the centre of the courtyard, strumming her guitar and singing in Chinese:

> *La-la-la, la-la-la*
> *Little wind, little wind,*
> *Slowly, slowly come on over*

"Are you Japanese or American?" Chen Ling asked, like they all did.
Neither, I told her.
"Ah, Canadian," she said, then added, like they all did, "Norman Bethune."
When she told me I had missed the lectures on how one literary journal managed to ignite the passion of the masses against their oppressors, I tried my best to look concerned. She said not to worry because the lessons on how some author gathered the hearts and soul of the people and used them to fuel the revolution were yet to come. I could still redeem myself with Old Teacher. A part of me wanted to tell her that Old Teacher would not know what modernism was if Gore Vidal kissed him on the lips. Before I could say anything, though, she asked me to the ballet.

"I have tickets for tomorrow night," she said. "Would you like to come?"
Somewhere in my mind, a yellow flag unfurled. But I also noticed for the first time that her waist was nice and narrow, her hips perfectly round and that maybe her face wouldn't be so bad without those glasses and if she fixed her teeth. Maybe I needed a change from sitting around all day and drinking a bottle of imported whisky every night. I looked at her and put my cigarette to my lips, then nodded almost imperceptibly.

"Great," she said, clapping. She told me to meet her in front of the theatre then ran off with the breeze.

The theatre was near the zoo, not too far from campus. The first thing Chen Ling did when we met was give me some unopened packs of *Fenghuang*. She said her father had recently stopped smoking and they were going to waste. When we got inside, she bought me an ice pop and a Coke. I washed down the ice pop with the Coke then lit a cigarette. She scolded me for smoking.

Then I had to endure two hours of watching *Giselle* with the Chinese. They said, "*Hao!*" when things went well, and sucked air through their teeth with a loud hiss when they recognized flaws in the performance. Some guy in tights jumped high and landed solidly. "*Hao!*" A girl resembling a Meissen figurine wobbled while holding her leg in the air. *Hiss.* Everything sounded louder in darkness.

And it was in the same darkness that I felt Chen Ling put her hand on my leg. "You know," I thought to myself, "this shit could get complicated awfully quick."

After the performance, she offered to buy me some sunflower seeds, but I declined, so instead she walked me to the bus stop.

"Did you like the performance?" she bubbled.

"It wasn't bad."

"It wasn't very good, was it?"

"Hmmmm?"

"The performers tonight were mostly trained during the Cultural Revolution. They learned the techniques, but theory back then was considered intellectualism and prohibited. It's better now, but we've a whole generation of dancers who know nothing of the meaning behind their movements."

I nodded gravely as if this was obvious from the performance we'd just witnessed.

I HAD TO ENDURE TWO HOURS OF WATCHING *GISELLE* WITH THE CHINESE. THEY SAID, "*HAO!*" WHEN THINGS WENT WELL, AND SUCKED AIR THROUGH THEIR TEETH WITH A LOUD HISS WHEN THEY RECOGNIZED FLAWS IN THE PERFORMANCE.

"Can I come over to your dorm room tomorrow?" she asked when we reached the terminal.

I furrowed my brow, letting her know I was pondering her question. I had to think quickly, but thinking quickly didn't help when you were falling fast down the side of a cliff.

"Okay," I said, and this made her laugh and clap her hands again.

It was late morning by the time something resembling a plan came to me. I straightened my room as best I could. Washed the whisky out of the tin mugs scattered on the floor. Actually made the bed.

The year before, when I was living at the Beijing Language Institute, I hadn't worried much about housecleaning. I was in love with a Greek Cypriot student with tanned legs and big brown eyes, and she with me. In addition to being bright enough to win a medical scholarship to China (there were no medical schools in Cyprus) she was also an impeccable cook and housekeeper.

Our affair was too good to last long. They assigned her to a medical school in Shanghai, while I remained in Beijing. She wrote faithfully, and I thought about her every night—usually in a drunken stupor, while the whitewashed walls spun around the bed.

But I still had the photographs. I dusted the one I kept framed and stood it at the centre of the bookshelf. I pulled a few more from my desk drawer—a couple of her alone, another of the two of us embracing—and pinned them on the wall. I had trouble meeting her silent gaze.

Chen Ling was right on time. She walked in like she owned the place and sat on the bed. She was scolding me for cutting class again when she noticed the photographs. Squinting as though they were cubist art, she stood and walked over to the one on the bookshelf.

"Is this your girlfriend?"

"No," I said, clearing my throat. "That's my fiancée."

Her face grew pale. For a second, I regretted my ploy because she looked like she might cause a scene. I didn't know what she might do, only that I didn't want to be around when she did it, especially if it was going to involve a lot of noise. But she only shook her head and whispered, "How could I have been so stupid?" She repeated this twice.

I wanted to laugh and tell her that it was a perfectly understandable misunderstanding, but she started for the door before I had the chance. She told me she had to go. When she closed the door behind her, I wondered for a fleeting moment what she might look like with her clothes off. Then I thought of how it might not be too early to open the bottle of Suntory that I'd recently bought at the Friendship Hotel.

The sun was still high but the bottle half-empty when she knocked on my door again.

"I'm sorry," she said, avoiding my stare. "I didn't realize you were engaged."

I waved my hand in front of my face, indicating it was already forgotten.

"I hope we can be friends. I wonder if you wouldn't come have lunch at my parents' house on Sunday?"

I thought about it. Surely we understood each other perfectly now. And I wasn't about to turn my nose up at a meal away from the dormitory cafeteria. "*Hao!*" she said, adjusting her glasses on her nose. Her smile was back. "*Hen hao!*"

Autumn was the most pleasant season in Beijing. Summers there were blistering, and winters bitter. Sandstorms blew in from the Gobi Desert in spring, covering everything in dust. But the air stayed still in the fall, and there was enough sunshine to add warmth to the perpetually grey architecture.

I felt good about remembering to buy flowers and cookies at the market before hopping on the bus. The engine was loud and made the floor rattle, but at least it wasn't crowded and people weren't fighting for seats. I sat by an open window, humming softly to myself as we passed by countless Mao jackets on bicycles:

> *Big ocean, where do you come from?*
> *And where do you wander to?*
> *Who knows your sadness?*
> *Who understands your loneliness?*

Chen Ling and her parents lived in a high-rise without any distinguishable features.

The bus dropped me off at the front, and Chen Ling waved at me from the entrance. She said, "You're late," but thanked me for the presents. She seemed nervous and as though she was in a hurry. The hallway leading to their apartment on the first floor was bare but clean.

No one was home. Nothing was on the stove, and the table was not set. She asked to take my coat, but I shook my head. I was suddenly feeling cold.

One wall of their living room was covered in black and white photographs. Age had stained the borders, like autumn leaves. The people from one picture to the next looked alike, but I couldn't be sure. There was one of a young couple holding a baby. I asked if they were her parents.

OUR AFFAIR WAS TOO GOOD TO LAST LONG. THEY ASSIGNED HER TO A MEDICAL SCHOOL IN SHANGHAI, WHILE I REMAINED IN BEIJING. SHE WROTE FAITHFULLY, AND I THOUGHT ABOUT HER EVERY NIGHT— USUALLY IN A DRUNKEN STUPOR, WHILE THE WHITEWASHED WALLS SPUN AROUND THE BED.

Some moments creep up on you when you're not looking. Fat tears began rolling down her pocked cheeks. "No," she murmured. "Those are my adoptive parents. My real parents are Japanese. I'm one of those orphans abandoned by Japanese parents when they left Manchuria. When I first saw you, I thought you were Japanese, so I thought you could help me look for my father and mother in Japan." She crumpled into a chair and began sobbing in earnest. "*I want my mama!!!*"

Foreign students at Beijing University, particularly those from the West, were used to being played. There was always some hustle—for foreign currencies, blue jeans, Beatles cassettes, porno magazines. Chen Ling was being more audacious than most. Even assuming she was just an infant when the Japanese evacuated north-eastern China after the Second World War, she would be close to forty years old. Her horrid glasses notwithstanding, she obviously was not half that.

Pulling herself together, she smiled and explained that she'd wanted to go to Japan for a while now. "In fact, I have some relatives in Japan who invited me to stay with them. But I just wrote and told them I was going instead to Canada with a boy I met at school."

My mind raced, searching for something to say. "What about lunch?" was the best I could do.

"Do you want to go somewhere?"

Both of us were adamant in our refusal to acknowledge the absurdity of the situation, so I told her I was going back to campus.

"Wait! I've got something for you!"

She ran into what looked like a bedroom and reappeared after a brief moment. "I want you to have a picture of me, but I don't have anything more recent than this."

It was another black and white photograph—this one of a beautiful little girl sitting on some rocks by the seashore. Despite her age, her pose was strangely seductive, inviting. Her eyes were wide, yet determined. Her confident smile seemed mismatched with her youth. For some reason, the bottom border of the photo had been trimmed off.

"I was really cute back then, wasn't I?" she asked.

I supposed she wanted me to assure her she was still cute, but she simply wasn't. And I was getting tired. I needed to be back in my dorm room. I needed a drink.

Chen Ling frequently came over to my room after that. Once, she wanted help with her English homework. Another time she wanted some foreign currency. One evening, as I helped her through her new vocabulary, I felt her hand on my knee again. I brushed it aside and tried to ignore her sobbing. "I implore you," she said, "to understand my feelings."

But I was not in a space where I could even understand my own feelings. After being in China for over a year, I was drowning in the country, in the brilliance and wonder contained in the tiniest minutiae of everyday living, like shopping for underwear and discovering that under those dreary uniforms, Chinese men wore floral boxer shorts.

By contrast, everything I'd lived through before coming here—all the things that awaited me back home—seemed tedious and unremarkable. The world as I'd known it no longer existed. Neither did the man I believed myself to be. It was like waking up after a deep sleep and not remembering anything. The only thing I knew was that daylight was painfully bright. So I buried my soul deep in myself and kept dousing it with alcohol. I refused to move from that comfortable place.

One night, my friend Mizutani invited me and a few Japanese students over to his room for dinner: curry cooked on a hot plate. Mizutani was from Japan and was an ardent follower of Nichiren Daishonin Buddhism. He kept an altar hidden in his closet, or so I'd been told by his exasperated French girlfriend, whom he'd tried to convert. But he kept his faith a secret from most people, and I didn't care about anything other than that he was a really good guy.

Winter was settling in, and we were dressed in layers of cotton and wool. We were drinking warm Five Star beer, smoking Mild Sevens and listening to Japanese pop music. Life didn't get much better, really.

Stirring the pot slowly with one hand, Mizutani threw me a small white packet with the other, saying he'd just bought it at the market the day before. Inside were black and white photographs of very good-looking men and women. They were classic Chinese movie stars, he explained. Sort of like bubble-gum cards without bubble-gum. Amused, I leafed through them until I came to one of a beautiful little girl sitting on some rocks by the seashore.

Someone said something funny, and the swelling laughter made the room seem bigger than it was. I fingered the edge of the photograph. It was the same face, same clothes, same alluring pose, only her name was inscribed on the bottom border and it wasn't Chen Ling. The curry bubbled noisily. Mizutani seemed pleased that I was so interested in his new buy. The others just seemed puzzled. I couldn't blame them, and for the first time, I understood that I couldn't blame Chen Ling either.

Rui Umezawa is the author of the novel The Truth About Death and Dying. *His short stories, essays and commentary have appeared in* Descant *magazine, the* Globe and Mail, *the* Toronto Star *and elsewhere. He was born in Tokyo and has lived in Italy, the American Midwest and Canada as well as China.*

COMING HOME
Jamie Zeppa

I am leaving Bhutan. Something is wrong with that sentence because no matter how many times I repeat it, it doesn't quite make sense. But here I am, getting into the car to go to the airport, heavy suitcases in the trunk and one-way tickets in the glove compartment. I turn for a last look at the yellow brick house that has been home. The windows are dark, and the door is wide open because there is nothing inside. Apparently, I no longer live there. And so, as completely nonsensical as it seems, the rest of it must be true as well: I am leaving, and tomorrow, this country that has for the last nine years been home and more than home (it has been a kind of dream) will no longer be mine either.

I tell myself I can turn around at any point. It's not too late to cancel the tickets, call the landlord, unpack the luggage, mend the marriage, stitch up the breach. It is entirely possible to stay, even now. All I have to do is assemble the words into a simple sentence: I've changed my mind. Or, I want to stay. But the words come out differently: "Well? What are we waiting for? Let's go." Tshewang, my soon-to-be ex-husband, helps our five-year-old son, Pema, into the car and then turns away so that he does not have to watch us drive off; and even as we are driving off, even as our former house disappears from view, even though Tshewang and I have talked this through a thousand times and have come to the same conclusion every time, I keep telling myself it's not too late. I can still turn the car around. There must be a way out of this departure, even though I can't see it, some secret passage that will lead me back in to the place I have lost.

But I drive on. Pema and I spend the night at Gangtey Hotel, a former palace on a hill crest overlooking the airport. At dawn, white clouds creep down from the dark ridges and fill up the valley with rain. If it rains hard enough, the flight will be delayed. But only if it rains forever will I not have to leave. The clouds shift and break and finally lift, and as we pass through customs, I feel I am repeating my departure from Canada nine years ago, step by step, thought by thought. As I hand over our passports: *I have no idea why I'm doing this.* As I fill out the visa forms: *It's not really leaving home, it's more like a holiday.* As I haul our suitcases onto the scales: *That is a hell of a lot of luggage for a holiday.*

Leaving Canada almost a decade ago, I expected my first experience of culture shock to be a sharply uncomfortable but quickly fading jolt. And the first waves were shocks to the system: there was the "fleas in the floorboards" shock and the "fried rice and chilies for breakfast" shock and the "monsoon has destroyed all the roads and there will be no mail for months" shock. I was in shock over my own stupidity, my head full of the traveller's lament: What am I doing here? I want to go home.

But as I adapted to life in a village that was three mountains and two landslides away from the nearest electric light, true culture shock came on like the succession of seasons, some mild and quite comfortable, others turbulent and intensely distorting. I passed through season after season, making friends, learning the language, becoming a Buddhist, falling in love. By the time I married my Bhutanese husband in the Thimphu District Court, Bhutan was home (and more than home, it was a dream and a kind of love). It was only when I visited Canada that I experienced the jarring, sickening, bottoming-out that comes from being lost in a foreign place.

But as I leave Bhutan this time, I know I am returning not to Canada-for-a-six-week-visit but to Canada-for-good. And this time, I will be ready for the phenomenon

I am leaving Bhutan. Something is wrong with that sentence.

experts call reverse culture shock: the despair at the material excess and crying-shame wastefulness of North American society, the noise and unrelenting rush, the complete inability of family and friends to understand where you've been and what you've seen and how wonderful it all was, blah blah blah. Bring it on, I will say. Let's go to the mall and get this over with.

I expect it to last a while, and so in the beginning, I am patient with my disorientation. But months and months later, I still cannot bear to think of the place I have lost, which was home and more than home (it was a kind of home in a dream of love). All the brightness and depth are gone from my days, as well as the raggedy, unregulated edges of life in Bhutan—unexpected stops, haphazard journeys, the kindness of strangers, the thousands of things still to be discovered and learned, and wordless connection in the most unfamiliar places. Now there are only flat, dull, polished surfaces, reflecting nothing. I take myself off to see a therapist. "I don't know what's wrong with me," I say. I explain that it's taking too long, it should have been over months ago. "It feels like grief," I say.

She says, "It is grief."

I meet a friend who has just returned to New York after eight years in Africa. She moves slowly and stiffly, like a victim of trauma. "Every view out of every window at home and at work is of one brick wall or another," she says. "How did you get through this?" I realize then that coming home is a long and very slow journey, and in my mind's eye, I see where I've been the last year and a half, since I returned. I would describe it like this: you get off the plane in your home country and get in your car and start driving. The view is dismal. All you can see are industrial estates and smokestacks and car parks. That's not all there is, but it's all you can see: grey sky, grey earth. Piles of smoking garbage, rusted metal. It's apocalyptic. Then, after months of driving through this wasteland, you hit a brick wall. A drab brick wall a thousand feet high in the middle of nowhere, and at eye level there is a sign. At last! A message! You get out of your car to read it. It says YOU ARE HERE.

You stand at the wall, waiting. Maybe the sign will say something else? Maybe it will scroll down and the next message will say YOU ARE HERE BUT NOT FOR LONG. Maybe it will turn into a door, and you will open it and walk through and be standing on the verge of blue mountains under a darkening sky. But it does not scroll down or change into a door. You give up and get back into the car. And now what?

You've come all this way to hit a brick wall, read a sign, and now you have to drive through the whole thing again. Because the first time you passed through it, you were thinking, "I do not belong here. I don't know where I am, but I am not home." The first time you passed through it, you thought you were on your way out. Now you know where you are (YOU ARE HERE) but this doesn't mean you are home yet.

After hitting the brick wall, I decide I need a more scenic route on this return journey back into my own country. I start with northern Ontario, which I claim to be from and yet know little about. Pema and I visit family and friends from Sault Ste. Marie to Temagami, but it is somehow not scenic enough. In fact, I have forgotten that I am supposed to be finding a way back in and have begun once again to look for a way out. With a child and a tiny budget, though, the options are limited. On the train north, my son asks me to tell him again why we are going to Moosonee. Because it is part of our province, I say, and it will be interesting and we should see it. But the real reason is I am hoping that I will find a beauty equal to the lost beauty of Bhutan, and the wildness and wilderness that all travellers seek when they leave home. Really, I am seeking the secret passageway out.

The train barrels through the night. Cramped in my seat, I search for a dark seam of sleep, waking frequently to see street lights shining into an empty parking lot. No wildness yet, but toward dawn, I open my eyes and see, very briefly, an orange moon sinking into an inky lake.

Of course, Moosonee is nothing at all like Bhutan. It is all long, low land and dark lines, water mixed into sky, and land mixed into water, black spruce and bush. We walk around Moose Factory Island, visit a church that once floated away, pick up fossils on the shore, and motor up the Moose River to the mouth of James Bay, where I listen, astounded (although surely this cannot be the first time I am hearing it), to the story of Henry Hudson's tragic end: After surviving the winter trapped in the ice of James Bay, he refused to turn the ship toward England and forced his starving crew to sail around and around the bay, looking for a way out. Not a way home but a way out. A non-existent secret passageway. Finally the crew mutinied. They put Hudson, his young son and a few loyal followers onto a boat and cut them loose. The crew sailed back to England, and Henry Hudson, his son and his friends were never heard from again. It is a terrible, haunting story in a wild and beautiful landscape, and I wonder why we always think there is nothing left to be discovered or told or learned at home.

My son is not sure what to make of the place. Outside the church that now has holes in the floor to allow it to fill with water instead of rising up and drifting off, someone asks him where he's from. He says the Himalayas. Then he looks around and shakes his head. "Well," he says. "I never thought I'd end up here." Neither did I, I have to admit, but that's the beauty of it, right there.

Jamie Zeppa's memoir, Beyond the Sky and the Earth: A Journey into Bhutan, *won the Banff Mountain Book Festival Award for Adventure Travel Writing. She won a Canadian Literary Award in 1996, and her letters from Bhutan were featured on CBC's* Morningside. *She lives in Toronto with her son.*

ACKNOWLEDGEMENTS

Working on *AWOL* has been a dream project come true. Thanks especially to the wonderful writers. We were incredibly lucky to work with you. To Amy: working with you has been an inspiration in itself. Thanks for being as clever and full of life as you are, and for making this so much fun.

Warmest personal thanks to Gav, great travel comrade, partner and friend; your love, support and brilliant ideas have meant so much. Deep thanks to Mum and Dad for giving me a love of travel and of books, for interest and encouragement, and for everything else; and to Duncan, adventurous and super-smart brother, for the good times in London. Thanks to Nana for coming to Canada and going snowshoeing.

For advice and ideas and help, many thanks also to Bryn Garrison, Cleo Paskal, Marq de Villiers, Greg Ioannou, Sam Hiyate, Patrick Hinchey, Gord Laird, Peter Padley, Meg Taylor and Bruce Westwood. Thanks to John Langford and Voyageur Quest for helping me stay sane and solvent during the editing. Thanks also to the amazing writers whose stories we couldn't use—we hope to have another chance in the future.

Finally, a huge thank you to Rox, Anne, Paul t., Pamela, Stacey and all the other brilliant people at Vintage Canada/Random House Canada for going AWOL with us, giving wise and stimulating feedback, invaluable promotion and generous support.

Jennifer Barclay

Co-editing this book has been one of the most fulfilling and gorgeous experiences of my life thus far. For this reason, I need to thank the following people: The ever-remarkable Jennifer Barclay for the absolute joy of sharing the giddiness, hard work and growing wisdom of this project with her. The brilliant writers involved with *AWOL* in all or some of its various stages; it has been an honour to work with each

ACKNOWLEDGEMENTS

of them. Susan Roxborough and Anne Collins for that first *AWOL* meeting that made me hyper for days, and for their unwavering commitment and guidance from there on in. Paul t. brooks, Pamela Murray and all the wise, wonderful people at Vintage Canada/Random House Canada who have had or will have a hand in this book's growth. Bill Douglas for his dedication and his mind-blowing sense of design and style—I actually *danced* when I saw his plans for *AWOL*. Gavin Mills, who was there from the very first *AWOL* porch conversation.

Sacha Gatien for instinctively knowing when I needed a break from my triple schedule. Nikki Pearson, our "big picture" talks have been invaluable, keeping all possibilities open. The WW women, Maurice and Cynthia Gatien, and Sam Hiyate for extra-special enthusiasm. Christine and Harry Brown and Edward Milton for Scotland-based hurrahs. Michael Holmes for love, insight and partnership through-out madcap times. Faye Logan for magical sisterly understanding that centres me. Finally, for the unconditional love and support of Robert and Ellen Logan through-out both my work on this book and *all* my life adventures, I have deeper gratitude than I have the words to properly express.

Amy Logan

And gone...